CW01171465

Qur'ānic Keywords

Qur'ānic Keywords

A Reference Guide

ABDUR RASHID SIDDIQUI

THE ISLAMIC FOUNDATION

Published by
THE ISLAMIC FOUNDATION,
Markfield Conference Centre, Ratby Lane, Markfield,
Leicestershire LE67 9SY, United Kingdom
E-mail: publications@islamic-foundation.com
Website: www.islamic-foundation.com

Quran House, PO Box 30611, Nairobi, Kenya

PMB 3193, Kano, Nigeria

Distributed by: Kube Publishing Ltd.
Tel: 44(01530) 249230, Fax: 44(01530) 249656
E-mail: info@kubepublishing.com

Copyright © The Islamic Foundation 2008/1429 H

All rights reserved. No part of this publication may be reproduced, stored in a retrieval system, or transmitted in any form or by any means, electronic, mechanical, photocopying, recording or otherwise, without the prior permission of the copyright owner.

British Library Cataloguing-in-Publication Data
Siddiqui, A. R.
Qur'anic Keywords: a reference guide
1. Koran – Concordances, English
I. Title II. Islamic Foundation (Great Britain)
297.1'22521

ISBN: 978-0-860374-42-8 *casebound*
ISBN: 978-0-860374-46-6 *paperback*

Typeset by: N.A.Qaddoura
Cover design by: Nasir Cadir
Indexing by: Yahya Birt

بسم الله الرحمن الرحيم

Contents

Transliteration Table vi

Foreword vii

Introduction x

Qur'ānic Keywords 1

Bibliography 275

Index of Arabic Terms 280

Index of English Terms 288

Transliteration Table

Arabic Consonants

Initial, unexpressed medial and final:

ء	ʾ	د	d	ض	ḍ	ك	k
ب	b	ذ	dh	ط	ṭ	ل	l
ت	t	ر	r	ظ	ẓ	م	m
ث	th	ز	z	ع	ʿ	ن	n
ج	j	س	s	غ	gh	هـ	h
ح	ḥ	ش	sh	ف	f	و	w
خ	kh	ص	ṣ	ق	q	ي	y

Vowels, diphthongs, etc.

Short:	ـَ a	ـِ i	ـُ u
Long:	ـَا ā	ـِي ī	ـُو ū
Diphthongs:		ـَوْ aw	
		ـَيْ ay	

Foreword

My esteemed colleague Abdur Rashid Siddiqui, author of this book, has asked me to write a short foreword on the assumption that I qualify to do so. Abdur Rashid Siddiqui is quite well known in the academic circle for authoring a number of books on a variety of subjects such as *Lift Up Your Hearts*, in two volumes, which is a collection of fifty-five Jumu'ah *Khuṭbahs*, and *Key to al-Fātiḥah* (The Opening Chapter of the Qur'ān) explaining its basic concepts. His *Key to Āl 'Imrān* attempts to present the synopsis of the Sūrah and expound its major themes. He has also edited a book entitled *Tazkiyah: The Islamic Path of Self-Development*. It is an anthology dealing with the purification of the inner soul. He has a passion for studying the Qur'ān and thus, he has spent his energy, time and efforts in trying to understand the Qur'ānic message in depth and then disseminating it to the general English readership, Muslim and non-Muslim alike. Through his writings on a variety of subjects related to the Qur'ān in one form or the other, he has received admiration and praise from the readers.

Muslims are fortunate that, by the grace of Allah, Arabic, the original language of the Revelation (*Waḥy*), is intact in its original form. Thus, the Arabic language in its purity shall remain in this world as long as the Qur'ān lasts. The ideal situation is that if one intends to grasp the full meaning and thrust of the Qur'ānic verses, one has to go back to the original language which, naturally, everyone cannot do. But, on the other hand, it is possible to gain the intended meaning and understand the general message and thrust of the Qur'ānic verses through translations. But to grasp the deeper complexities and infinite dimensions of the verses does require expertise and mastery over major sciences of the Qur'ān, *Ḥadīth*: Sayings of the Prophet (peace be upon him), and Islamic jurisprudence in addition to thorough knowledge of the Arabic language.

With the same objective in mind, the author's present work, *Qur'ānic Keywords: A Reference Guide*, explains fully the intended meanings of a variety of important Qur'ānic words and terminologies. This latest book is the result of many years of hard work. The author has selected over 140 major Qur'ānic terms and has explained them in simple English in order that those who do not know Arabic well and do not have access to the original sources will be able to grasp the intended meanings and thrust of these words and terms. Sometimes it is difficult to translate into English certain Qur'ānic words and terms exactly as these appear in the original Arabic text. However, it is possible to convey the real intended meaning of these terms into English by explaining them in some detail. It is noteworthy that the author has used authentic original and secondary sources in order to explain and convey the intended meaning. Here two examples will be more than sufficient to show how the author has been able to convey the intended meanings of the Qur'ānic words listed in the book.

The word *Ghayb* has often been translated into English as "unseen". But this is a weak translation and does not convey the real intended meaning (see for instance 2: 3 where the word *Ghayb* occurs). The author has translated and explained correctly that the intended meaning of the word *Ghayb* is things which human senses cannot perceive. This is exactly what the Qur'ān aims to convey. Likewise, the translators of the Qur'ān into English have translated the word *Taqwā* in various ways. Some say it means fear of Allah, and some say it is duty to Allah, while others have translated it as piety and other similar renderings. The author has correctly explained its intended meaning, that it means a perpetual consciousness of Allah's presence in one's mind as this consciousness of Allah's presence reminds a believer constantly of his/her accountability to Allah in the Hereafter. Otherwise how would one differentiate and distinguish between the meanings of the words *Khashyah* (2: 74) and *Taqwā* if both of these are translated as fear?

The author has ably explained in the Introduction the methodology and arrangement he has employed in dealing with the subject and has indicated the sources he has used in this book. The book contains two indexes, one for Arabic and the other for English terms. A bibliography at the end contains a long list of original and secondary sources which the author has used in the preparation of this book. This book will help the general English reader to understand the Qur'ānic verses better. The task has been made even easier by arranging the listed terms in alphabetical order. In fact, the book is a valuable addition to the Qur'ānic literature in English and it is worth having in every Muslim home as it can also be used as a reference book. The author deserves our praise and gratitude for this timely book. May Allah reward him for his hard work and sincerity.

Syed Salman Nadvi

Visiting Professor of Islamic Studies,
Markfield Institute of Higher Education,
Leicester, UK.
March 23rd, 2007

Introduction

Thankful praise be to Allah, the Most Gracious, the Most Merciful for sending down His Blessed Book for the guidance of human beings. Peace and Blessings be on our beloved Prophet who conveyed the Message of Allah to humanity. The need to understand the Qur'ānic message and guidance so that these can be implemented in one's life is of paramount importance. It is for this reason that a few years back I compiled a preliminary publication explaining the words in Sūrah al-Fātiḥah.[1] This attempted to understand the basic concepts. My intention was to cover the whole of the Qur'ān and, *Alḥamdulillāh*, and after five years I was able to fulfil this task. In my earlier book I have given the reasons for using this approach to understanding the Qur'ān for those who rely solely on English translations. Some relevant passages are reproduced here.

Reasons for This Compilation

Every science and discipline has its own vocabulary and terminology. A person lacking familiarity with the technical words used to expound that science will fail to grasp the essence of the message conveyed. The Holy Qur'ān revealed by Allah *subḥānahū wa ta'ālā* is the guidance for mankind until eternity. It was revealed in the Arabic language at a particular time during mankind's history. Those living in the West today, in different cultural and linguistic traditions, who try to understand it

---

1. *Key to al-Fātiḥah: Understanding the Basic Concepts*. Leicester, UK: The Islamic Foundation, 2001.

and reflect upon it without an adequate knowledge of Arabic, are really handicapped in reaching the essence of its message.

Translations help in overcoming language barriers, but no matter how faithfully accomplished, translations can never capture the true meaning and import of the ideas of the original. Encountering this very difficulty, one of the eminent translators of the Qur'ān into English, Mohammad Marmaduke Pickthall, frankly admitted in his Foreword to the *Meaning of the Glorious Koran* that "The Koran cannot be translated. That is the belief of old-fashioned Sheykhs and the view of the present writer." What Pickthall is trying to convey is that a mere literal rendering, word for word, will not help the reader understand the true meaning of the Qur'ān. Commentaries (*Tafāsīr*) to some extent, provide some means of overcoming this problem, but unfortunately there are as yet not many good ones available in English.

To alleviate this problem, I think explanatory notes on some of the basic keywords employed in the Glorious Qur'ān will be helpful. What do we mean by keywords? How can they help towards a better understanding of the Qur'ān? To answer these questions we need to look at the process by which a language is changed to give new meanings to old words. The study of any language reveals that words may gradually acquire very different meanings from their original use. For example, words like *culture*, *industry* or *family* used to convey different concepts in earlier centuries than what we mean by them today. This is discussed extensively by a distinguished sociologist, Raymond Williams, in his book, *Keywords: A Vocabulary of Culture and Society.* After the Second World War, when the author was released from the army and returned to Cambridge to resume his studies, he and his old friend noticed so many changes in the English language that it was as if younger students did not speak the same language as their elders. He observed: "Yet it had been, we both said, only four or five years. Could it really have changed that much? Searching for examples we found that some general attitudes in politics and religion had altered, and agreed that these were important changes. But I found myself preoccupied by a single word, *culture,* which I was hearing very much more often..." (p. 12). This led him to the development of *Keywords* in which he wrote notes on about 125 such words.

The dominant vocabulary in the modern world is that of the secular-Christian West. The direct political hegemony of the West may have shrunk, but its ideas and its ideology still rule the world. Thus, the vocabulary that prevails today is the vocabulary of Western ideology and its institutions. The perceptive mind of Khurram Murad has observed this and he also has identified the importance of keywords. In his Introduction to Sayyid Mawdūdī's *The Islamic Movement: Dynamics of Values, Power and Change,* he writes:

> Vocabulary, however, is not defined by the dictionary alone; that may well be only a surface meaning. Each keyword carries within it a deeper world of meaning. It has its own epistemology, its anthropology and ecology; its psychology and sociology, its politics and economy and its history and ethos – all acquired from the culture within which it develops. For words do not exist in isolation from man and his society. So the language of contemporary culture embodies the culture of Western language. (p. 14)

This is very well illustrated by Urdu and Hindi, which are linguistically and grammatically the same language, but represent two totally different cultures by their use of keywords. The words *ghusl* and *ashnān* both mean 'to take a ritual bath' but there is a world of difference in their meaning for a Muslim and a Hindu.

Thus, in order to understand the message of the Qur'ān we have to clarify the concepts which each Qur'ānic term conveys in the language with which we are familiar. Unless these concepts are fully understood we may be just skipping over the surface. One of the reasons why the Muslim *Ummah* at large, despite its reverence for the Qur'ān, has failed to be inspired by its message, is the lack of appreciation of what the message really means. I would like to quote Khurram Murad again, who has described this problem very succinctly in his Introduction to the work cited above:

> For example, at one time, *Lā ilāha illā Llāh* possessed the *meanings* which could shake its hearers. Today it can be proclaimed without causing even a stir, even in the realm of false *ilahs* (gods). Can such words regain their power without being understood in the contemporary context? Perhaps translating the original meaning of the Qur'ān in a language within which Muslims live today is the most critically important task the Ummah has been challenged to address. (pp. 16–17)

It is very difficult to take up this challenge. Perhaps there are more qualified people in all respects who will attempt to bridge this gap. What I intend to do is to provide brief notes on some of the keywords of the Qur'ān. I hope that these will help to clarify and provide understanding about the dynamic ideas portrayed in the Qur'ān.

Some Important Sources

I have used the following sources extensively in compiling these notes. These have helped me immensely in developing my understanding of the Qur'ān as well. Amīn Aḥsan Iṣlāḥī's *Tadabbur-i-Qur'ān* is a monumental work of eight volumes in Urdu. Its unique contribution to *tafsīr* literature is that it provides the logical explanation regarding the internal arrangement of the verses of the Qur'ān as well as the relationship of each *sūrah* to its preceding and subsequent *sūrah*. Iṣlāḥī also provides plenty of notes on the meaning and etymology (origin and history) of words.

Sayyid Abul A'lā Mawdūdī's *Tafhīm al-Qur'ān* is his *magnum opus* of six volumes in Urdu. Sayyid Mawdūdī's translation in contemporary Urdu idiom attempts to do justice to the beauty of the Qur'ān. It is an immense treasure-house of knowledge providing a systematic exposition of social, political, economic and legal teachings.

Sayyid Mawdūdī also wrote a very valuable book on the *Four Key Concepts of the Qur'ān*. His explanation of these four terms, namely *Ilāh*, *Rabb*, *'Ibādah* and *Dīn*, provide valuable insights into the real message of the Qur'ān.

Imām al-Rāghib al-Iṣfahānī's *Al-Mufradāt fī Gharīb al-Qur'ān* is an indispensable work for understanding Qur'ānic vocabulary. It has been translated into several languages. Its value lies in providing brief definitions of different shades of meaning in which words are used. I also found Mustansir Mir's *Dictionary of the Qur'ānic Terms and Concepts* very useful. I will not try to duplicate the work he has already done. There may be some overlap but I will try to focus on a few keywords which I hope will open the way to a better understanding of the Qur'ān. Other works that I have consulted are listed in the Bibliography.

I have used 'Abdullāh Yūsuf 'Alī's translation of the Qur'ān throughout this book, except in a few places where other translations seemed more appropriate.

Methodology and Arrangement

I have selected over 140 Qur'ānic keywords which cover the basic concepts of the Qur'ān. In the Arabic language most words stemmed from a trilateral verb form and from this root other words are formed. A derivate retains the basic meaning of its root. I have given the root of each word and its different shades of meanings, followed by brief analysis of the concept and related issues if any. In discussing each keyword I have also included synonyms and antonyms as well as other words derived from the root to help the reader to understand the concept better. Thus, in all over 250 words are discussed in this work. I have incorporated all the words of Sūrah al-Fātiḥah which appeared earlier as a separate publication. As this is basically a compendium of conceptual terms, I have omitted all personal names, place names, natural phenomena, flora and fauna as well as historical events.

Terms are arranged in alphabetical order of the transliterated Arabic letters. For each word, at least five Qur'ānic references are given to help readers in their own study. For ease of reference there are indexes of both the Arabic and English terms.

Concluding Remarks

I could not have accomplished this work without the help and guidance of my many learned friends. Professor Syed Salman Nadvi read my manuscript thoroughly and made many invaluable corrections and suggestions which I have incorporated in the text. He was also kind enough to write a Foreword at my request. I am most grateful for his generous help. Professor Abdul Raheem Kidwai suggested the inclusion of a few more keywords and recommended refinements on the general layout of the book. Mawlana Iqbal Ahmad Azami and Mokrane Guezzou critically looked at the Arabic words and their meaning and checked the diacritical marks. Professor Khurshid Ahmad helped in clarifying certain concepts about which I was uncertain. I am most grateful and sincerely thank them for their help. My thanks are due to Ms. Pat Harper for copy-editing the book. I have benefited from her advice. I would also like to thank Nasir Cadir for the cover design and N. Qaddoura for typesetting and the staff of Kube Publishing for undertaking its production. Last, but not the least, I am most grateful to Dr. Manazir Ahsan for the final checking of the manuscript and diacritical marks.

I feel very humble that one who is so deficient in knowledge and good deeds should undertake this immense task of explaining the vocabulary of the Glorious Qur'ān. Yet, I feel that there is a need for such a work. Furthermore, I hope that those who are more knowledgeable and competent will provide their valuable comments and suggestions to help improve this effort. I pray and hope that Allah in His Boundless Mercy accepts my very humble effort. May He open up our hearts to receive guidance from His Book.

Leicester **Abdur Rashid Siddiqui**
12 Rabīʿ al-Thānī 1427
30 April 2007

Qur'ānic Keywords

'Abd [عبد]
see *'Ibādah*

'Adhāb [عذاب] (Punishment)

Meanings
Lexicographers differ about the exact root of this word. *'Adhāba al-rajul* is a person who has lost his appetite and ability to sleep due to the intensity of thirst. Hence *Ta'dhīb* means to keep someone hungry and awake. Another opinion is that this word is derived from *'adhb* meaning sweet and that from this comes the word *'adhdhabtuhū* which means I have deprived someone of the pleasures of life. Yet another opinion is that its origin is *al-ta'dhīb* which means to flog someone with lashes. All these meanings have the common theme of deprivation of the necessities and pleasures of life as well as the infliction of pain and suffering. A fourth opinion is that the word is derived from *'adhb*, meaning to stop, as punishment stops the criminal from re-offending. (*Lughat al-Qur'ān*, vol. 4, p. 262)

Analysis
'Adhāb usually refers to divine punishment. Punishment meted out by an Islamic state is called *ta'zīr*, a term which includes punishments which may not have been mentioned in the Qur'ān. Whereas *Ḥudūd*

punishment is sanctioned by Allah but carried out by an Islamic state. The word *Ḥudūd* comes from *ḥadd* meaning a barrier which prevents two objects meeting each other. The punishment deters a person from committing the same act again. *Ḥudūd Allāh* are the limits set by Allah which should not be transgressed (al-Baqarah 2: 229). The Qur'ān has provided the punishments for adultery, murder, theft, false allegation of unchastity and rebellion.

According to the Qur'ānic teachings, man is responsible for his acts. Thus, he should be accountable for them and is required to face the consequences arising from his actions. That crimes should be punished is a universally accepted principle and is enshrined in the criminal codes of all countries. However, there may be variation in the administration of punishment. Jurists agree that the punishment should fit the crime. The more severe the crime the more stringent should be the punishment.

One obvious purpose of punishing the offender, as we have seen above, is retribution. But the other purpose is to reform the offender. For example while in prison one will have time to reflect and reform oneself. The other purpose is to deter potential wrong-doers from committing such deeds. Thus, the aim of the imposition of punishments is to reform society and establish law and order.

It should be noted that there are certain actions that are not indictable under the criminal law such as backbiting, jealousy, lying, hurting someone's feelings and many minor moral lapses. However, these could be punished by Allah in the Hereafter, where each individual has to give an account of his deeds (al-Zalzalah 99: 8). Of course, all sins are wiped out by sincere repentance, as Allah is Most Kind and Most Merciful.

Allah may inflict punishment for disbelief, acts of gross injustice and tyranny in this world as well as in the Hereafter. Those who rejected the call of the prophets in the past and indeed persecuted them were in the end destroyed in this world by floods, storms and thunder. The Qur'ān extensively narrates the stories of the people of Nūḥ, Pharaoh, 'Ād, Thamūd and others to warn humanity of the dire consequences of rejecting the true faith. As there is no messenger of Allah to come after the last messenger, the Prophet Muḥammad (peace be upon him), Allah now inflicts only selective punishments to warn mankind to take heed.

The Agents of Divine Punishments

Everything in this universe is under Allah's control so He can use any of His creation to inflict punishment. The people of Nūḥ were destroyed by flood, Pharaoh and his army were drowned in the sea. 'Ād were overrun by a fierce storm. Thamūd were annihilated by a thunder, the people of Lūṭ were destroyed by severe earthquake, and the army of Abrahah and his herd of elephants were decimated by a flock of tiny birds through pebbles. Thus, by Allah's command any agency can create havoc and destroy strong structures as well as powerful armies.

The final punishment will be in the Hereafter. Hellfire awaits those whose deeds in this world deserve that they face eternal damnation.

Synonyms

The most common word used for divine punishment is *'adhāb* (350 times). The other word is *jazā'*, which means requital or recompense. This is a neutral word and used both for reward and punishment. In the sense of punishment it is used 100 times. The word *'iqāb* (2: 211) is also used for punishment and penalty. The least-used word is *nakāl* (5: 38 and 73: 12) which means exemplary punishment or warning.

References

'Adhāb: 2: 10; 22: 2; 32: 14; 37: 9; 44: 12. *Jazā'*: 2: 85; 5: 38; 9: 26; 10: 37; 12: 25. *'iqāb*: 2: 196 and 211; 3: 11; 5: 2; 6: 165. *Nakāl*: 2: 66; 5: 38; 73: 12; 79: 25.

See also *Thawāb*

'Adl [عدل] (Justice)

Meaning

The literal meaning of *'Adl* is to divide into exactly two equal parts so that there is no disparity between them. Justice requires the firm will and determination to give each one his due. In the Qur'ān some other words are used to convey the same meaning as *'adl*, for example the word *qisṭ* (equity, fairness) and *mīzān* (balance). Like *'adl*, *qisṭ* means to be equal; *al-qisṭās* means a measuring scale. The same meaning is conveyed by the word *mīzān*, which comes from *al-wazn* meaning weight; *mīzān* is the instrument to determine the weight of something. *'Adl* also means compensation, as in Sūrah al-Baqarah (2: 48).

The Importance of *'Adl*

Justice is one of the attributes of Allah. One of His ninety-nine names is *al-'Adl* meaning the Just and He will judge everyone justly (Ghāfir 40: 20). Similarly His *Kalimah* (Word) "*is perfect in truthfulness and justice*" (al-An'ām 6: 115). It is stated in the Qur'ān that the whole universe is established on the basis of a harmonious balance. Hence human beings should not transgress and create imbalance.

> *And the Firmament has He raised high, and He has set up the Balance (of justice) in order that you may not transgress (due) balance. So establish the weight with equity, and do not make the balance deficient.*
>
> (al-Raḥmān 55: 7–9)

The establishment of justice and equity within human society is in consonance and harmony with what Allah has already established in the universe.

It is also evident from the study of the Qur'ān that the specific purpose for sending down the prophets and scriptures was that there should be justice in society.

Indeed We sent our Messengers with clear signs and sent down with them the Book and the Balance (of right and wrong) so that people might conduct their affairs with justice.

(al-Ḥadīd 57: 25)

The Commandment of Justice

In Sūrah al-Naḥl a comprehensive set of instructions is given:

Allah commands justice, the doing of good and compassion to kith and kin, and He forbids all shameful deeds and wickedness and rebellion: He instructs you that you may receive admonition.

(al-Naḥl 16: 90)

The first commandment from Allah in this verse is to do justice. Being just is the fundamental injunction obligated on human beings. The Qur'ān upholds justice as an absolute value. In human affairs it is imperative that dealings with others be on the basis of fairness and equity. The concept of justice, equity and fair dealings is one of the basic tenets of morality that is imbued in all human beings. Regardless of religion, race or nationality, human beings throughout history have admired and praised justice and fair play and despised injustice and inequity.

Justice should encompass the entirety of human affairs including the family, the community, and the nation as well as the assembly of nations. In personal life one should treat all one's children equally. If one cannot do justice among one's wives one should be content with one wife only (al-Nisā' 4: 3). In business and economic affairs dealings should be fair and just (al-An'ām 6: 152), and there should be no double standards for giving and receiving (al-Muṭaffifīn 83: 1–3). This commandment prohibits adulteration and the selling of fake merchandise. In one's dealings one should speak justly (al-An'ām 6: 152) and not be swayed by self-interest or concern for one's relations. One should not be influenced by rich and powerful people or by compassion for someone's poverty (al-Nisā' 4: 135). One should not deviate from the path of justice out of enmity and hatred either (al-Mā'idah 5: 8).

Judicial Proceedings

Allah has assigned a special responsibility to those who have to administer justice. In Sūrah al-Nisā' there is a specific decree:

> *Allah commands you to deliver whatever you have been entrusted with to their rightful owners and whenever you judge between people, judge with justice. Most excellent is what Allah exhorts you to do. Allah hears all and sees all.*
>
> (al-Nisā' 4: 58)

Thus giving false evidence, perjury, is designated as one of the major sins. It is considered so serious that it ranks after *shirk* (associating someone or something with Allah).

The Muslim *Ummah* is instructed to settle disputes among two factions of the believers with fairness and equity. When there is disagreement between two groups of Muslims, the instruction is to:

> *Make peace between them with justice and be fair for Allah loves those who are fair (and just).*
>
> (al-Ḥujurāt 49: 9)

Inter-Faith Relations

It is imperative not to follow one's own desires when inviting others to Islam. Instead one should say:

> *I believe in the Book which Allah has sent down; and I am commanded to judge justly between you. Allah is our Lord and your Lord. For us (is the responsibility for) our deeds, and for you for your deeds. There is no contention between us and you. Allah will bring us together, and to Him is (our) final goal.*
>
> (al-Shūrā 42: 15)

This verse instructs that one should convey the message fully without discrimination, and that all human beings should be judged on the same footing.

Certain Exceptions

Justice demands that all human beings should be treated fairly. However, this does not mean that there should always be equality among them in all matters. Of course, there are some basic civil rights in respect of which all citizens are to be treated equally, for example the right to vote. But there will be inequality in the remuneration of those who work in different fields or positive discrimination in favour of the disabled and oppressed. Attempts to create artificial equality are not practical nor desirable. The Islamic teachings are that everyone should have equal rights and opportunity in the social, economic and political fields and that everyone should be treated justly.

References

'Adl: 2: 282; 4: 58; 16: 90; 49: 9; 65: 2. *Qisṭ*: 3: 18; 4: 135; 5: 8 and 42; 6: 152. *Mīzān*: 6: 152; 7: 85; 11: 85; 55: 8; 57: 25.

'Afw [عفو]

see *Maghfirah*

'Ahd [عهد] (Contract, Agreement, Pact)

Meaning

Al-'Ahd (pl. *'uhūd*) means to protect or take care of something. Hence, a binding promise, a promise that should be fulfilled is called *'ahd*. In the Qur'ān the word is often used for fulfilling one's obligation to Allah. The other word also used with the same meaning is *Mīthāq*. Its root is *WTHQ* which means reliability and trust and is translated as a covenant. Thus, it indicates permanence and it is used for important issues in which both parties have fully committed themselves to observe the agreement. The word is commonly used for treaties between nations.

In the Qur'ān, the most important meaning of *'ahd* and *mīthāq* is man's covenant with Allah, whereby man binds himself to worship Him to the exclusion of all other animate or inanimate beings or objects. In return Allah promises man's spiritual and material well-being as well as his salvation in the Hereafter.

The First Covenant

The first covenant which human beings entered with Allah was before their birth. It is recorded in the Qur'ān thus:

> *And (remember) when your Lord brought forth from the Children of Ādam from their loins their descendants, and made them testify concerning themselves, (saying): "Am I not your Lord?" They said: "Yes, we testify." (This) was, lest you should say on the Day of Resurrection: "Of this we were unaware."*
>
> (al-A'rāf 7: 172)

According to *aḥādīth* this incident took place at the creation of mankind. After the creation of the Prophet Ādam (peace be upon him) angels were asked to bow down before him and man was proclaimed vicegerent on Earth. All mankind was brought forth and this covenant took place so that mankind has no excuse of not knowing their obligations. To reinforce this Allah promised to send His prophets to remind people of their covenant. Hence, this covenant will be presented as testimony on the Day of Judgement to prove that Allah has fulfilled His part of the agreement. It is also logical that as vicegerent and representative of Allah on earth, man should take an oath of allegiance. As this oath is taken individually each person is responsible to Allah for this. One cannot plead ignorance of one's obligations.

The question may be raised that since this "covenant" is not in our conscious memory, how can it be cited as testimony against us? This is an instinctual covenant which may not be in man's conscious memory but everyone by instinct knows the difference between good and evil. This awareness can be sharpened or destroyed by man's own inclinations and actions. This is also true of our potential capabilities as well. These potentialities have to be activated by external factors such as education and training. Hence, these can be preserved or obliterated. The task of the prophets throughout human history was to revive the memory of this covenant.

Covenants through the Prophets

These covenants were made to reinforce the instinctual covenant through the agency of the Prophets. These covenants through the Prophets were either oral or in written form. The Qur'ān makes several references to them. For example Banū Isrā'īl were reminded: "*Fulfil your covenant with Me as I fulfil My covenant with you*" (al-Baqarah 2: 40); and again they were told: "*And remember We took your covenant and We raised above you Mount Sinai (saying): 'Hold firmly to what We have given you...'*" (al-Baqarah 2: 63). Further on, yet another covenant is mentioned: "*And remember We took a covenant from the Children of Isrā'īl (to this effect): worship none but Allah...*" (al-Baqarah 2: 83). The Ten Commandments given to the Prophet Mūsā (peace be upon him) established the covenant wrought in stone. Similar scriptural covenants in written form are mentioned in the Bible (Old and New Testaments) and the Qur'ān.

Some Specific Covenants with the Prophets

The Qur'ān also narrates several specific covenants Allah has taken from His Messengers. For example about the Prophet Ādam (peace be upon him) it is mentioned: "*We had already, beforehand taken the covenant of Ādam, but he forgot: and We found on his part no firm resolve*" (Ṭā Hā 20: 115). The other covenants mentioned are with the Prophets Ibrāhīm and Ismā'īl in (al-Baqarah 2: 125) and with the Prophets Nūḥ, Ibrāhīm, Mūsā, 'Īsā and Muḥammad (peace be upon them) in (al-Aḥzāb 33: 7) and (al-Shūrā 42: 13).

General Contracts

Great emphasis is given on fulfilling the promises and contracts one enters into in daily life whether domestic or commercial. Man's life on this earth is full of covenants, contracts and agreements either explicit (business transactions) or implicit (marriage contracts). The general Qur'ānic command is to fulfil them (al-Naḥl 16: 91). One is accountable for them on the Day of Judgement (al-Isrā' 17: 34).

References

'Ahd: 2: 27; 3: 77; 13: 20; 16: 91; 17: 34. *Mīthāq*: 2: 83; 3: 81; 4: 92; 8: 72; 13: 20.

Ahl al-Kitāb [أهل ٱلكتاب]

see *Kitāb*

Ajal [اجل] (The Appointed Time)

Meaning

Ajal means date, deadline, and time of death, hence the appointed time. To emphasize this last meaning, in some Qur'ānic verses the expression used is *Ajal Musammā* (fixed period of time). The *Ajal* as a keyword refers to the fixed period of time allotted to an individual or a nation or the whole universe. The *Ajal* indicates the finiteness of the time for everything in this universe. When that time arrives there cannot be any delay. This message is repeated in several verses of the Qur'ān. For example: "*To every people is a term appointed: when their term is reached, not an hour can they cause to delay, nor (an hour) can they advance (it in anticipation)*" (al-A'rāf 7: 34). (See also Yūnus 10: 49 and al-Naḥl 16: 61.) The same is true of an individual: "*But to no soul does Allah grant respite when the time appointed (for it) has come; and Allah is well acquainted with (all) that you do*" (al-Munāfiqūn 63: 11). The fate of this universe is the same: "*We have not created heavens and the earth and all between them but for just ends...*" (al-Aḥqāf 46: 3). Although death will overtake everything, it is not the end. There will be resurrection and accountability and the life in the Hereafter will be eternal.

The word *Ajal* is also used in the Qur'ān in its ordinary meaning: for example in contracts or other legal issues when time is appointed for the performance of certain acts (al-Baqarah 2: 282; al-Qaṣaṣ 28: 28).

Synonyms

al-'Aṣr means era, time, period, epoch. As it signifies the speed with which time passes its better translation is 'fleeting time'. It usually refers to the time that has passed. Unlike *al-Dahr* which also means time, epoch, age, and refers to destiny and fate.

Sūrah al-'Aṣr indicates that man should pay heed to quickly passing time and try to save himself from the loss in the Hereafter. One should take the short span of life to do good deeds and enjoin truth and patience. (al-'Aṣr 103: 1–3).

Whereas the pagan Arabs deified "*al-Dahr*" and used to say: "*What is there but our life in this world? We shall die and we live, and nothing but Time can destroy us.*" (al-Jāthīyah 45: 24), the Prophet (peace be upon him) advised them not to abuse *al-Dahr* (Time) as Allah Himself is Time.

References

Ajal: 7: 34; 11: 3; 14: 44; 29: 5; 71: 4. *al-'Aṣr*: 103: 1. *al-Dahr*: 45: 24 and 26: 1.

See also *Mawt*

Ākhirah [آخرة] (The Hereafter)

Meaning

The word *Ākhirah* is derived from *Ākhir* which means last, ultimate, end and close. Its opposite is *Awwal* which means first and foremost. The two blessed names of Allah are *Al-Awwal* and *al-Ākhir*. They indicate that Allah is eternal with no beginning and no end – as stated in the *Book of Revelation*: "I am the Alpha and the Omega, says the Lord God Almighty, who is, who was, and who is to come" (Revelation 1: 8).

Often *al-Ākhirah* is used as the opposite of *Dunyā*, meaning this world in which we live, *Ākhirah* will come later hence it is called the Hereafter. Sometimes *al-Ākhirah* is used in conjunction with *al-dār* as *al-Dār al-Ākhirah* (the Last Abode).

Al-Ākhirah: the stages

Many graphic words are used in the Qur'ān to depict the horror and calamity of that Day. Some of these words are:

al-Qāri'ah	the Calamity
al-Zalzalah	the Earthquake
al-Ṣā'iqah	the Blast
Yawman Thaqīlā	the Hard Day
Al-Yawm al-Muḥīṭ	the Encompassing Day
Yawm al-Faṣl	the Day of Separation
al-Ṭāmmah al-Kubrā	the Great Disaster
al-Ḥāqqah	the Reality
Yawm al-Dīn	the Day of Judgement
Yawm al-Ḥaqq	the True (inevitable) Day
Yawm al-Ḥisāb	the Day of Reckoning
Yawm al-Khurūj	the Day of Exodus (from the graves).

Al-Ākhirah is a composite term which includes the following stages

- *Al-Sā'ah* which means the Hour, that is, the Hour of Resurrection. "*They ask you about the Hour – 'When will be its appointed time?'*" (al-Nāzi'āt 79: 42). The Qur'ān provides the answer: "*With Him is the knowledge of the Hour*" (al-Zukhruf 43: 85). Sūrah al-Qamar states that it is very near: "*The Hour is the time promised to them and the Hour will be most grievous and most bitter.*" (al-Qamar 54: 1 and 46). This will be heralded by the sound of the Trumpet. "*The Trumpet* (al-Ṣūr) *shall be blown: that will be the day whereof warning had been given.*" (Qāf 50: 42)
- The Resurrection (*al-Qiyāmah*) when humanity in its entirety will stand up for accountability of their deeds before Allah. It is

called *Yawm al-Ḥisāb* (the Day of Judgement) or *Yawm al-Jazā'* (the Day of Recompense).

- The final result will separate people. Those successful will attain an everlasting life of pleasure in *Jannah*. Those doomed will live in eternal damnation in Hell.

The *Ākhirah* with *Tawḥīd* (the oneness of God) and *Risālah/ Nubuwwah* (Prophethood) are the three main components of *Īmān* (faith). The *īmān* in the *Ākhirah* is, of course, a part of *al-Īmān bi'l-Ghayb* (Belief in things which we cannot perceive by our senses). Hence, in both the Qur'ān and *aḥādīth* there is a detailed description of all the events that will take place in the Hereafter so as to convince the believers and strengthen their faith.

Proof of the Hereafter

The Qur'ān often uses the simile of rain to explain how it is possible to resurrect dead bodies. Just as after a shower of rain, dead earth becomes covered with greenery so can Allah resurrect the dead (Qāf 50: 11; al-'Ankabūt 29: 20; al-Ḥajj 22: 5-6).

The Qur'ān also argues that the presence of conscience (*nafs*) in human beings presupposes that one can instinctively distinguish between right and wrong (al-Shams 91: 7). We see that the physical laws do take effect in this world but not the moral laws. For example fire burns but telling a lie does not harm.

As to the ability of Allah to bring about resurrection, the Qur'ānic argument is, if He is able to create not only human beings but the whole universe in the first place why should it be difficult for Him to recreate them? (Yā Sīn 36: 79; al-Aḥqāf 46: 33).

Some of the prophets, including the Prophet Ibrāhīm (peace be upon him) were shown how Allah brought the dead to life (al-Baqarah 2: 259–260). Similarly the story of *Aṣḥāb al-Kahf* related in *Sūrah* 18 is presented as historical evidence to prove that people can be raised again after sleeping for about three hundred years.

The Necessity of *al-Ākhirah*

Al-Ākhirah is necessary so that true justice can be done. In this world pious people suffer and do not reap a full reward for their actions. Similarly evil persons triumph and often do not receive full punishment for their deeds. Allah, who is Just, wants full justice to be done and everyone to be fully recompensed. Why is there such a long delay in meting out this justice? There are two reasons: one, this world is *Dār al-Imtiḥān* (a place of test or trial – (al-Mulk 67: 1–2)) and only at the conclusion of the test are the papers marked and the results announced. Second, the benefits of good deeds one does are reaped by succeeding generations and similarly the evil practices devised by an individual continue to have repercussions for a long time. The effects of all the good and evil deeds will have to be accumulated in order to reward or punish those who started them in the first place. This can be done only when the whole world comes to an end, only then can the full account of deeds be measured. Thus, in this world people will be tested, and in the *Ākhirah* they will be either rewarded or punished as the case may be.

References

Ākhirah: 2: 4; 4: 77; 40: 39; 59: 3; 87: 17. *al-Sā'ah*: 43: 85; 54: 1 and 46; 79: 42.

'*Ālam* [عالم] (Universe)

Meaning

The word '*Ālam* (pl. '*Awālim*, '*Ālamūn*, '*Ālamīn*) derives from '*LM*. The word '*Ilm* also comes from the same root. '*Ālamūn* in its noun form means that apparatus or entity through which one acquires knowledge about other things. Our universe provides knowledge about our Creator, hence it is called *al-'ālam*. It is for this reason that the Qur'ān instructs us to reflect upon the universe.

> *Behold! In the creation of the heavens and the earth and the alternation of night and day there are indeed signs for people of understanding.*
>
> (Āl 'Imrān 3: 190)

> *Do they not look at the sky how We made it, and there are no flaws in it? And the earth – We have spread it out, and set thereon mountains standing firm and produced therein every kind of beautiful growth (in pairs) – to be observed and as a reminder for every penitent human being.*
>
> (Qāf 50: 6–8)

Since *'Ālam* means this world, its plural *al-'Ālamīn* refers to several other worlds. Similarly, if *'Ālam* refers to this universe then its plural refers to other solar systems and the existence of very many galaxies in addition to our own. According to some *mufassirūn* (commentators), *al-'Ālamīn* refers to different species such as angels, *jinns* and human beings. The word *'Ālamīn* is used 73 times in the Qur'ān. By looking at the verses where it occurs and the context in which it is used, all the above meanings are possible. Thus, when *Banū Isrā'īl* were told that "*I preferred you over* al-'Ālamīn" (al-Baqarah 2: 47), it means all contemporary nations. By referring to the Prophet (peace be on him) "*as a mercy for al-'Ālamīn*" (al-Anbiyā' 21: 107), the Qur'ān means that he is a mercy for all creatures including mankind.

It is pertinent to note that here Allah is referred to as "Lord of the Worlds". This attribute of Allah means that every creation needs nourishment and provision and that only Allah can provide this. This also highlights the Islamic belief that Allah is the Cherisher and Sustainer of the Worlds, that He is not the deity of any particular race, nationality or tribe as was the belief of polytheists and even of *Banū Isrā'īl*, though they were supposed to be monotheists.

References

'Ālam: 2: 47; 3: 97; 7: 121; 28: 30; 32: 2.

Allah [الله]

The Personal Name

The word Allah is used with the highest frequency in the Qur'ān. It is the personal name of the Creator of the Universe. The root of this word is *ALH* and by adding *al* it becomes Allah – a proper noun. However, there is another opinion, which according to *Al-Qāmūs* is the correct one, is that Allah is a non-derivated noun.

Words that derive from this Arabic root have the following meanings, which illustrate some of the attributes of Allah.

Meanings

The word Allah has five meanings. These were discussed by Sayyid Mawdūdī extensively and also mentioned in *Mufradāt* by Imām al-Rāghib al-Iṣfahānī.

A. To be bewildered or perplexed

No one is able to perceive and comprehend the exact nature of Allah. The human mind has always remained astonished and bewildered about Him. The Holy Qur'ān says:

> *There is nothing whatever like unto Him, and He is the One Who hears and sees (all things).*
>
> (al-Shūrā 42: 11)

In order to know Allah, the Prophet (peace be upon him) advised us to "reflect on the creation of Allah and not to think about His personality".

(Ibn 'Ābbās, *al-Targhīb wa al-Tarhīb*)

B. To get satisfaction or to find comfort from someone's company or by seeking his protection

It is only when a person establishes a true relationship with Allah that he attains satisfaction and contentment.

Those who believe and whose hearts find satisfaction in the remembrance of Allah: for without doubt in the remembrance of Allah do hearts find satisfaction.

(al-Ra'd 13: 28)

C. To have intense attachment and love for somebody or something
All creatures love their creator. Being the Supreme Creator, Allah infuses the feeling of affection and love among His creation. In the Qur'ān Allah says:

But those of faith are overflowing in their love for Allah.

(al-Baqarah 2: 165)

D. To be hidden or to remain concealed
It is obvious that Allah cannot be seen or perceived by anyone:

No vision can grasp Him. But His grasp is over all vision: He is above all comprehension.

(al-An'ām 6: 103)

Although we cannot perceive Allah, as mentioned above, Allah is very close to us. Allah says:

For We are nearer to him than (his) jugular vein.
(Qāf 50: 16)

E. To worship someone
The person who deserves to be worshipped should be the One who can fulfil the needs of the worshipper and give him satisfaction. It is only Allah who provides all the necessary provisions for all His creatures to survive, and He is the One who fulfils their needs and gives them satisfaction. Thus, He is the One who should be worshipped.

All these meanings have a logical relationship with each other. The concept of Allah evokes intense love and awe that compels the entire universe to bow down before Him in submission. As He is the sole Creator He should be worshipped exclusively and obeyed without reservation. Worship without obedience is the negation of His Sovereignty. His remembrance is the source of satisfaction and comfort. He is the sole Sovereign, the Mightiest, the Greatest and His Rule should override all human affairs.

The word Allah is unique and almost incapable of translation into any other language. The English word 'God' with a capital 'G' does not convey the array of meanings outlined above. Allah is the personal name of the Ultimate Reality in this Universe. Thus, there cannot be any plural of this word in the way 'God' becomes 'gods'; nor has it a feminine form as 'goddess' or 'goddesses'.

Tawḥīd

The Oneness of Allah (*Tawḥīd*) is the central theme of the Qur'ān. The name Allah is used exclusively for the One who created the heaven and the earth and everything in this universe. Arabs before the revelation of the Qur'ān also considered Allah in this sense. Their worship of deities stemmed from their belief that such deities had some influence in the domain of Allah. The Qur'ān repudiates this idea vehemently. The Qur'ān also categorically refutes duality (the ancient Persian concept that there is one God of Good and another God of Evil) and the Christian concept of the Trinity. The Sovereignty of Allah demands that His Rules and Commands be enforced upon the entire universe including mankind. The submission of man to His Rule and to His Will and the readiness to live in compliance with His Commands is Islam.

Other Attributes

According to a *ḥadīth* the Holy Prophet (peace be upon him) said:

> Verily, there are ninety-nine names of Allah, whosoever recites them shall enter Paradise.
>
> (Bukhārī and Muslim)

These names are collectively known as *al-Asmā' al-Ḥusnā* (the most beautiful names) and some are mentioned in the Qur'ān in the following verses: al-Baqarah 2: 255; al-Ḥadīd 57: 1–6 and al-Ḥashr 59: 22–24. These Names express Attributes of Allah. They lead us to the proper understanding of our relationship with our Creator. They also provide a focal point for us to contemplate upon His attributes and, thus, fashion our lives according to them. However, the most repeated names of Allah are the Merciful (*al-Raḥīm*) and the Most Compassionate One (*al-Raḥmān*). They express the immensity of Divine Mercy for everything that is in the universe.

References

Allah: 2: 255; 17: 110; 24: 35; 57: 1–6; 59: 22–24; 112: 1–4.

'Amal [عمل] (Action, Deed)

Meaning

'Amal is from the verb *'Amila* which means doing, acting, action and activity. Hence *al-'Amal* is an action performed by a human being. This word is not usually used for actions done by animals. *'Amal* is used for both good and bad deeds.

Analysis

The predominant use of *'Amal* is in conjunction with *Ṣāliḥāt* meaning good, righteous and pious acts. It often follows the affirmation of the faith. The faith and pious deeds are often mentioned together in the Qur'ān. The paramount importance of this combination can be appreciated by the fact that both these terms are used 64 times together in the Qur'ān. Whereas the faith is the inner conviction, good deeds are its manifestations, both are integrally related. The faith should lead to good action otherwise it lacks commitment. Conversely those performing good actions are expected to have faith. In Sūrah al-Balad after description of such deeds as the freeing of slaves, feeding the poor and helping orphans and the down-trodden it is said: "*Then he became one of those who believed and enjoined patience and enjoined deeds of kindness and compassion*" (al-Balad 90: 17).

'Amal is used in conjunction with bad deeds (*Sayyi'āt*, sing. *Sayyi'ah*) as well (al-Qaṣaṣ 28: 84 and Ghāfir 40: 40). It should be noted that both the good and evil deeds are being recorded (al-Infiṭār 82: 11–12) and on the Day of Judgement a person will be rewarded or punished according to his deeds (al-Zalzalah 99: 6–8). Whereas the minimum reward of a good deed is tenfold (al-An'ām 6: 160) "*the doers of evil are only punished (to the extent) of their deeds*" (al-Qaṣaṣ 28: 84).

The Qur'ān mentions many attributes of *Ṣāliḥīn* (those who do good deeds) as well as specific statements about such deeds. The most comprehensive narration in this respect is in verse 177 of Sūrah al-Baqarah. Some major evil deeds are mentioned in Sūrah al-Isrā' 17: 23–38.

Synonym

Fi'l also means activity, action and performance. Unlike *'amal* which is a conscious act, *fi'l* can be done without knowledge and intention. Thus this word is usually attributed to acts done by animals. However, it is also used in the Qur'ān for good or bad human actions (al-Baqarah 2: 197; al-Nisā' 4: 30 and al-Mā'idah 5: 67).

References

'Amal: 3: 195; 5: 90; 11: 46; 25: 23; 35: 10. *Fi'l*: 7: 155; 16: 33 and 35; 21: 59; 89: 6.

Amānah [أمانة] (Trust)

Meaning

The root of *Amānah* is *AMN* meaning to be faithful, reliable and trustworthy. It is usually used when dealing with people and implies delivering to them whatever they have entrusted to others. It means honesty in everyday transactions and fulfilling one's obligations as instructed in Sūrah al-Baqarah 2: 283 and Sūrah al-Anfāl 8: 27. This noble quality is one of the characteristics of true believers (al-Mu'minūn 23: 8 and al-Ma'ārij 70: 32).

Analysis

As a keyword *amānah* is not just limited to mutual dealings but covers a very wide spectrum. The instruction in Sūrah al-Nisā' is: "*Allah commands you to render back your trusts to those to whom they are due*" (4: 58). Here *amānah* implies an office of trust (i.e. religious, communal and political leadership). This responsibility should not be given to immoral, incompetent and corrupt people. Important and responsible office should be entrusted only to those who are capable of undertaking the burdens of such positions. The use of the word *amānah* for official responsibilities conveys the concept that these are entrusted by Allah and it is to Him people will be accountable as well. The word *amānah* for the offices of responsibility is also used in *aḥādīth*. When the Prophet (peace be upon him) was asked when would be the Day of Judgement? He replied: "When *amānah* will be destroyed." He was asked, "What is meant by the destruction of *amānah*?" He said: "When the affairs (of government) are entrusted to incompetent people." This means that giving political leadership and authority to the incapable, or immoral, untrustworthy and impious people leads to the downfall and destruction of civil society.

The use of the word *amānah* is similar in Sūrah al-Aḥzāb: "*We did indeed offer the trust to the Heavens and the Earth and the Mountains but they refused to undertake it being afraid thereof. But man undertook it; he was indeed unjust and foolish*" (al-Aḥzāb 33: 72). Here the concept of *amānah* is the role of being a trustee or vicegerent of Allah which requires free-will and the ability to obey or disobey. This undertaking given to man is an *amānah* and it requires people to fulfil their obligations and be accountable to Allah in the Hereafter. To emphasize the gravity of such an undertaking Allah has shown that the heavens and the earth as well as the grand mountains declined to accept this challenge because it is a trial they found themselves incapable of doing justice to. Of course, we cannot understand the mode of their refusal or maybe this is narrated in the form of a parable. Having accepted this role of *Khilāfah* (vicegerent), man should be mindful of this *amānah* otherwise he will be foolhardy.

References

Amānah: 2: 283; 4: 58; 8: 27; 23: 8; 33: 72.

Amr [أمر] (Order, Command)

Meaning

Amr (pl. *Awāmir*) means order, command and instruction. When *Amr* is used for acts of Allah it manifests His supreme inventive power. Allah is the Creator and hence it is He who is Sovereign and His commands are instantaneously executed: "*Our command is but a single (act) like the twinkling of an eye*" (al-Qamar 54: 50) and "*Verily when He intends a thing His Command is 'Be' and it is*" (al-Baqarah 2: 117; Āl 'Imrān 3: 47 and Yā Sīn 36: 82). All the creations in the universe are under Allah's command as He is the Creator. It is He who should govern (al-A'rāf 7: 54). Some of Allah's commands are carried out by angels, particularly Jibrīl who is designated as *al-Rūḥ* and *Amr* (al-Isrā' 17: 85); his descent on the Night of Power (*Laylat al-Qadr*) with Allah's command is recorded in Sūrah al-Qadr 97: 4.

Amr is also used in the legal sense for an ordinance or decree as well as the sovereign power exercised by a government. Although obedience to Allah and His Messenger (peace be upon him) is paramount, people are also required to obey the commands of those who are in authority – *Ulū al-Amr* (al-Nisā' 4: 59). Hence, legislation or a code of law is a collection of *al-Awāmir wa al-Nawāhī* (commands and interdictions).

See also *Ḥukm*

al-Amr bi al-Maʿrūf wa al-Nahy ʿan al-Munkar **(Enjoining Good and Forbidding Evil)**

This is one of the most important injunctions imposed on an individual Muslim as well as the Muslim *Ummah* as a whole. Its importance can be gauged by the fact that it is repeated at least nine times in the Qur'ān.

MAʿRŪF

*Maʿrūf*s root is *ʿRF*, to know, to recognize to perceive. Hence *Maʿrūf* is something that is well-known, universally recognized and generally accepted. In Qur'ānic terminology it means all good deeds that human beings recognize as wholesome and desirable: for example, helping the poor and destitute, widows and orphans, the sick and infirm, or establishing peace and harmony in society. Muslims are ordered that they should actively get involved in the social betterment of the society in which they live.

MUNKAR

The opposite of *Maʿrūf* is *Munkar*. Its root is *NKR* which means not to know, to have no knowledge, to deny. Hence *Munkar* means disagreeable, objectionable and detestable acts which human beings abhor. Such acts are abusing others, wrongful acts, misappropriation, pride, miserliness and shameful and lewd acts. Such acts and behaviour should be checked and stopped. If one is not in a position to stop such an act physically then one should verbally condemn it and if even this is not possible then at least feel abhorrence in one's heart. This, according to a *ḥadīth*, is the lowest degree of *īmān*. (Muslim)

References

Amr: 2: 117; 3: 47; 7: 54; 36: 82; 54: 50. *al-Amr bi al-Maʿrūf wa al-Nahy ʿan al-Munkar*: 3: 104 and 114; 7: 157; 9: 67 and 71.

Anfāl [أنفال] (Spoils of War)

Meaning

Anfāl, the plural of *Nafl*, is specifically used for the booty or spoils of war. (Another word, *Nafl* or *Nāfilah* (pl. *Nawāfil*), means to do more than is required by one's duty or obligation and it is used for supererogatory performance of *'Ibādah* like in prayers, fasting and charity by the believers for the sake of Allah.)

It is instructive to note that after the Battle of Badr, when for the first time questions arose about the distribution of the spoils, the Qur'ān used the word *Anfāl* instead of *Maghānim* (sing. *Maghnam*). This is another word for the booty and spoils of war and is used elsewhere in the Qur'ān (al-Nisā' 4: 94; al-Fatḥ 48: 15, 19, 20). In Sūrah al-Anfāl its verbal form *ghanimtum* is used (al-Anfāl 8: 41, 69). What is being conveyed is that there is no point wrangling about the spoils of war since it is entirely for Allah to decide about their distribution, as they are a gift from Him. This was a major conceptual reform because the purpose of *jihād fī sabīl Allāh* is not to acquire the spoils.

Distribution of *Anfāl*

Sūrah al-Anfāl (8: 41) lays down the law for distribution of the spoils. All spoils collected by soldiers should be banked with the commander or ruler. One-fifth of the spoils belong to Allah and His Messenger and his relatives, the orphans, the needy and the wayfarer. The other four-fifths is to be distributed among the soldiers taking part in the fighting.

The basic purpose of the share of Allah and His Messenger (peace be upon him) is for promoting Islamic teachings and religion. As the Prophet (peace be upon him), being the Head of State, received no remuneration to support him and his family, this share was for their sustenance.

Distribution of *Fay'*

The spoils that are obtained without warfare are called *Fay'*. The Qur'ān uses its verbal form *Afā'a* as in al-Ḥashr 59: 6–7. It literally means "one that has come back (or returned) on its own". In *Fay'* there is no share for the soldiers as no combat took place. After the expulsion of the Jewish settlements around Madīnah the spoils thus acquired were termed *Fay'* and its distribution is laid down in Sūrah al-Ḥashr: "*What Allah has bestowed on His Messenger (and taken away) from the people of the townships belongs to Allah, to His Messenger and to kindred and orphans, the needy and the wayfarer*" (al-Ḥashr 59: 7). No specific shares of the beneficiaries are fixed. These depend on the prevailing circumstances and were left for the Head of State to decide.

References

Anfāl: 8: 1. *Maghānim*: 4: 94; 8: 41 and 69; 48: 15, 19 and 20. *Fay'*: 59: 6 and 7.

'Arsh [عرش]

see *Istiwā'*

'Aṣr [عصر]

see *Ajal*

Āyah [آية] (Sign)

Meanings

The word *āyah* (pl. *āyāt*) has many meanings such as: sign, token, mark, miracle, wonder, marvel, prodigy, model, example and paragon. Hence, the word *āyah* is used in different meanings in the Qur'ān. Its wide usage can be gauged by the fact that *Āyah* and its derivatives occur 385 times in the Qur'ān.

Usage

A. VERSES OF THE REVEALED BOOK

As a keyword, *āyah* is often used for the Qur'ānic verses. The reason is that each verse is (a sign from Allah establishing) the Qur'ān's divine origin. People are urged to reflect on the Qur'ānic verses to attain insight.

"*A Messenger who rehearses to you the* āyāt *of Allah containing clear explanations, that he may lead forth those who believe and do righteous deeds from the depth of darkness into light*" (al-Ṭalāq 65: 11). One of the tasks of Allah's Messenger was to recite to the people Qur'ānic verses. "*Allah did confer a great favour on the believers when He sent among them a Messenger from among themselves reciting unto them the* āyāt *of Allah, purifying them and teaching them the Book and wisdom, while before that they had been in manifest error*" (Āl 'Imrān 3: 164). This verse occurs twice in Sūrah al-Baqarah (2: 129 and 151) and also in Sūrah al-Jumu'ah (62: 2).

B. PROOF AND EVIDENCE

The other extensive use of the word *āyah* is for providing proof and evidence of the existence of a Creator and of the inevitability of the Hereafter. For this purpose, the entire universe and the creation including man himself are used as signs confirming and vindicating these truths and realities. "*Behold! In the creation of the heavens and the earth, and alternation of night and day, there are signs for persons of understanding*" (Āl 'Imrān 3: 190). Looking at the universe one observes that it is continuously changing. Whatever changes cannot be permanent thus the universe will not last for ever. In Sūrah al-Naḥl (16: 11–13) the following are mentioned as signs for those who reflect and possess wisdom: corn, olives, date palms, grapes, fruits, night and day, the sun, the moon and the stars, and things of varying colours on this earth. Similarly in Sūrah al-Rūm (30: 20–23) the following are mentioned as Allah's signs: the creation of man from dust, the creation of his mate and of mutual love, the creation of heaven and earth, the variations of human languages and colours, as well as sleep during the night and the quest for Allah's bounty during the day. All these signs are reminders that prove Allah's existence and His benevolence towards human beings.

Man is also reminded to reflect on himself as there are Allah's signs therein. "*Soon will We show them Our signs in the universe in their own selves until it becomes manifest to them that this is the truth*" (Fuṣṣilat 41: 53).

C. MIRACLES

The miracles shown to people or performed by the prophets are termed *Āyah*. For example: the birth of the Prophet ʿĪsā (Maryam 19: 21); the camel sent to the Thamūd people (al-Aʿrāf 7: 73); the nine clear signs given to the Prophet Mūsā (al-Isrā' 17: 101); the saving of the drowned body of Pharaoh (Yūnus 10: 92) and many other miracles performed by other prophets.

See also *Muʿjizah*

D. SIGNS AND INDICATIONS

The word *āyah* is used for the specific sign or indication given about the occurrence of a future event; for example the Prophet Zakarīyā (peace be upon him) was reassured by a sign that a son would be born to him in his old age (Maryam 19: 10). Similarly the defeat of the Quraysh in the Battle of Badr, paving the way for the triumph of Islam, was termed as an *Āyah* (Āl ʿImrān 3: 13).

Muḥkamāt and *Mutashābihāt*

There are two types of Qur'ānic verses: those that are clear in their meanings and those that are ambiguous. "*He it is Who has sent down to you the Book; in it are verses basic and fundamental (of established meaning); they are the foundation of the Book; others are not of well-established meaning*" (Āl ʿImrān 3: 7). This of course does not mean that all verses fall into these two types only; these two kinds of verses are in contradistinction to each other. The *muḥkamāt*, basic or fundamental, verses are the foundation of the Book. Then, there are other verses called *mutashābihāt*, allegorical or ambiguous, whose meanings are not well established, as they relate to the things that cannot be perceived by human beings. No one can fathom their real meaning except Allah. However, we are required to believe in all of them.

Those whose hearts are perverse turn their backs on the facts clearly stated in the Qur'ān. Instead, they try to unravel those verses that are ambiguous by ascribing to them their own meanings. Often they search the enigmatic verses for hidden meanings. On the contrary, those people who are firmly rooted in knowledge and purity of heart, in order to receive guidance concentrate on those verses that are clear and unambiguous. Many sects that developed in the past and still exist today base their religion on *Bāṭin,* hidden meanings, with the result that they lead themselves and others astray into misguidance.

References

Āyah: 2: 129; 3: 190; 16: 11; 30: 20; 41: 53; 65: 11.

'Azm [عزم]

see *Irādah*

Baghy [بغي] (Rebellion)

Meaning

Baghā means to surpass, to outrage and to transgress; hence *Baghy*, from this root, means oppression, unjust and rebellious acts. Instead of adopting a path of moderation one resorts to infringing others rights' by unlawful acts. Ḥāfiẓ Ibn al-Qayyim says that *baghy* usually refers to usurping the rights of fellow human beings.

Analysis

According to Imām al-Rāghib al-Iṣfahānī, because its original meaning is to surpass, *Baghy* can be of two types. One, which is praiseworthy, is where someone does more than is required of him in good deeds: for example, someone not only does justice but tries to reach the status of *Iḥsān* or in addition to obligatory prayers performs *nawāfil.* However, the word is never used in this sense. The other type of *baghy* relates to oppression and transgression by insurrection and rebellion. In the Qur'ān the word is used in its latter meaning. Whenever *baghy* is used to mean rebellion it is always used with the preposition *'alā.*

The derivates of the word *baghy* are used in Sūrah al-Ḥujurāt for the rebellion and transgression by one group of Muslims after a peace pact was procured between the two factions of Muslims. The instruction given is "*but if one of them transgresses beyond bounds against the other, fight the one that transgresses until it complies with Allah's command*" (al-Ḥujurāt 49: 9).

Baghy means a whore or prostitute because they overstep the limit of chastity; the word is used in this sense in Sūrah Maryam: "*O sister of Hārūn! Your father was not an evil man nor was your mother an unchaste woman*" (Maryam 19: 28).

References

Baghy: 7: 33; 16: 90; 42: 37; 49: 9.

Balā' [بلاء]

see *Fitnah*

Barakah [بركة] (Blessing)

Meanings

Barakah means to kneel down or to make a camel kneel down so that it is firmly in place. The word's other meaning is to bless or to invoke blessing. In this latter meaning *barakah* and its derivatives are used 32 times in the Qur'ān, either as a noun or as a verb. In the Qur'ān this word is overwhelmingly used for spiritual and immaterial prosperity. The following five meanings are narrated by eminent lexicographers:

a. Growth, increase and advancement, especially in crops and cultivation (al-A'rāf 7: 96)
b. Dignity, exaltation and high status
c. Permanence and continuity of blessings, as in Sūrah Hūd 11: 73 for household of the Prophet Ibrāhīm (peace be upon him)
d. The increase and upsurge in goodness and benevolence (al-Isrā' 17: 1)
e. Auspiciousness and prosperity.

Words from the Same Root

Barakāt, the plural of *Barakah*, is widely used to denote that something is endowed with Allah's blessings. "*If the people of the towns had but believed and feared Allah, We would indeed have opened out to them (all kinds of) blessings*" (al-Aʿrāf 7: 96). It is also used for the tidings of grace and blessings given by angels to the household of the Prophet Ibrāhīm (peace be upon him) (Hūd 11: 73). This prayer of blessing for the Prophet (peace be upon him) is recited in *Tashahhud* and *Ṣalāt*.

The word *Bāraknā* (We have blessed) is used to convey the meaning that Allah, the Almighty, has showered His benediction on *Bayt al-Maqdis* and its precincts and consecrated it (al-Isrā' 17: 1). This word is used in several other *sūrahs* in this meaning.

Mubārak means a thing that is full of blessings and goodness. The Qur'ān is called *Mubārak* in several verses so is *Laylat al-Qadr*. This indicates that all five meanings mentioned above are embodied in this blessed Book and night.

The blessings from Allah are not perceivable and cannot be felt. They are manifested by different means, such as an increase in goodness. This is called *Barakah* (pl. *Barakāt*).

Tabāraka denotes that Allah is the Blessed One and He is the one Who bestows benediction and goodness (al-Mulk 67: 1; al-Furqān 25: 1, 10 and 61 and many other places as well).

References

Barakah: 7: 137; 17: 1; 25: 61; 41: 10; 67: 1.

Barzakh [برزخ] (Barrier)

Meaning

According to Imām al-Rāghib, the word *barzakh* came into Arabic from the Persian word *pardah* (barzah) which mean a barrier. The literal meaning of *Barzakh* is interval, gap, break, as well as partition, barrier or obstruction. It is used in the sense of barrier in Sūrah al-Raḥmān:

"*The two bodies of flowing water meeting together: between them is a barrier which they do not transgress.*" (al-Raḥmān 55: 19–20); there is a similar reference in Sūrah al-Furqān (25: 53).

As a key concept the word *barzakh* means an interval or a break between individual death and resurrection. At present there is a barrier between the deceased and the living. This barrier prevents the dead returning to this world; thus they will stay on the other side of it until the Day of Judgement (al-Mu'minūn 23: 100).

Analysis

According to the Qur'ān and *aḥādīth*, the period of stay in the *barzakh* will give the foretaste of the things to follow. Conversations between the angels and the person approaching death as recorded in the Qur'ān give a vivid description of what happens in *barzakh* (al-Naḥl 16: 28–29). Those who went through their lives in transgression and wrongdoing will face torments in *barzakh*. We are told "*The people of the Pharaoh are exposed to fire every morning and evening*" (Ghāfir 40: 46). In contrast those who lived and died for the cause of truth, like the person mentioned in Sūrah Yā Sīn who was martyred while he was pleading with his people to obey the Prophets, will be rewarded and honoured (36: 26). The pleasure and pain which one will experience in *barzakh* will be real in the sense that one will feel in full consciousness.

References

Barzakh: 23: 100; 25: 53; 55: 20.

Bāṭil [باطل] (Falsehood)

Meanings

The root of *Bāṭil* is *BṬL* meaning to be or to become null and void, invalid, false, vain, futile, ineffective, worthless and obsolete. Hence *Bāṭil* means something baseless, a lie, falsehood or deception. Its opposite is *Ḥaqq* which means truth, correctness and rightness.

The word *bāṭil* is used with several different shades of meaning in the Qur'ān:

a. Falsehood as against truth (al-Baqarah 2: 42; Āl 'Imrān 3: 71)
b. Illegal acts such as the misappropriation of goods and property belonging to others (al-Baqarah 2: 188; al-Nisā' 4: 29 and 161; al-Tawbah 9: 34)
c. False deities whom some people believe in and invoke for help (al-'Ankabūt 29: 52 and 67; Luqmān 31: 30)
d. Worthless and futile religion which is destined to be destroyed and annihilated by the force of truth (al-Isrā' 17: 81; Sabā' 34: 49)
e. Purposeless and fruitless exercise (Āl 'Imrān 3: 196; Ṣād 38: 27).

Analysis

There are forces of evil that try to overcome the truth by misleading people and alluring them to falsehood and untruth. These can assume the forms of gods and goddesses or false ideologies or ways of life. The Qur'ān emphasizes that falsehood cannot succeed against the truth. Allah will make the truth triumph over falsehood "*as falsehood by its nature is bound to perish*" (al-Isrā' 17: 81). It may be possible for truth to be suppressed for a time and falsehood may seem to be prevailing but this would be a temporary situation as truth will always come back and restore the balance whereas falsehood is bound to perish.

The other thing to note is that the pure falsehood will never succeed and hence falsehood carries with it some grains of truth to enable it to prevail for a short time. There are many systems and isms prevalent in the world; despite their defective and false premises they prevail as they include some elements of goodness. But in the end they are destroyed as the Qur'ān says: "*Nay, We hurl the Truth against falsehood, and it knocks out its brain, and behold, falsehood does perish*" (al-Anbiyā' 21: 18).

References

Bāṭil: 2: 42; 9: 34; 31: 30; 34: 49; 38: 27.

See also *Ḥaqq*

Bay'ah [بيعة] (Oath of Allegiance, Pledge)

Meaning

Bay'ah is from *Bā'a* which means to sell or to make a contract. It is used commonly together with *Shirā'*, which means to purchase or to buy. In these senses the words *Bay'ah* and *Shirā'* are used in several places in the Qur'ān. From its use for a commercial transaction the word *Bay'ah* also means an agreement, contract, commercial transaction, bargain or business deal. Nowadays this word is also used in the special meaning of taking an oath of allegiance or pledging loyalty. There are a few instances in the Qur'ān where *bay'ah* is used in this sense.

The *Bay'at al-Riḍwān*

The most well known is the *Bay'at al-Riḍwān*. This pledge was made during the Treaty of Ḥudaybīyah with the Makkans. It was rumoured that 'Uthmān ibn 'Affān, the envoy of the Prophet, (peace be upon him) was killed by the Makkans. This *Bay'ah* was made by the Companions each placing a hand upon the hand of the Prophet and pledging that they were ready to lay down their lives in any encounter with the Makkans. This pledge in fact was with Allah as the Messenger is Allah's representative. The Companions' act of loyalty and bravery was praised in the Qur'ān (al-Fatḥ 48: 10 and 18).

The *Bay'ah* taken from the Immigrant Women

This is a pledge that the Prophet (peace be upon him) was asked to take from the women who migrated from Makkah (then a pagan society) to the Muslim society of Madīnah. They were required to make six specific undertakings as mentioned in Sūrah al-Mumtaḥinah (60: 12).

The *Bay'at al-'Aqabah al-Ūlā wa al-Thāniyah*

These two *bay'ah* were taken in the 10 and 11 Nabawī (year of Prophethood) from the delegation of the people who came from Yathrib (later renamed Madīnah) and accepted Islam on the invitation of the Prophet (peace be upon him). Their pledge was that they would defend the Prophet and Muslims as their own kinfolk and provide them refuge in Yathrib. This *bay'ah* was taken in two succeeding years from the delegations from

Yathrib at a place outside Makkah in the Valley of 'Aqabah. Thus, they were named the *Ūlā* (first) and *Thāniyah* (second) *Bay'ah*. The details of these *bay'ah* are to found in the books of *Sīrah*.

The *Bay'ah* to the *Khalīfah*

In *aḥādīth, Sīrah* and history books, there is mention of another kind of *bay'ah*, a pledge that is given to a *khalīfah*. This is purely to accept the political authority of the *khalīfah*. As there was no system of electing a head of state, when a *Khalīfah* was appointed in consultation with the tribal chiefs and persons of integrity, a *bay'ah* taken on his hand was a symbolic act of allegiance that legitimized his rule. This *bay'ah* cannot be compared with *bay'ah* given to the Prophet (peace be upon him).

Bay'ah to a *Pīr* or a *Murshid*

This *bay'ah*, prevalent among some Muslims, is based on the juridical rule of analogy (*qiyās*). This is a *Bay'ah* of obedience to the *Murshid* or *Pīr* (spiritual guide) for following the teachings of Islam. Similar *Bay'ah* is also given to the *Amīr* (head) of some Islamic organizations. These are based on the analogical precedents as the Prophet (peace be upon him) often took *Bay'ah* of obedience from his Companions.

References

Bay'ah: 9: 111; 48: 10 and 18; 60: 12.

Bid'ah [بدعة] (Innovation)

Meaning

Bada'a means to invent, to originate, to create or to bring into existence. Thus, the word *Badī'* is used as one of the attributes of Allah, the Creator of Heavens and Earth (al-Baqarah 2: 117; al-An'ām 6: 101).

From this root the word *bid'ah* is derived. It means inventing something novel in religion, which is neither consonant with the rules of *Sharī'ah* nor practised by the Prophet (peace be upon him) or his Companions. In this sense *Bid'ah* comes to mean a blameworthy innovation and heresy.

Analysis

The term *Bid'ah* is attributed only to those acts of *'Ibādah* which have no basis in the Qur'ān or the *Sunnah*. These may have been introduced under the false assumption that they would gain Allah's pleasure. The implication of *Bid'ah* is serious: that Islam was incomplete and thus a new addition was needed.

In Sūrah al-Ḥadīd Allah criticized the introduction of monasticism by Christians, although this was invented to seek Allah's pleasure by devoting oneself completely to His worship. "*But the monasticism which they invented for themselves, We did not prescribe for them*" (al-Ḥadīd 57: 27). As celibacy and monasticism are against human nature, the Christians were not able to observe them as it ought to be observed. This practice led many into moral corruption. Human beings are required to establish Allah's *Dīn* which needs courage, resistance to evil, firmness and discipline. It is only by such deeds that justice can prevail. Retiring into seclusion does not solve human problems.

In Muslim society *Bid'ah* came in the form of pseudo-Sufism. The establishment of monasteries (*Khānqāh*) promoted seclusion, meditation, austerity and abstinence. The Prophet (peace be upon him) has said: "The evil deeds are innovations and every *bid'ah* (new thing) is spurious and misguided" (Muslim). In another *ḥadīth* the Prophet is reported to have said: "He who innovates something in this matter of ours [i.e. *Dīn*] that is not of it will have it rejected" (Bukhārī).

Reference

Bid'ah: 57: 27.

Birr [بِرّ] (Righteousness)

Meanings

Barra means to be reverent, to be dutiful, and to be kind or devoted. *Birr* means reverence, obedience or righteousness. The word *Birr* is used for fulfilling a promise, loyalty and discharging the rights of others. The word "rights" is used here in a very wide sense and includes the rights of

Allah as well as those of parents and also the rights and obligations one incurs from entering into a contract or transaction.

Usage

A very important verse called *Āyat al-Birr* (al-Baqarah 2: 177) defines the concept of *Birr* very well. It is a comprehensive term embracing all the basic beliefs as well as the acts of worship and obedience. The verse starts thus: "*It is not* al-birr *that you turn your faces towards east or west (in prayers)*". It then enumerates all the beliefs followed by the rights of kinfolk and of the disadvantaged people in society. Then specific acts of worship – *ṣalāh* and *zakāh* – are mentioned followed by a long list of obligations which is concluded by reminding the believer of the importance of fulfilling one's covenants and of remaining patient (*ṣābir*) in times of extreme poverty, sickness and during wars. The Qur'ānic verdict on those who are endowed with these virtues, is that they are really truthful and pious people.

Birr is often used in conjunction with *taqwā*, a fact that indicates their close relationship; their opposites are *ithm* (sin) and *'udwān* (transgression). "*You help one another in* al-birr *(virtue, piety) and* al-taqwā *(righteousness, God-consciousness) but help you not in* al-ithm *(sin) and* al-'Udwān *(transgression)*" (al-Mā'idah 5: 2). This explains that *birr* covers all acts of righteousness and good deeds but in its specific meaning it requires fulfilling one's responsibilities and obligations as sanctioned by the *sharī'ah*.

The phrase *birr bi wālidayihi* means that one is obedient to one's parents as opposed to being unruly. It is said about the Prophet Yaḥyā (peace be upon him): "*He was devout and kind to his parents and he was not overbearing or rebellious*" (Maryam 19: 13–14).

The attainment of obedience to Allah demands purity of intention and willingness to spend and give in His way what one covets most. In Sūrah Āl 'Imrān it is specifically mentioned that: "*By no means shall you attain righteousness* (al-birr) *unless you give (freely) of that which you love most*" (Āl 'Imrān 3: 92). As the wording is very general it could include everything – one's life, time, skills and talents as well as possessions.

Al-Birr is one of the Most Beautiful Names (*al-Asmā' al-Ḥusnā*) of Allah. This means that Allah fulfills all His promises and gives rewards as well. Thus, in Sūrah al-Ṭūr it is said: "*Truly it is He Who is* al-Barr *and* al-Raḥīm." (al-Ṭūr 52: 28).

Other Words from this Root

Barr and *Bārr* (pl. *Abrār* and *Bararah*). *Abrār* is used in the Qur'ān to mean righteous and pious beings (Āl 'Imrān 3: 193 and 198; al-Insān 76: 5; al-Infiṭār 82: 13; al-Muṭaffifīn 83: 18 and 22).

Bararah is used in the sense of reverent and dutiful. In Sūrah 'Abasa the attributes 'pious' and 'just' are used of the honourable scribes (angels) ('Abasa 80: 16)

References

Birr: 2: 117; 3: 92; 5: 2; 19: 14; 52: 28.

Bukhl [بخل]

see *Infāq*

Dahr [دهر]

see *Ajal*

Ḍalāl, Ḍalālah [ضلال، ضلالة]

(Deviation, Error)

Meaning

Ḍalāl, Ḍalālah are the opposite of *Hudā* and *Hidāyah*. *Ḍalla* means to lose one's way, to go astray, to deviate from the straight path. Therefore *Ḍalālah* is the opposite of *Hidāyah* (guidance) and means misguidance. It embraces all aspects of straying from the right path whether intentionally or by mistake or ignorance.

Iḍlāl, from the same root, means misguiding, deceiving and misleading. In many verses in the Qur'ān it is mentioned that Allah guides whoever He likes and misguides whoever He wants:

> *Such is the guidance of Allah: He guides therewith whom He pleases, but such as Allah leaves to stray, can have none to guide.*
> (al-Zumar 39: 23)

But this is not an arbitrary act on the part of Allah. As all acts of Allah are based on justice and fairness those who are misguided are responsible for their own misguidance. This is explained in many places in the Qur'ān. Those who are prone to evil render themselves incapable of benefiting from Divine Guidance:

> *Those who believe know that it is truth from their Lord; but those who reject faith say: 'What means Allah by this similitude?' By it He causes many to stray and many He leads into the right path; but He causes not to stray except those who forsake (the path).*
> (al-Baqarah 2: 26)

> *Allah will establish in strength those who believe, with the Word that stands firm, in this world and in the Hereafter; but Allah will leave, to stray, those who do wrong. Allah does what He wills.*
> (Ibrāhīm 14: 27)

> *Thus Allah leaves the unbelievers to stray.*
> (al-Mu'min 40: 74)

From the above verses it is clear that *Fāsiq* (sinner), *Ẓālim* (oppressor) and *Kāfir* (non-believer) are led astray because of their rejection of the Path of Righteousness. In the Holy Qur'ān mention is also made of Christians who strayed from the Right Path:

> *Say: "O People of the Book! Exceed not in your religion the bounds (of what is proper), trespassing beyond the truth, nor follow the*

vain desires of people who went wrong in times gone by – who misled many, and strayed (themselves) from the even Way.”
(al-Māʾidah 5: 77)

References

Ḍalālah: 1: 7; 3: 164; 40: 25; 42: 18; 67: 9.

Ḍarar [ضرر]

see *Iḍṭirār*

Daʿwah [دعوة] (Invitation)

Meaning

Daʿwah is derived from *Daʿā* which means to call or to invite. Hence *Daʿwah* means invitation. This invitation could be *daʿwah ilā al-khayr* (calling people towards good) which is performed by all the prophets (Nūḥ 71: 5), or it could be insinuation by Satan to allure people to his way (Ibrāhīm 14: 22).

Analysis

The prophets throughout the ages performed the duty of calling people towards Allah's way. As the Prophet Muḥammad (peace be upon him) was the last prophet, this duty was transferred to the Muslim *Ummah*. “*You are the best of people, evolved for mankind, enjoining what is right, forbidding what is wrong and believing in Allah*” (Āl ʿImrān 3: 110).

The Qur'ān has provided the methodology of *daʿwah* by giving the basic guidance. The first duty is to invite oneself to surrender to the will of Allah as explained in the following verse: “*Who is better in speech than one who calls (others) to Allah, works righteousness, and says: ‘I am of those who bow to Islam’*” (Fuṣṣilat 41: 33). The second is to invite the whole society to live in submission to the will of Allah. These two processes continue simultaneously.

The other comprehensive advice is given in Sūrah al-Naḥl: "*Invite (all) to the Way of your Lord with wisdom and beautiful preaching; and reason with them in the best and most gracious manner possible*" (al-Naḥl 16: 125). Thus, one has to know the psychology of the addressees. It is essential to respect their feelings and avoid hurting their dear and emotional attachments. One should choose the appropriate time and place to present the message. Of course the message has to be varied according to the competence of the addressees. If people are getting bored one should stop. If someone argues, one should not try to win the argument thus humiliating him. One can win the hearts of people by not retaliating and by continuing to be patient (Fuṣṣilat 41: 34–35).

Da'wah is a long and tiring process. One cannot achieve success very quickly. It needs a lot of patience and perseverance. Even then it may not bring any result. People often give up in despair, but one should realize that one's responsibility is only to convey and explain the message, one cannot change people's hearts if they do not want to change themselves. It is only Allah who can give guidance to whom He wishes, provided one who seeks guidance is sincere only then he will be guided. The Prophet Nūḥ (peace be upon him) preached for 950 years yet his wife and one of his sons did not accept Islam. Similarly the father of Ibrāhīm, the wife of Lūṭ, and Abū Ṭālib, uncle of the Prophet, died without accepting Islam.

References

Da'wah: 12: 108; 14: 22; 16: 125; 41: 33; 71: 5.

See also *al-Indhār wa al-Tabshīr*

Dhikr [ذِكر] (Remembrance)

Meaning

The word *Dhikr* (pl. *Adhkār*) comes from *dhakara* which means to remember, to recall and to recollect. Hence *dhikr* means remembrance, recollection, reminiscence and memory. It is an important term in the Qur'ān, signifying remembrance of Allah.

Analysis

Dhikr has to be at three levels. First, the seat of *Dhikr* is *Qalb* (heart). One should be conscious of the presence of Allah as much as possible: as the Qur'ān reminds us: "*Be not among those who are forgetful*" (al-A'rāf 7: 205).

Second, we should recite His praise and His glory with our tongues. This *Dhikr* should be with humility and reverence, without loudness of voice whether sitting, standing or laying down on our sides in the mornings or evenings, day or night (Āl 'Imrān 3: 191). All other acts of *'Ibādah* are quantified, for example the times of Prayers, the days of fasting or the amount to be paid in *Zakāh*. But for *Dhikr*, Allah has set no limits. In several places in the Qur'ān, believers are exhorted to do *Dhikr* as much as possible (al-Aḥzāb 33: 41; al-Jumu'ah 62: 10). It is the attribute of the hypocrites that they do not remember Allah and they pray without sincerity of heart.

Finally, when the word *Dhikr* is mentioned, the imagery of someone rolling his fingers on *Tasbīḥ* comes to mind. But according to the Qur'ān, one's whole life should be full of *Dhikr*. The *Dhikr* should be integrated into one's activities. This *Dhikr* should be with *Fikr* (reflection) as the *āyah* of the Qur'ān expounds: "*People who remember Allah, standing, sitting, and lying down on their sides and contemplate the creation in the heavens and the earth*" (Āl 'Imrān 3: 191). Of course the best form of *Dhikr* is *Ṣalāh* (Prayer). As the purpose of Prayer is to remember Allah, the Holy Qur'ān says: "*Establish* Ṣalāh *for My remembrance*" (Ṭā Hā 20: 14). Thus, *Dhikr* should be integrated within our everyday activity. Remembrance of *Ākhirah* is also part of the *Dhikr* of Allah. *Dhikr* is only fruitful when one assimilates it with one's concern about one's accountability in the *Ākhirah*. The best way to remember *Ākhirah* is to remember death which one sees every day.

Unwitting forgetfulness is a basic human weakness and the *Dhikr* and *Ṣalāh* are the reminders to cure this weakness. There are many *Adhkār* prescribed throughout day and night to remind one of Allah and His bounties.

The Qur'ān itself is referred to as *al-Dhikr al-Ḥakīm* (Āl 'Imrān 3: 58) and in many verses it is called *Dhikr* (al-Anbiyā' 21: 50; Ṣād 38: 49 and 87;

al-Qalam 68: 52). The Qur'ān is *Dhikr* as it reminds us of our covenant with Allah for His worship and obedience as well as of our responsibility in this world.

Words from the Same Root

Tadhkirah, *Tadhkīr* and *Dhikrā* are synonyms of *Dhikr*. They also mean reminder and remembrance. *Dhākir* is the person who engages himself in the *Dhikr*.

References

Dhikr: 3: 41; 33: 21; 62: 10; 73: 8; 87: 15.

Dīn [دين]

Meanings

The word *dīn* is derived from *dāna*, meaning to be recompensed, judged and obeyed. It also means to profess or to follow a pattern. The word *dīn* is used in four different ways in the Qur'ān:

a. Judgement, recompense, appraisal
b. Worship and obedience
c. Law, Constitution
d. System of beliefs, code of life of which religion is a part

As happens in all languages, a word can have several meanings but the context in which it is used defines its exact import. The same is the case with *dīn*.

A. When *dīn* is used in combination with *Yawm* (Day) as in *Yawm al-Dīn*, it is translated as the Day of Judgement or the Day of Reckoning. This refers to *Ākhirah* (the Hereafter) when people will be brought before their Lord and He will dispense justice according to their deeds in this world. This Day is graphically portrayed in Sūrah al-Infiṭār:

> *And what will convey unto you what the Day of Judgement is? Again, what will convey unto you what the Day of Judgement is? A Day on which no soul has power at all for any (other) soul. The (absolute) command on that Day is Allah's.*
>
> (al-Infiṭār 82: 17–19)

B. *Dīn* also conveys the meaning of surrendering sincerely to the Sovereignty of Allah. This is mentioned in several places in the Qur'ān:

> *And they have been commanded no more than this: To worship Allah, offering Him sincere devotion* (Dīn) *being true in faith…*
>
> (al-Bayyinah 98: 5)

> *To Him belongs whatever is in the heavens and on earth. And to Him is the obedience* (Dīn) *due always: then will you fear other than Allah?*
>
> (al-Naḥl 16: 52)

> *Say: "It is Allah I serve with my sincere and exclusive devotion* (Dīn)."
>
> (al-Zumar 39: 14)

C. In some instances in the Qur'ān, *Dīn* is used to denote the law or the constitution of a country. When it refers to the *Sharīʿah*, it is termed as the *Dīn* of Allah. It could also refer to the laws of a country. Thus in Sūrah Yūsuf reference is made to the prevailing Egyptian law:

> *Thus, We planned for Yūsuf. He could not take his brother by the law* (dīn) *of the king except that Allah willed it (so).*
>
> (Yūsuf 12: 76)

In prescribing punishment for adultery, however, the reference is to the *Sharīʿah*:

Flog each of them with a hundred stripes. Let not compassion move you in their case, in a matter prescribed by Allah.

(al-Nūr 24: 2)

D. By far the most common use of the word *dīn* is for a system of beliefs or code of life or religion. However, it should be noted that Allah has not used the word "religion" – a very common word – as this has a very narrow and limited meaning usually referring to rites and rituals, whereas *dīn* is a comprehensive term that embraces all aspects of life. Thus, in Islam, *Dīn* is a keyword and a technical term to denote the whole array of meanings pertaining to the system of beliefs as well as to a complete code of life. Thus, it is not possible to translate this into a single word in other languages.

According to Islamic belief, the only *Dīn* acceptable in the sight of Allah is Islam. This is stated categorically:

This day I have perfected your Dīn *for you and completed My favours upon you, and chosen for you Islam as your* Dīn.

(al-Mā'idah 5: 3)

Dīn *before Allah is Islam* (complete submission to His Will).

(Āl 'Imrān 3: 19)

If anyone desires Dīn *other than Islam, never will it be accepted of him; and in the Hereafter he will be in the ranks of those who have lost (all spiritual goods).*

(Āl 'Imrān 3: 85)

However, no one is forced to accept Islam against his wishes. Human beings have the freedom to choose their own way of life:

There is no compulsion in Dīn.

(al-Baqarah 2: 256)

> *To you be your* Dīn *and to me mine.*
>
> (al-Kāfirūn 109: 6)

The implication of this verse is that there cannot be any compromise between my and your religion.

Analysis

DĪN AS A WAY OF LIFE

In Islamic terminology, *al-Dīn* is that way of life in which Allah is recognised as the Sovereign, the Master and the Lord to whom human beings should surrender, submit, abase and humble themselves. He should be accepted as the Lord of Reward and Punishment in the *Ākhirah*.

Islam is the name of this *Dīn*. This is the only *Dīn* that is acceptable to Allah as the verses quoted above from Sūrah Āl 'Imrān clearly proclaim. Thus, three obligations stand out from the various meanings of *al-Dīn*:

a. to acknowledge Allah as the Lord, the Master and the Ruler;
b. to obey and serve only Him;
c. to be accountable to Him, to fear only His Punishment and to seek only His Pleasure.

Within the meaning of *Dīn*, the obedience to Allah's Messengers is implied. For Allah's commandments are conveyed to human beings through His Books revealed to His Messengers. Thus, when the repentance of Ādam and Ḥawwā' (peace be upon them) was accepted and they were sent down on Earth as a *Khalīfah* (vicegerent), Allah commanded them:

> *Get you down all from here and, if, as is sure, there comes to you Guidance from Me, whosoever follows My guidance, on them shall be no fear, nor shall they grieve.*
>
> (al-Baqarah 2: 38)

The same message is reiterated to human beings in Sūrah al-Aʿrāf:

> *O you Children of Ādam! Whenever there come to you Messengers from amongst you, rehearsing My Signs unto you – those who are righteous and mend (their lives) – on them shall be no fear nor shall they grieve.*
>
> (al-Aʿrāf 7: 35)

Allah has given human beings the freedom of choice either to accept His Guidance or to reject it. This is unlike Allah's other creations, who instinctively obey Him:

> *Do they seek other than the* Dīn *of Allah? – while all creatures in the heavens and on earth have willingly or unwillingly bowed to His Will (accepted Islam), and to Him shall they all be brought back.*
>
> (Āl ʿImrān 3: 83)

DĪN: THE UNIVERSAL WAY OF LIFE FROM THE BEGINNING UNTIL ETERNITY

Dīn has remained the same for human beings throughout history. All Messengers of Allah from Ādam (peace be upon him) to Muḥammad (peace be upon him) conveyed the same Message: "*So fear Allah and obey me.*" This verse is repeated several times in Sūrah al-Shuʿarā' (26: 108). This was the message of all Messengers. However, detailed laws and regulations (*Sharīʿah*) changed as the human race went through the different stages of its history.

THE MEANING OF *SHARĪʿAH*

Sharīʿah literally means a way or a path and more specifically the way to a watering place. In Islamic terminology, it means that after accepting Allah's *Dīn*, the way to be followed, as shown by the Guidance from Him and His Messenger, is the *Sharīʿah*. This is the Path and the Guidance for humankind for its success and salvation in this world and in the Hereafter.

> *To each among you have We prescribed a Way* (Sharī'ah) *and an Open Way.*
>
> (al-Mā'idah 5: 48)

> *Then, We put you on the (right) Way* (Sharī'ah)*: so follow you that (Way) and follow not the desires of those who know not.*
>
> (al-Jāthiyah 45: 18)

Thus, *Sharī'ah* is the Divinely ordained system or code of conduct to guide mankind straight to the Path of Peace in this world and to bliss in the Hereafter. The affairs of this world are viewed by the Lawgiver in the light of the interest of the other world – a better one and everlasting. This is the difference between divine law and human laws that are concerned with the interests of this world alone.

THE DIFFERENCE BETWEEN *DĪN* AND *SHARĪ'AH*

The key difference is that while *Dīn* always was, has been and still is one and the same, many *Sharī'ahs* were revealed. Some were subsequently replaced or altered but there was no change in the *Dīn*. All Prophets and Messengers (peace be upon them all) presented the same *Dīn* but their *Sharī'ah* varied to some extent. For example, the prescribed ways of performing prayers and observing fasts were different under the *Sharī'ah* of earlier Prophets. The rules of cleanliness and codes of marriage, divorce and inheritance were also different. Thus, *Dīn* remained the same throughout whilst the precise details of following it have differed.

References

Dīn: 1: 3; 2: 132; 3: 19; 12: 76; 61: 9. *Sharī'ah*: 5: 48; 42: 13 and 21; 45: 18.

Du'ā' [دعاء] (Supplication)

Meaning

The word *Du'ā'* is derived from *Da'ā* which means to call or to summon. In many verses of the Qur'ān the word *Da'ā* is used in its dictionary meaning (Fuṣṣilat 41: 33; al-Anfāl 8: 24). However, *Du'ā'* (pl. *Ad'iyah*) means invocation of Allah, supplication, request and plea to Him.

Analysis

The Qur'ān has explained the attributes and character as well as *adab* (manners) of making *du'ā'* in a number of places: "*Call on your Lord with humility and in private for Allah loves not who trespass beyond bounds. Do no mischief on the earth after it has been set in order, but call on Him with fear and longing (in your hearts). For the mercy of Allah is (always) near to those who do good*" (al-A'rāf 7: 55–56). In Sūrah al-Isrā' it is said: "*Neither speak your prayer aloud nor speak it in a low tone, but seek a middle course between*" (17: 110).

Du'ā' is the embodiment of one's humility before his Lord. One reposes one's trust and hopes in divine help and mercy, and in this situation of complete submission and surrender, whatever words come from one's heart is *du'ā'*. When this *du'ā'* is accompanied by *'amal ṣāliḥ* (testifying good deeds according to *du'ā'*) and is expressed with utter helplessness and humility it is expected to be responded to by Allah's mercy and forgiveness. On the contrary, making *du'ā'* casually and as a ritual without real commitment is of no avail.

The *Du'ā'* occupies a pivotal position in Islam, as *du'ā'* in fact is a form of *'ibādah* (worship). The Prophet (peace be upon him) said: "*al-Du'ā'* is really *al-'ibādah*" and in another *ḥadīth* he said: "*al-Du'ā'* is the essence of *al-'ibādah*" (Tirmidhī). Muslims are required to make *du'ā'* only to Allah and to seek His help and call upon Him. Most of the rites performed in all our *'ibādah* consists of *du'ā'*. Believers should always seek Allah's help, His *tawfīq* (grant of success), His guidance and mercy to traverse through life.

Some Misconceptions about the *Du'ā'*

There is a common misconception about the *du'ā'*. Many people think that certain specific words uttered are magical in themselves, and that repeating them a certain number of times on certain days, or at specific auspicious times, will bring about the desired result. The other common misconception is that if *du'ā'* does not seem to be accepted in the precise manner as was requested that means it has been rejected by Allah and leads one to get disheartened and despair. This thinking is a reflection of the business mentality, the Prophet (peace be upon him) has given this guidance: "Whoever asks Allah his prayer is always accepted: either he receives the benefit in this world or it is saved for him in the Hereafter or some of his sins are forgiven provided he has not asked for some sinful thing or for severing relationship or for getting quick results" (Tirmidhī). The reason is that it is Allah who knows whether what one has asked for is really suitable for the person; either He will accept what is being asked for, or give one a better result than what was requested, or He will not accept and instead grant one a reward in the Hereafter. Allah Himself has asked us to make *du'ā'* and He promised to answer all who call upon Him. "*I am indeed close (to them): I listen to the prayer of every supplicant when he calls upon Me*" (al-Baqarah 2: 186). Hence, one should be hopeful and keep faith in Allah's mercy.

However, if one's prayers are not answered then one should also scrutinize one's life-style. If one does not fulfil one's obligations imposed by *Sharī'ah* and does not care whether one's earnings are lawful or unlawful then utterance of a few words of prayer will not fulfil the aims of *du'ā'*. This is well illustrated by a *ḥadīth* in which the Prophet (peace be upon him) told of a person who was on a long journey in a dishevelled state and covered in dust, who stretched both his hands towards the sky calling: "O My Lord! O My Lord" while his condition was that his food was unlawful, his drink was unlawful and his dress was unlawful. "He was being nourished by *ḥarām* (unlawful) means. How could his prayer be granted?" (Muslim).

The Auspicious Times for *Du'ā'*

Although *du'ā'* can be made at any time during the day or night, certain days and times are indicated by the authentic *aḥādīth* as auspicious. They are: *Laylat al-Qadr*, the day of *'Arafah*, early morning before dawn, certain times on Fridays, at the time of breaking the fast, during the *Ḥajj*, after completion of reading the Qur'ān and between saying the *Adhān* and the *Iqāmah*. Although *du'ā'* can be made in any language, if one chooses a *du'ā'* mentioned in the Qur'ān and *aḥādīth* one can hope that these will be more effective.

References

Du'ā': 2: 186; 3: 38; 17: 11; 27: 62; 54: 10.

Dunyā [دنيا] (World)

Meaning

Danā means to be near or to be close as well as to be low or lowly. From this root comes the word *Adnā* meaning nearer, closer, situated lower down, inferior or of less significance; its feminine form is *Dunyā*. The word *Dunyā* is used for this world as it is closest to one's life as opposed to the life of the Hereafter. It is also considered to be base and low in comparison to the Hereafter. *Dunyā* refers to everything on this earth.

Characteristics of *Dunyā*

IMMEDIATE AND PERCEPTIBLE

As compared to the *Ākhirah, Dunyā* is more immediate and perceptible, whereas the *Ākhirah* is distant and hidden. For this reason *Dunyā* is referred to as *al-'Ājilah* (fleeting life). "*Nay, but you love the fleeting life, and leave alone the Hereafter*" (al-Qiyāmah 75: 20–21; al-Insān 76: 27).

TRANSITORY

The Qur'ān has often emphasized that this world is transitory and perishable as compared to the *Ākhirah* which is to remain forever. "*Nay (behold) you prefer the life of this world. But the Hereafter is better and more enduring.*" (al-A'lā 87: 16–17) As man by nature is impatient (al-Anbiyā' 21: 37) he loves haste and things that are achievable hastily. For this reason he pins his hopes and efforts on transitory things which do not endure for long but he neglects things of lasting value, which come slowly but surely but can only be seen in the Hereafter.

GLITTERING AND ALLURING

This world and its adornments attract people to the life of joy and pleasure and of play and amusement (al-An'ām 6: 32). However, these worldly goods and chattels which one is so proud to collect and display are in fact only deceptions (Āl 'Imrān 3: 185). And these worldly possessions only provide a little enjoyment (Āl 'Imrān 3: 197).

In Sūrah al-Ḥadīd an apt simile is given to explain the utter futility of this alluring world. "*Know you (all) that the life of this world is but play and amusement, pomp and mutual boasting and multiplying (in rivalry) among yourselves, riches and children. Here is a similitude; how rain and the growth which brings forth delight to (the hearts of) the tillers soon withers. You will see it becomes yellow. Then it becomes dry and crumbles away*" (al-Ḥadīd 57: 20).

Yet this *Dunyā* is also called *Dār al-Imtiḥān* (a place of test) where one has to work hard in order to reap the reward from Allah; otherwise by neglecting one's duties one becomes liable for the punishment in the Hereafter. There is a saying of the Prophet (peace be upon him) that this world is the farmland for the Hereafter.

References

Dunyā: 4: 77; 6: 32; 11: 15; 20: 72; 35: 5.

Faḥshā', Fāḥishah [فحشآء، فاحشة] (Immorality, Shameful and Indecent Deeds)

Meaning

Faḥusha means to be monstrous, to be excessive, atrocious, obscene and indecent. Etymologically from this root, *Faḥshā'* and *al-Fāḥishah* (pl. *Fawāḥish*) have connotations of indecency and excessiveness. *Al-Fāḥisha* is the Qur'ānic term for obscenity and indecency. It means everything that exceeds its limit. However, it is mainly associated with sexual immorality and those acts that human beings instinctively find repulsive. Such vices include adultery, fornication, homosexuality, nudity and pornography or any other obscene act.

Analysis

The Qur'ān enjoins Muslims to refrain from all the immoral and indecent acts whether open or secret (al-An'ām 6: 151 and al-A'rāf 7: 33). Some of the shameful and immoral acts also have legal and social sanctions as they are offences against society and are universally considered abominable. Then there are certain acts in which one may indulge in private but will feel ashamed if this comes to public knowledge, such as watching pornography or looking at someone with lust which the Qur'ān describes as treachery of the eyes (Ghāfir 40: 19).

To save society and oneself from this flood of immodesty, and shameful and evil deeds, Allah has endowed human beings with natural modesty, shyness and bashfulness. In Islamic terminology this is called *al-ḥayā'*. In essence, it is a feeling in one's heart that keeps one from indulging in evil deeds that may cause embarrassment. It is very close to what is termed "one's moral conscience" in Western society. If one has no conscience one can perform and do whatever one likes without any care for what society might think. Conversely, someone with a conscience will feel ashamed to do any evil deed even if no one is watching. The Prophet (peace be upon him) emphasized this on many occasions: "*Ḥayā'* and *īmān* are two companions that go together. If one of them is lifted, the other is also lifted" (al-Ḥākim). It is very obvious from this *ḥadīth* that a person who has no *ḥayā'* lacks faith as well. In another *ḥadīth* the Prophet (peace be upon him) is reported to have said: "*Al-ḥayā'* is part of *īmān*" (Muslim).

Al-Ḥayā' is the first line of defence against obscenity. It safeguards one from committing indecent acts as our conscience stops us from indulging in vice. As the Prophet observed: From the words of the previous prophets that the people still find are: "If you feel no shame, then do as you wish" (Bukhārī). This means that the importance of and emphasis on modesty has been passed on from earlier prophets. This is the legacy which humanity inherited from time immemorial. It means that modesty or shame is the criterion for whether or not one should do something. If one is satisfied that there is no shame in doing something one should do it. But if there is reason to be ashamed in doing such a thing then one should refrain.

References

Faḥshā': 2: 268; 7: 28; 12: 24; 24: 21; 29: 45. *Fāḥishah*: 3: 135; 4: 22; 17: 32; 29: 28; 33: 30.

Falāḥ [فلاح] (Salvation)

Meaning

Falaḥa means to split, cleave and hence to plow and to cultivate. Therefore a farmer is called *Fallāḥ*. There is a famous Arabic saying, *al-Ḥadīd bi'l ḥadīd yuflaḥ*, meaning iron is cleft with iron. From this root *falāḥ* means permanent prosperity, happiness and salvation. The word *Falāḥ* is exclusively used for salvation in the Hereafter, whose achievement is the ultimate goal of a Muslim. The other word used in the Qur'ān for salvation is *al-Fawz*. This also means success, triumph, victory, attainment and accomplishment. Both these words are used to indicate the final achievement of one's goal that is the real success.

Analysis

Falāḥ depends on the purification of soul: "*Those will attain* Falāḥ *who purify themselves*" (al-A'lā 87: 14) and "*Truly he succeeds that purifies it (soul)*" (al-Shams 91: 9). *Falāḥ* is bound to follow with good deeds as mentioned in Sūrah al-Mu'minūn (23: 1–11) and Sūrah al-Ḥajj (22: 77). Good deeds include acts of *'ibādah* as well as concern for the social virtues and actions. Thus, *Adhān* five times a day from every mosque calls believers for *Ṣalāh* and also conveys the tidings about attaining *Falāḥ* as well.

The ultimate aim of an individual is to attain the pleasure of Allah and salvation in the life Hereafter. This does not negate success in this world. In the Qur'ān the success of an individual in the *Ākhirah* is declared to be the real success and is termed *Fawz* and *Falāḥ*. "*Only he who is removed far from the Fire and admitted to the* Jannah *will have attained success*" (Āl 'Imrān 3: 185). "*For those who believe and do righteous deeds will be Gardens beneath which rivers flow. This is the great salvation (the fulfillment of all desires*" (al-Burūj 85: 11).

For the success of the believers in this world, the Qur'ān uses the terms *Fatḥ* (victory) and *Nuṣrat* (support). "*Verily We have granted you a manifest victory*" (al-Fatḥ 48: 1). "*When comes the help of Allah and victory*" (al-Naṣr 110: 1). "*And another (favour will He bestow) which you do love – help from Allah and a speedy victory*" (al-Ṣaff 61: 13). The verse before this identifies the real success. "*He will forgive you your sins and admit you to Gardens beneath which rivers flow, and to beautiful mansions in gardens of eternity: that is indeed the supreme achievement*" (al-Ṣaff 61: 12).

Everyone will be accountable individually on the Day of Resurrection. One's intention, determination, efforts and struggle will be scrutinized. The *Ummah* as a social body whose mission is to be a witness unto mankind, enjoining good and forbidding evil, has the responsibility to use its resources in such a way that individuals can succeed in achieving their aims. It is quite possible, and indeed has happened, that individuals have failed. We know many prophets and righteous people whose struggles in this world did not achieve success and yet they will be honoured in the Hereafter. It is also possible that the political entity in the form of an

Islamic state may succeed in this world but some individuals may fail to achieve *Fawz* and *Falāḥ*.

The opposite of *Falāḥ* and *Fawz* is *Khusrān*, meaning to incur loss, suffer damage, to go astray and lose one's way. The greatest loss is for the unbelievers as the Qur'ān points out: "*Truly those in loss are those who lose their own souls and their people on the Day of Judgement: Ah! That is indeed the (real and) evident loss*" (al-Zumar 39: 15). The word *Khāba* (to fail) is used as opposite of *aflāḥa* in Sūrah al-Shams (91: 9–10).

References

Falāḥ: 2: 5; 23: 1; 58: 22; 87: 14; 91: 9.

Faqr [فقر] (Poverty)

Meaning

Faqr means poverty and *Faqīr* (pl. *Fuqarā'*) means poor, needy or a pauper. Imām al-Rāghib has identified four uses of the word *al-Faqr*:

1. lack of the basic necessities of life. In this sense not only man but everything else in this universe is *Faqīr* (Fāṭir 35: 15).
2. being unable to fulfil all the requirements of one's needs (al-Baqarah 2: 273).
3. one's dependence on Allah for His bounties (al-Qaṣaṣ 28: 24).
4. *Faqr al-Nafs* means avarice for wealth which leads one to the brink of *kufr* as opposed to *Ghanā' al-Nafs* which gives contentment.

Analysis

Everyone who is dependent on others for a livelihood is a *Faqīr*. This dependence may be the result of one's permanent infirmity or old age or being unemployed or ill for a short period. Such dependent persons include widows and orphans. The antonym of *Faqīr* is *Ghanī*. Hence, the one who is not *Ghanī* is *Faqīr*. Such a person may not beg for his needs out of self-respect; hence others are encouraged to help because such a person is more deserving of help (al-Baqarah 2: 273). *Fuqarā'* are entitled to receive a share from *Zakāt* and *Ṣadaqāt* (al-Baqarah 2: 271; al-Tawbah 9: 60).

Synonyms

Miskīn means one who is needy; such a person is unable to earn his livelihood because of his helplessness and lack of determination. Being incompetent, his needs are greater than that of a *Faqīr* because he suffers from *Faqr* as well as from *Maskanah* (hopelessness or extreme poverty). Believers are encouraged to feed and help the *Miskīn*. Like a *Faqīr*, a *Miskīn* has a share from *Zakāt* and *Ṣadaqāt*.

Sā'il comes from *Sa'ala* which means to ask or to request, and *sā'il* means both a questioner and a beggar. In this latter sense it is the synonym of *Faqīr* and *Miskīn*. Hence one is encouraged to help those who seek help (al-Baqarah 2: 177; al-Dhāriyāt 51: 19; al-Ma'ārij 70: 25). Of course, if one is not in a position to help, then one should politely deal with this situation but should not repulse them (al-Ḍuḥā 93: 10).

Maḥrūm means one who is deprived of wealth and prosperity, possibly by some misfortune. This may be due to a change in one's circumstances, either through suffering a business setback or through being a victim of natural disaster. Like *Miskīn* and *Sā'il* such a person should be helped so that he can again be able to establish himself (al-Dhāriyāt 51: 19; al-Ma'ārij 70: 25).

References

Faqr: 2: 268; 9: 60; 22: 28; 35: 15; 59: 8. *Miskīn*: 17: 26; 30: 38; 68: 24; 89: 18; 107: 3. *Sā'il*: 2: 177; 51: 19; 70: 25; 93: 10. *Maḥrūm*: 51: 19; 56: 67; 68: 27; 70: 25.

Fasād [فساد] (Corruption)

Meanings

Fasād means to upset the balance either by exceeding the limit or reducing it. The word is derived from *fasada* which means to be or to become bad, rotten, decayed, wicked, corrupt and perverted. Thus, the word *fasād* is used in the Qur'ān in a wide range of meanings: disorder, corruption, mischief, riot, and anarchy. Its opposite is *ṣalāḥ* which means goodness, usefulness, righteousness, peacefulness. The word *iṣlāḥ* comes from the same root, meaning restoration, betterment, and improvement. In many verses of the Qur'ān these two words are used to illustrate the two contrary attitudes and frames of mind. "*Do no mischief on the earth after it has been set in order*" (al-A'rāf 7: 56 and 85); "*When it is said to them: 'Make no mischief on the earth,' they say: 'Why, we only want to make peace'*" (al-Baqarah 2: 11). Similarly the active nouns *Mufsid* (one who corrupts) and *Ṣāliḥ* (one who is virtuous and pious) are used in the Qur'ān to highlight the contrast in these two personalities.

Analysis

As many shades of meaning are included in the word *Fasād*, it can take many forms. It may be moral corruption, physical destruction, unlawful acts, social injustice and riots. Allah has set the universe in (right) balance; hence man should not transgress the (due) balance (al-Raḥmān 55: 7–8). The Qur'ān presents this well-ordered and regulated universe as an argument for the existence of one God only because "*If there were, in the heavens and the earth, other gods besides Allah, there would have been chaos* (Fasād) *in both*" (al-Anbiyā' 21: 22). It is human beings who create mischief on land and sea by transgressing the limits set by Allah (al-Rūm 30: 41) and by destroying crops and cattle (al-Baqarah 2: 205). The other sort of mischief is killing innocent people such as the killing of Jewish children by Pharaoh (al-Qaṣaṣ 28: 4).

In addition to physical mischief there is moral corruption which damages the fabric of society. Thus, many nations that continued to create havoc by transgressing Allah's laws and refusing to follow the teachings of their prophets and indeed persecuting them instead, were destroyed by Him. It is Allah's *sunnah* to purge the *fasād* by bringing about changes in regimes (al-Baqarah 2: 251).

References

Fasād: 2: 205; 8: 73; 28: 83; 30: 41; 89: 12.

Fawz [فوز]

see *Falāḥ*

Fay' [فئ]

see *Anfāl*

Fi'l [فعل]

see *'Amal*

Firdaws [فردوس]

see *Jannah*

Fisq [فسق] (Wickedness)

Meaning

Fasaqa means to stray from the right path, to deviate from goodness, to act unlawfully, sinfully, immorally. Thus, in Islamic terminology a *Fāsiq* (active participle from *Fisq*, whose plural is *Fāsiqūn, Fussāq* and *Fasaqah*) means a person who has deviated from the path of *Sharī'ah*. Although *Fisq* can be applied to someone committing any act of deviation, it is usually applied to those who commit grave sins. Sometimes it is applied even to those who are unbelievers as they transgress the rational and natural laws. Hence, the disobedience of Satan is termed *Fisq* (al-Kahf 18: 50).

Analysis

In the Qur'ān *Fisq* is used as the opposite of *Īmān*. For example one who persists in disobeying the commands of Allah leads him to *Fisq* (deviation). "*Is then the man who believes no better than the man who is rebellious and wicked? They are not equal*" (al-Sajdah 32: 18).

It is the *Sunnah* of Allah that He provides guidance to those who seek such guidance. Those who deliberately try to distort the signs of Allah are the *Fasaqah*, and they are deprived of Allah's guidance (al-Baqarah 2: 26). "*When they went wrong, Allah let their hearts go wrong. For Allah guides not those who are rebellious transgressors*" (al-Ṣaff 61: 5).

The *Munāfiqūn* (hypocrites) are described as *Fāsiqūn* in Sūrah al-Tawbah, and their characteristics are vividly enumerated: "*The hypocrites, men and women, (have an understanding) with each other: They enjoin evil, and forbid what is just, and are close with their hands [i.e. they are miserly]. They have forgotten Allah, so He has forgotten them. Verily the hypocrites are rebellious and perverse* (Fāsiqūn)" (al-Tawbah 9: 67). Hence, the Prophet was told it was of no use his seeking forgiveness for them as: "*Allah will not forgive them. Truly Allah guides not rebellious transgressors*" (al-Munāfiqūn 63: 6).

Unlike the unbelievers, *fāsiqūn* and *manāfiqūn* are still part of the Muslim society. Therefore, Muslims are forewarned to be careful in dealing with them. For example, if some news is brought by them, it should be carefully checked for its authenticity before taking any action (al-Ḥujurāt 49: 6). If they are proved to be fabricating evidence against chaste women, their testimony should never be accepted (al-Nūr 24: 4).

References

Fisq: 2: 197; 5: 3; 6: 121; 17: 16; 49: 7.

Fitnah [فتنة] (Trial)

Meanings

Fatana means to put a piece of gold in a crucible and heat it in order to test whether it is pure gold or contains impurities. It is used in this sense in Sūrah al-Dhāriyāt: "*(It will be) a day when they will be tried (and tested) over the Fire*" (al-Dhāriyāt 51: 13). The other meanings of *Fatana* are: (a) to subject to temptations or trials; (b) to charm, fascinate, captivate; (c) to torture, torment; (d) to create tumult or discord.

The word *Fitnah* which comes from this root means temptation, trial, charm, intrigue, sedition, riot, disorder, or civil strife.

Analysis

The word *Fitnah* is used in at least the following four different meanings:

A. TRIAL

One of its meanings is a test or trial. In this sense it is a synonym of the word *Balā'*. The root of the word *Balā'* also means to test, to try or to afflict. Hence, *Balā'* means trial, tribulation, visitation, affliction, distress or misfortune.

The purpose of the creation of the universe as well as of life and death, according to the Qur'ān, is the trial of human beings. Allah wants to find out who is the best in his deeds (al-Mulk 67: 1; Hūd 11: 7). The life on the earth consists of a series of trials. These trials can take many forms, and each human being as well as each nation is tried in different ways. These include:

1. through one's own family, which is called *Fitnah* as also is affluence (al-Anfāl 8: 28; al-Taghābun 64: 14–15).
2. suffering and adversity, fear and famine (al-Baqarah 2: 155).
3. temptations (Yūsuf: 12: 23–24).

A trial is an essential requirement to test the sincerity of one's *Īmān*. The path of Islam is the path of struggle. People will not be left alone just by saying that they believe. They will be tested to establish whether their belief is superficial or rooted firmly in their hearts and manifested in their actions. The Qur'ān mentions this fact in several places in order that one should not be perturbed when these trials come and instead remain steadfast in one's *Īmān*: "*Do people think that they will be left alone on saying, 'We believe', and that they will not be tested? We did test those before them, and Allah will certainly know those who are true from those who are false*" (al-'Ankabūt 29: 2–3). (See also al-Baqarah 2: 214 and Āl 'Imrān 3: 142.)

It was only after going through severe trials, tests and untold sacrifices that the Prophet Ibrāhīm (peace be upon him) was granted the honour of the title "The Leader of Mankind" (al-Baqarah 2: 124).

Unbelievers are also tested so that they may turn to Allah and repent. This test is not necessarily effected by imposing some misfortune. It may be conducted by giving them plenty of worldly goods. The believers are warned not to be dazzled by glitter of their wealth; as Allah says: "*through this We test them...*" (Ṭā Hā 20: 131).

B. PERSECUTION

The word *Fitnah* is also used for the persecution of believers. The persecution by Pharaoh of Banī Isrā'īl (Yūnus 10: 83), and of the believers by the *Aṣḥāb al-Ukhdūd* (the makers of the pit fire) (al-Burūj 85: 10), is termed *Fitnah*. In this sense the *Fitnah* is regarded as worse than killing and warfare (al-Baqarah 2: 191 and 217).

C. TEMPTATION

One of the methods used by Satan or his agents is to seduce people by alluring them so that they deviate from the right path (al-A'rāf 7: 20; al-Isrā' 17: 73).

D. BURNING

This is the literal meaning of the word *fitnah* as stated above. It is used in this meaning in several places in the Qur'ān (85: 10).

References

Fitnah: 2: 102; 8: 25; 17: 60; 21: 35; 85: 10; *Balā'*: 2: 49; 14: 6; 44: 33; 67: 2; 89: 15 and 16.

Fiṭrah [فطرة] (Nature)

Meaning

One of the meanings of the verb *faṭara* is to make, to create, to bring into being, or to endow with something. *Fāṭir* is the term used to express Allah's creative power. "*Praise be to Allah, Who created (out of nothing) the heavens and the earth*" (Fāṭir 35: 1).

Fiṭrah means natural disposition, temperament, constitution, innate character or instinct. In the Qur'ān it refers to human nature, which is essentially good.

Analysis

There is an inborn sense of morality in all human beings. Throughout the ages certain qualities have been warmly approved of by society, while others have been consistently condemned. People by instinct appreciate truthfulness, charity, courage, honesty, hospitality, loyalty, sympathy, fidelity, justice and many other good qualities. Equally, they disdain hypocrisy, bigotry, injustice, falsehood, betrayal, infidelity, cowardice, cruelty and rudeness. When they become part of the collective behaviour of society, the personal moral values bring about a just, compassionate and morally upright society and state. This is summed up as: "*By the soul and the proportion given to it. And its enlightenment as to its wrong and its right*" (al-Shams 91: 7–8).

Fiṭrah is the duty imposed by Allah on human beings as it is stated in the Qur'ān: "*So set your face steadily and truly on the faith: (establish) Allah's handiwork according to the pattern which He has made for mankind. No change (let there be) in the work (created) by Allah*" (al-Rūm 30: 30). Yūsuf 'Alī maintained that this verse indicates that man is created innocent, pure, true, free, inclined to right and virtue, and endued with true understanding about his own position in the universe and about Allah's goodness, wisdom and power (*The Meaning of the Holy Qur'ān*, note 3541, p. 1016).

Allah in His mercy has given us the basic instincts to differentiate between good and evil. But human affairs are much more complex and need more precise guidance. Hence, through His messengers and prophets Allah guided humanity in all ages as promised to the Prophet Ādam (peace be upon him) and his progeny (al-Baqarah 2: 38). Verse 30 of Sūrah al-Rūm quoted above is preceded by the injunction: "*To set your face steadily and truly to the (true) religion*". This signifies that religion is not an imposition on human beings but the fulfilment of their basic need. Thus, the Qur'ān refutes those who assert that man is shaped by his environment. Instead man is created in the best of moulds (al-Tīn 95: 4). A *ḥadīth* of the Prophet (peace be upon him) reports that he said: "Every child who is born of *Fiṭrah* (natural disposition), it is his parents who later convert him to be Christian, Jew or fire worshipper" (Bukhārī and Muslim).

Reference

Fiṭrah: 30: 30.

Fu'ād [فؤاد]

see *Qalb*

al-Furqān [الفرقان] (The Criterion)

The word *Furqān* comes from *Faraqa* which means to separate, to divide, or to make distinction or differentiate. *Furqān* means something that separates right from wrong, the criterion, the proof, and the evidence. The *Furqān* is something that distinguishes truth from falsehood. This distinction can be based on some internal evidence that is supported by a rational judgement or a logical argument, or it could be observed from factual events. In this sense the *Furqān* is one of the proper names of the Qur'ān. In the first verse of Sūrah al-Furqān Allah says: "*Blessed is He Who sent down al-Furqān to His servant...*" (al-Furqān 25: 1). This means that the Qur'ān is the criterion by which one can judge what is right and what is wrong. The word *al-Furqān* is also applied to the Old Testament in several places in the Qur'ān (al-Baqarah 2: 53; Āl 'Imrān 3: 4; al-Anbiyā' 21: 48).

The day of the Battle of Badr is called *Yawm al-Furqān*, as this was the first decisive battle between the powers of good and evil. With the defeat of evil in this battle, it became evident who was following the path of truth. This battle was also a test of those who proclaim the faith (al-Anfāl 8: 41).

If a believer is God-conscious and tries to follow the path of truth by refraining from evil deeds then Allah will endow him with ability to discern for himself what is right and what is wrong. This inner light will guide him through the vicissitudes of life. This granting of the *Furqān* is mentioned thus: "*O you who believe! If you fear Allah He will grant you a criterion...*" (al-Anfāl 8: 29).

References
al-Furqān: 2: 53 and 185; 3: 4; 21: 48; 25: 1.

See also al-Qur'ān

Ghaḍab [غضب] (Wrath)

Meaning
One of the literal meanings of *al-Ghaḍab* is hardness. Hence a hard rock is called *ghaḍabah* and a deadly poisonous snake is called *Ghaḍūb*. The other meaning is to be angry or enraged, thus, anger is called *Ghadab* and an angry person is referred to as *Ghaḍbān*. *Ghaḍab* is a relative state and varies in intensity. The hardness of a rock, the poison of a snake and the anger of a human being differ in their manifestation but all possess a quality of extremism. Allah is above feelings and sensations that we experience; thus, we cannot really comprehend the quality of His anger.

Analysis
The word *Ghaḍab* signifies anger, displeasure and wrath. Those who incurred Allah's wrath are those who were deprived of His Favours and received punishment:

> *Thus they (Jews) have drawn on themselves Wrath upon Wrath, and humiliating is the punishment of those who reject Faith.*
>
> (al-Baqarah 2: 90)

> *They (Jews) were covered with humiliation and misery; they drew on themselves the Wrath of Allah.*
>
> (al-Baqarah 2: 61)

It is instructive to note that the word *maghḍūb 'alayhim* in Sūrah al-Fātiḥah is used impersonally and means that the Jews' actions are responsible for Allah's Wrath. Thus, the Jews either rejected the *Sharī'ah* of Allah or, if they accepted it, they tried to distort it or mould it to suit their own desires. Thus, they incurred Allah's Wrath. Their worst crime was to conceal the Truth. For this they were deprived of Allah's Blessings and incurred His Curse which is signified by the word *La'nah.*

> *Those who conceal the clear (signs) We have sent down, and the Guidance, after We made it clear for the People in the Book – on them shall be Allah's Curse, and the curse of those entitled to curse.*
> (al-Baqarah 2: 159)

The causes that incur Allah's Wrath are deviation from the Path of Righteousness after receiving Divine Guidance and favours, and people's following their own base desires. It is important to know why this disease afflicts and prevents people from following the Way of Truth. One factor is their own inclinations, desires and self-interests, and the other is the corrupt environment that surrounds them. These disrupt their relation with Divine Guidance, and thus they follow their own whims and desires. All corruption and deviation in *Dīn* starts from these diseases. Thus, in several places, the Qur'ān instructs the People of the Book:

> *O People of the Book! Why do you reject Allah's Signs when you yourselves are there as witnesses. O People of the Book! Why do you mix truth with falsehood and knowingly conceal the truth?*
> (Āl 'Imrān 3: 70–71)

> *Say: "O People of the Book! Exceed not in your* Dīn *the bounds (of what is proper), trespassing beyond the truth, nor follow the whims and desires of people who went wrong in times gone by – who misled many and strayed (themselves) from the Right Way."*
> (al-Mā'idah 5: 77)

Thus, one of the supplications of the Prophet (peace be upon him) narrated by 'Abdullāh ibn 'Umar (may Allah be pleased with both of them) is:

> O Allah! I seek Your refuge from forfeiture of Your Favours, displacement of Your concern for my well-being, and from sudden descent of Punishment and Your Wrath and Anger
>
> (Ṣaḥīḥ of Muslim)

The other supplication taught to us by the Qur'ān is:

> *Our Lord! (they say) "Let not our hearts deviate now after You have guided us..."*
>
> (Āl 'Imrān 3: 8)

References

Ghaḍab: 2: 61; 7: 71; 16: 106; 24: 9; 42: 16. *al-Maghḍūb*: 1: 7.

Ghanīmah [غنيمة]

see *Anfāl*

Ghayb [غيب] (Non-Perceptible)

Meaning

Ghayb comes from *Ghāba* which means absence, hidden, invisible or concealed. *Ghayb* is something that is hidden, concealed, or one that is transcendental. It is also applied to the supernatural or Divine secret. This word is commonly translated as "the Unseen"; perhaps a better translation, as suggested by Muhammad Asad, should be "that which is beyond the reach of human perception". Thus, *Ghayb* means things that human beings cannot perceive through natural means of attaining knowledge: that is, through one's senses, intuition, reason or logic. *Ghayb* are things beyond the range of human perception and as such cannot be proved or disproved by scientific methods. One can only know about them through the information provided by the prophets. In contrast, the Qur'ān uses the term *Shahādah* for the realm that is present and evident. Allah alone is the One, who is *'Ālim al-Ghayb wa al-Shahādah* (He knows the non-perceptible and that which is visible and perceptible) (al-An'ām 6: 73).

Analysis

Al-Īmān bi al-Ghayb is part of the Islamic creed. Allah, the events of the Hereafter, the real nature of time and the existence of spiritual forces are non-perceptible by the human senses and intellect. We are required to believe in them on the testimony of the prophets who were informed about them through revelation by Allah.

The same is true of other areas as well, such as past events where human beings are incapable of recording them that far back in history: For example, the creation of Ādam and Ḥawwā' (peace be upon them), their stay in paradise and their descent on earth, as well as histories of earlier messengers and prophets (Āl 'Imrān 3: 44).

This also applies to future events, which are only in Allah's knowledge: "*Say: None in the heavens or on earth except Allah knows what is non-perceptible; nor can they perceive when they shall be raised up (for) judgement*" (al-Naml 27: 65). (See also Yūnus 10: 20; Hūd 11: 123; al-Naḥl 16: 77.)

Al-Ghayb is also applicable to events happening in the present, but which limited human senses cannot encapsulate. "*With Him are the keys of the non-perceptible, that none knows but He. He knows whatever there is on the earth and in the sea. Not a leaf does fall but with His knowledge*" (al-An'ām 6: 59).

Even the messengers and prophets did not possess knowledge of the *Ghayb*: "*Say: I tell you not that with me are the treasures of Allah, nor do I know what is non-perceptible nor do I tell you I am an angel. I but follow what is revealed to me*" (al-An'ām 6: 50 and a similar verse in Hūd 11: 31). However, Allah does inform His messengers of the non-perceptible when He wants to and in whatever portion of the *ghayb* He wants to give them (al-Jinn 72: 26–27; al-Taḥrīm 66: 3).

The Qur'ān categorically refutes the Arabian mythology that the *Jinns* have access to *al-Ghayb* and that through them soothsayers are able to predict future events (al-Jinn 72: 8–9). This is further illustrated by the helplessness of the *Jinns* who did not realize the death of the Prophet Sulaymān (peace be upon him) and continued their assigned task (Sabā' 34: 14).

References

Ghayb: 2: 3; 6: 59; 16: 77; 34: 3; 59: 22.

Ghusl [غسل]

see *Ṭahārah*

Hady [هدي]

see *Nusuk*

Ḥajj [حج] (The Pilgrimage)

Meaning

Ḥajja means to intend to visit someone or somewhere that is the object of reverence, veneration, respect or honour. In the terminology of the *Sharī'ah* it is the pilgrimage to the Ka'bah during certain specific days in the month of Dhū'l-Ḥijjah.

The Institution of the *Ḥajj* and Its Rites

In accordance with the command of Allah, the call for *Ḥajj* was first given by the Prophet Ibrāhīm (peace be upon him). Ever since, this call has been proclaimed every year; it has been carried on for the last four thousand years. Muslims from all over the world, using different modes of transport, assemble on the plain of 'Arafāt responding:

> Here I am O Allah, here I am. Here I am. You have no partners, here I am. Verily all praise and Dominion is Yours, and You have no partner.

The performance of the *Ḥajj* is one of the five pillars of Islam. It is obligatory for all adult Muslims who are financially well off and physically fit to undertake this journey once in a lifetime.

One is required to don a pair of the unstitched white sheets of cloth called *Iḥrām*, thus eliminating all differences of culture, race, class, nationality and age. The state of *Iḥrām* also imposes many restrictions on pilgrims.

The Rites of *Ḥajj* symbolically re-enact many of the events in the lives of the Prophet Ibrāhīm, his wife Hājir and their son Ismāʿīl (peace be upon them). The *Ḥajj* ceremonies start on the 8th of Dhū'l-Ḥijjah with pilgrims doing the *Ṭawāf* (circumambulation) of the Kaʿbah seven times. This is followed by doing *saʿy* (a swift walk) between the hillocks Ṣafā and Marwah which are now incorporated in the Masjid al-Ḥarām. Pilgrims then proceed to Minā, which is about five miles from Makkah. After an overnight stay there they move to ʿArafāt on the 9th of Dhū'l-Ḥijjah and spend the whole day in prayers and supplications, returning after the sunset for a stop-over in Muzdalifah for the night and finally back to Minā to perform the rest of the rites, including the sacrifice of an animal, the shaving or clipping of their hair, the stoning at three pillars (*Jamarāt*) and the performance of another *Ṭawāf* of the Kaʿbah. The *Ḥajj* ceremonies finish by the 12th or 13th of Dhū'l-Ḥijjah.

The rituals performed during the *Ḥajj* create bonds of brotherhood among Muslims and as such the *Ḥajj* manifests the unity of the *Ummah* as one family. It also eliminates all differences of race, colour, language, nationality and social status. The *Ḥajj*, if performed with purity of intention and sincerity, will be acceptable to Allah and will absolve all sins. All the prescribed rituals create spirituality and closeness to Allah and thus rejuvenate one's *īmān*.

'Umrah

'Amara means to thrive, to prosper or to flourish and it also means to visit or to meet. The word *'Umrah* from this root is used for a specific *'Ibādah* of visiting the Ka'bah. The *'Umrah*, for this reason, is called the minor *Ḥajj*. Unlike the *Ḥajj*, the *'Umrah* need not be performed at a particular time of the year. It can be performed any time except during the designated *Ḥajj* period. It has fewer rituals, and they are all performed within the Masjid al-Ḥarām. Of course the wearing of the *iḥrām* is compulsory for the *'Umrah* also.

References

Ḥajj: 2: 189 and 196; 3: 97; 9: 3; 22: 27. *'Umrah*: 2: 158 and 196.

See also *Nusuk*

al-Ḥalāl wa al-Ḥarām [الحلال والحرام]

(The Lawful and the Unlawful)

Meanings

Ḥalla means to untie, to unbind, to unfasten or unravel. From this meaning of "to untie a knot" it is used idiomatically to mean to make something lawful or permissible. The word *Ḥalāl* means that which is lawful, permitted or permissible. Its opposite is the word *Ḥarrama* which means to forbid, prohibit or disallow, and the noun *Ḥarām* means that which is unlawful or prohibited.

General Principles

In the *Sharī'ah* the basic principle is that all things and all acts are lawful. Nothing is *Ḥarām* except those things that are declared unlawful by Allah and His Messenger. In some cases lawful acts are clearly mentioned as permissible: "*This day are (all) good things made lawful for you*" (al-Mā'idah 5: 5). In other cases a different mode of expression is used which makes it clear that act is permissible. For example: "*It is no sin…*" (al-Baqarah 2:

158, 198, 229, 230, 233, 234, 235, 236, 240, and 282 and many other places where this expression is used).

Similarly some acts are clearly designated as unlawful: "*Forbidden for you are...*" (al-Mā'idah 5: 3). These words are followed by a long list of unlawful food and prohibited acts. As a general rule all acts for which there is a prescribed punishment are unlawful. In Islam the sphere of prohibited things is very small, whereas that of permissible things is vast.

However, one legal principle of *Fiqh* in this respect should also be noted. If something is unlawful, then whatever leads to it is likewise prohibited. Hence, the *Fuqahā'* have established the criterion that whatever is conducive to or leads towards the *Ḥarām* is itself *Ḥarām*. For example, sex outside marriage is unlawful: hence scant clothing, nudity, pornographic images, obscene songs, free mixed gatherings and other similar things are also considered unlawful.

Although *Ḥalāl* and *Ḥarām* are clearly identified, there may be some doubtful things as well. The advice in this respect is to avoid them. This is exemplified by the *ḥadīth* of the Prophet (peace be upon him) which states:

> That which is lawful is clear and that which is unlawful is clear and between the two of them are doubtful (or ambiguous) matters about which not many people are knowledgeable. Thus, he who avoids these doubtful matters certainly clears himself in regard to his religion and his honour. But he who falls into doubtful matters falls into that which is unlawful.
>
> (Bukhārī and Muslim)

The advice in such doubtful matters is that as an act of piety they should be avoided.

Some Exceptions to the General Rules

Although there are strict rules of *ḥalāl* and *ḥarām*, in exceptional circumstances, when it is a matter of saving a life, it is permissible to consume the prohibited items of drink and food in quantities sufficient for survival. This concession is specifically mentioned in the passage of the Qur'ān which lists unlawful things: "*But if one is forced by necessity, without wilful disobedience nor transgressing due limits – then is he guiltless for Allah is Oft-Forgiving, Most Merciful*" (al-Baqarah 2: 173). This is repeated in other places as well. On the basis of these verses, the *Fuqahā'* have derived the principle that "necessity removes restrictions".

See also *Iḍṭirār*

Other Words from the Same Root

al-Masjid al-Ḥarām or *al-Ḥaram:* The reason for calling the Grand Mosque of Ka'bah by this name is because its sanctity is inviolable and thus it is declared holy and sacred.

al-Shahr al-Ḥarām: Four months (Rajab, Dhū'l-Qa'dah, Dhū'l-Ḥijjah and Muḥarram) are designated as the sacred and holy months for performing the *Ḥajj* and *'Umrah*. Arabs used to perform *'Umrah* in Rajab, but now *'Umrah* can be performed anytime of the year apart from the time of the *Ḥajj*. They are declared *Ḥarām* because it is not lawful to wage war during these months.

Iḥrām: In order to perform the *Ḥajj* or *'Umrah*, pilgrims have to don two unsewn pieces of cloth, called *Iḥrām*. In the state of *Iḥrām* many acts are unlawful, such as the clipping of hairs and nails and the use of perfume etcetera.

References

Ḥalāl: 2: 168; 5: 88; 8: 69; 10: 59; 16: 116. *Ḥarām*: 5: 87; 7: 157; 9: 37; 10: 59; 24: 3. *al-Masjid al-Ḥarām*: 2: 144 and 191; 9: 7 and 28; 17: 1. *al-Shahr al-Ḥarām*: 2: 194 and 217; 5: 2 and 97.

Ḥalf [حلف]

see *Qasam*

Ḥamd [حمد] (Thankful Praise)

Meaning

Ḥamd is usually translated as praise, but gratitude is also an integral part of its meaning. The more accurate translation would be "grateful praise". The other word often used for gratitude is *shukr.* But there is a difference in their meanings. *Ḥamd* is more expansive than *shukr*. Whereas *shukr* is an expression of gratitude by its recipient towards the benefactor, *Ḥamd* is an acknowledgement that someone embodies the excellent qualities of beneficence and radiates blessings and benedictions. Thus, it is exclusively used for Allah, as He alone can be the object of *Ḥamd.*

Words from the Same Root

One of Allah's Attributes is *Ḥamīd.* It means that He alone is the One who deserves to be praised or to whom one should be grateful. *Maḥmūd* also comes from the same root and its meaning is very similar to *Ḥamīd.* However, there is a subtle difference in their meanings: *Maḥmūd* is the one who is actually being praised whereas *Ḥamīd* is the one who deserves praise whether he is being praised or not.

Two other words also derived from *Ḥamd* are *Aḥmad* and *Muḥammad.* These are the blessed personal names of the Prophet (peace be upon him) and are mentioned in the Qur'ān. They also signify the characteristics of our beloved Prophet (peace be upon him). Aḥmad is the name which the Prophet ʿĪsā (peace be upon him) used in his prophecy:

> *And remember, ʿĪsā, the son of Maryam, said: "O Children of Isrāʾīl! I am the Messenger of Allah (sent) to you, confirming the* al-Tawrāt *(which came) before me, and giving glad tidings of a Messenger to come after me, whose name shall be Aḥmad."*
>
> (al-Ṣaff 61: 6)

Aḥmad is the superlative form, which means he is the most highly praised among the Prophets. *Muḥammad* means the one whose character and manners are highly praiseworthy.

Significance

It is significant that the first word of the opening chapter of the Qur'ān starts with *al-Ḥamd.* It implies that man's natural response to the numerous blessings that he receives from Allah should be grateful praise. The universe is full of His bounties that serve mankind. This should generate feelings of gratitude towards their Creator. Thus, it was the consistent practice of the Prophet to start his *Khuṭbah* (sermon) with *Ḥamd.* It is the recommended practice of all scholars of Islam to begin lectures and talks with *Ḥamd.* It is also pertinent to note that the Qur'ān mentions that believers who have done righteous deeds and are guided by their Lord will be rewarded with eternal bliss in Paradise. They will say:

> *'Glory to You O Allah!' and 'Peace' will be their greeting therein! and the end of their call is* al-Ḥamdu Lillāhi Rabb al-'Ālamīn – *'Grateful praise be to Allah, the Cherisher and Sustainer of the Worlds.'*
>
> (Yūnus 10: 10)

This implies that the whole life of a believer should revolve around gratitude for, and acknowledgement of, the mercy of the living embodiment of blessings and benediction.

This is what the angels do:

> *And you will see the angels surrounding the Throne (Divine) on all sides, singing glory and praise to their Lord.*
>
> (al-Zumar 39: 75)

References

Ḥamd: 1: 1; 6: 1; 7: 43; 10: 10; 18: 1. *Ḥamīd*: 14: 1; 31: 12; 35: 15; 42: 28; 85: 8. *Maḥmūd*: 17: 79. *Aḥmad*: 61: 6. *Muḥammad*: 3: 144; 33: 40; 47: 2; 48: 29.

See also *Shukr*

Ḥanīf [حنيف] (Upright Person)

Meaning

Ḥanafa means to turn or incline towards something. *Ḥanīf* (pl. *ḥunafā'*) is a person who has abandoned and cut himself off from all other ways in order to concentrate on and follow fully Allah's path. Thus it means a true believer, one who scorns the false creeds surrounding him and professes the true religion.

Analysis

The Qur'ān uses the word *Ḥanīf* repeatedly in connection with the Prophet Ibrāhīm (peace be upon him) as he was truly an upright person in all his dealings and sincerely followed the path of monotheism and completely submitted to the obedience of Allah. As he was viewed as the spiritual head of all Jews, Christians as well as the *Mushrikūn* (idolaters), the Qur'ān emphasizes that the Prophet Ibrāhīm (peace be upon him) was not a Jew, Christian or idolater but a *Ḥanīf*, totally devoted to the worship of one God (Āl 'Imrān 3: 67 and 95; al-Baqarah 2: 135).

Before the advent of the Prophet (peace be upon him), some people still followed the creed of the Prophet Ibrāhīm (peace be upon him), by avoiding all forms of polytheism and accepted monotheism yet did not follow the Jewish and Christian doctrines.

References

Ḥanīf: 2: 135; 3: 3 and 67; 4: 125; 6: 79; 98: 5.

Ḥaqq [حق] (Truth)

Meanings

Ḥaqq is one of those words that are used in many different meanings in the Qur'ān. It is derived from *ḥaqqa* meaning to be true, to be right or correct as well as to confirm. It also means to be obligatory, imperative or incumbent upon someone. This word is used in the following meanings in the Qur'ān:

1. As Allah is the ultimate reality and truth He is *al-Ḥaqq*. "*Then they all shall return to Allah, their True Protector, surely His is the command and He is the swiftest in taking account*" (al-An'ām 6: 62). The emphasis is that the Reality, the Truth is only the True One and human beings come from Him and will return to Him. "*Such is Allah, your real Cherisher and Sustainer: apart from the Truth what (remains) but error?*" (Yūnus 10: 32). Here Allah's handiwork and wisdom are referred to as the Real Truth so that man should turn to Him.
2. As the Hereafter is also a reality, it is called "*Yawm al-Ḥaqq*" – the Day of Sure Reality (al-Naba' 78: 39). When unbelievers sought the confirmation of *Qiyāmah*, the Prophet was asked to confirm; "*Yes, by my Lord it is the* Ḥaqq *(Truth)*" (Yūnus 10: 53).
3. As Allah is *al-Ḥaqq*, everything which emanates from Him is also *Ḥaqq*. In this sense the Qur'ān is *Ḥaqq* (al-Baqarah 2: 26; al-Mā'idah 5: 84; Yūnus 10: 94 and al-Ra'd 13: 1). So is the Messenger of Allah (peace be upon him) who is sent down as *Ḥaqq* and as a bearer of glad tidings and warnings (al-Baqarah 2: 119). So also is the *Dīn* which is the way of life prescribed by Allah. It is called "*Dīn al-Ḥaqq*" (al-Tawbah 9: 33; al-Fatḥ 48: 28; al-Ṣaff 61: 9).
4. The word is used for any statement or act that is in conformity with reality and hence is in fact true. The opposite of this is falsehood (*Bāṭil*). Allah has created the universe with a purpose and in true proportion; this is the truth (al-Zumar 39: 5; al-Ḥijr 15: 85).
5. *Ḥaqq* is used in the legal sense as right due to someone: for example the right of the needy in the wealth of rich people (al-Dhāriyāt 51: 19; al-Ma'ārij 70: 24); making a will as an obligation (al-Baqarah 2: 180) or making provision for divorced women (al-Baqarah 2: 241); rights of one's relatives (al-Isrā' 17: 26).
6. The word *Ḥaqq* is applied to the due process of law which is undertaken to determine guilt or otherwise. This procedure is

Ḥaqq: "*Take no life, which Allah has made sacred, except by way of justice and law*" (al-An'ām 6: 151; al-Isrā' 17: 33).

References

Ḥaqq: 6: 62; 9: 33; 13: 1; 39: 5; 78: 39.

See also *Bāṭil* and *Ṣidq*

Ḥarām [حرام]

see *al-Ḥalāl wa al-Ḥarām*

Ḥasad [حسد] (Envy)

Meaning

Ḥasada means to envy or to be jealous or resentful, and the noun *Ḥasad* means envy or jealousy. *Ḥasad* can be defined as disliking and hating another person for having the bounty that Allah has bestowed on him. This could be wealth, knowledge, honour or prestige, or any other favour or blessing. The envier (*Ḥāsid*) wishes that these bounties should be taken away from the envied person and awarded to him or at least that person should be deprived of them. However, only wishing that one should also be endowed with such bounties does not constitute *Ḥasad*. Indeed, believers are encouraged to compete with one another in the acts of righteousness (al-Muṭaffifīn 83: 26).

The Evils of *Ḥasad*

Satan is the arch-enemy of humankind. He was envious because the Prophet Ādam was given special blessing and knowledge by Allah because all the angels were ordered to prostrate before him. Satan's response was envy and pride, and his refusal to prostrate himself earned him eternal damnation. In Sūrah al-Falaq believers are taught to seek Allah's refuge from the evil of the envier, a term which is firstly applicable to Satan and then to others also (al-Falaq 113: 5).

Similarly *Ahl al-Kitāb* (the People of the Book) were expecting that the last prophet would be from Banū Isrā'īl. When this favour was bestowed on Banū Ismā'īl, however, they became envious and wanted Muslims to return to disbelief (al-Baqarah 2: 109; al-Nisā' 4: 54).

Ḥasad can penetrate and wreck the closest of blood relationships, as shown in the story of two sons of the Prophet Ādam (peace be upon him) as narrated in Sūrah al-Mā'idah (5: 27–31). As mentioned by Ibn Kathīr, it was envy of his brother, that his brother's sacrifice was accepted and his was not, that led one son to kill his own brother.

The story of the brothers of the Prophet Yūsuf (peace be upon him) is very similar. His brothers were jealous of their father's love for Yūsuf and hence plotted to get rid of him (Yūsuf 12: 8–10).

A *ḥadīth* warns about the evil of *Ḥasad* very graphically: "*Ḥasad* eats away one's good deeds just as fire swallows a dry wood." (Abū Dāwūd)

Safeguarding against *Ḥasad*

One should put one's trust in Allah and be assured that no one will be able to harm him. Seeking Allah's refuge by reciting the last two *sūrahs* of the Qur'ān is recommended by the Prophet (peace be upon him) to safeguard the believer not only from *Ḥasad* but from all other evils as well. Of course one should not bear any grudge against the envier, and one should repel evil with goodness. Finally, one should always repent to Allah and seek His forgiveness and try to form a close relationship with Him.

References

Ḥasad: 2: 109; 4: 54; 48: 15; 113: 5.

Ḥasanah [حسنة]

see *Iḥsān* and *Sū'*

Hawā [هوىٰ] (Lust)

Meaning

Hawā means to drop down, to fall down or to tumble. In Sūrah al-Najm it is used for the setting of the star (al-Najm 53: 1). From this root the noun *Hawā* (pl. *Ahwā'* and *Hawāyā*) also means love, affection, craving, lust or pleasure. In the Qur'ān it is also used for the base desires. It is said about the Prophet (peace be upon him) "*And he speaks not of his own desire*" (al-Najm 53: 3). This refutes the argument of those who allege that the Qur'ān is the composition of the Prophet himself. Both meanings of the word *Hawā* are used in close proximity in Sūrah al-Najm.

Lustful desires drag down a person from his honoured and respectable position and disgrace him, and ultimately in the *Ākhirah* they lead him into *Hāwiyah* (the bottomless pit of the blazing fire) (al-Qāri'ah 101: 9–11)

Analysis

Allah has created human beings innocent and pure with an inclination towards virtue and righteous conduct. They are endowed with goodness, wisdom and power. By making them His vicegerents Allah has raised their status above the angels. Of course, the vicegerency also gave them will and discretion. They are given a choice of following the path of obedience to Allah or of following their own whims and desires. Those who follow the latter debase themselves as the lowest of the low. These are the ones who have made their desires their deity; thus their hearts are sealed and they cannot be guided.

> *Have you seen him who takes as his god his own vain desire, and Allah has sent him astray despite his knowledge, and has sealed up his hearing and his heart and has set up a covering on his sight? Who, then will guide him after Allah (has withdrawn guidance)? Will you not then be admonished?*
>
> (al-Jāthiyah 45: 23)

The orderliness of the heavens and the earth and their sustained existence is the consequence of the fine balance that Allah has fashioned.

It is not the outcome of the whims and caprice of people. "*If the truth had been in accord with their desires, truly the heavens and the earth, and all therein would be in confusion and corruption*" (al-Mu'minūn 23: 71).

References

Hawā: 4: 135; 38: 26; 53: 1 and 3; 79: 40.

Ḥayā' [حياء]

see *Faḥshā', Fāḥishah*

Hidāyah [هداية]

see *Hudā*

Hijrah [هجرة] (Migration)

Meaning

The literal meaning of *Hajara* is to leave someone or something. It means to emigrate, to give up, or to disassociate, and to part company with someone. In this sense *Hijrah* means to leave or avoid something and to move from one thing to something else. In the terminology of the *Sharī'ah* it means that a believer leaves a place where it has become very difficult and dangerous for him to practise his *Dīn* and preserve his faith and moves to another place that is more secure for him.

The Historical Context

During the life of the Prophet (peace be upon him), persecution by the Quraysh in Makkah forced Muslims to emigrate to Abyssinia (modern-day Ethiopia). Later, Muslims migrated to Yathrib (later named Madīnah), as did the Prophet (peace be upon him). When the Islamic state was established in Madīnah it became obligatory on all Muslims to migrate there. Those who, despite having means and ability to migrate from

Makkah to Madīnah, did not do so were not considered true Muslims. The emigration became the proof of their faith (al-Nisā' 4: 89). Those Muslims who did not migrate to Madīnah, were told that the Islamic state owed them no duty of protection (al-Anfāl 8: 72).

After the conquest of Makkah this specific form of *Hijrah* was abolished as Makkah became part of the Islamic state. This ruling is based on a *ḥadīth* of the Prophet (peace be upon him) in which it is said: "There is no *Hijrah* after the conquest of Makkah but there remains *Jihād* and intention" (Bukhārī and Muslim). This does not mean that there cannot be any occasion for *Hijrah* at all. Another *ḥadīth* states: "*Hijrah* will not be discontinued so long as there is *Jihād*" (Aḥmad). Situations may always arise when a believer finds himself forced to emigrate to save his *dīn*.

The *Hijrah* of the Prophet (peace be upon him) to Madīnah in 622 CE marks the beginning of the Islamic calendar, as this marks the establishment of the Islamic state in Madīnah.

Characteristic Features of the *Hijrah*

The *Hijrah* is considered as a noble and difficult form of sacrifice. It is not easy to cut off all the ties with one's relations and friends and leave one's means of livelihood and emigrate to a different city or country and live among strangers. But this is what many prophets did when they were rejected by their own people. The *Hijrah* of the Prophets Ibrāhīm and Lūṭ are mentioned in detail in the Qur'ān. Allah has promised great rewards for those who emigrate with the aim of safeguarding their *Dīn*. "*Those who believe and suffer exile and strive in the cause of Allah as well as those who give them asylum and aid – these are (all) the real believers. For them is the forgiveness of sins and a provision most generous*" (al-Anfāl 8: 74). This aspect of the *Hijrah* is very important for Muslims living in the West to consider.

The *Hijrah*: a Different Concept

As *Hijrah* in its literal meaning is to abandon something, hence leaving evil and turning to good is also considered as *Hijrah*. Making a conscious effort to leave and abandon the path and the company of those who are transgressing the divine laws and to migrate towards a good and righteous society is also a *Hijrah*. The Prophet is reported to have said: "A *Muhājir* (migrant) is one who avoids what Allah has prohibited" (Bukhārī).

Of course, the *Hijrah* will always remain an integral part of the Islamic society. The Prophet (peace be upon him) said: "I command you to perform five duties that Allah has ordered me to do. Be with *al-Jamāʿah* (the Muslim Community), *Al-Samʿ* (listening attentively), and *al-Ṭāʿah* (obeying diligently), and *al-Hijrah* (migrating from evil society to a noble society) and *al-Jihād* (struggling in the Way of Allah)" (Tirmidhī). This means that the *Hijrah* will always remain obligatory for Muslims. This *Hijrah* will be primarily in the sense as explained above.

References

Hijrah: 2: 218; 3: 195; 8: 72; 9: 20; 22: 58.

Ḥikmah [حكمة] (Wisdom)

Meanings

Ḥakama is to pass judgement or to express an opinion, and *al-Ḥukm* is to give a decision about something. Thus, *Ḥikmah* means that knowledge that provides profound insight and the ability to give accurate judgement.

In Sūrah al-Baqarah it is said: "*those to whom* al-Ḥikmah *is granted receive indeed a bounty overflowing*" (2: 269). This verse occurs in the course of a passage encouraging believers to spend in Allah's way and not to be deceived by the tricks of Satan, who threatens poverty if one gives away one's money in charity. In this context *al-Ḥikmah* is that bounty which safeguards a person from following the path of Satan, so that instead of miserliness one spends one's wealth generously in good causes.

In Sūrah al-Naḥl believers are instructed to "*Invite all to the way of your Lord with wisdom and beautiful preaching and argue with them in ways that are best and gracious...*" (16: 125). Here *al-Ḥikmah* means logical arguments and convincing proofs.

Analysis

One of the blessings of *Ḥikmah* is the ability to arrive at a balanced and correct judgement. Its other benefits are enabling one to acquire a chaste moral life and a civilized approach in personal and social affairs. It is for this reason that the word *Ḥikmah* is used to indicate maturity in reason and virtuous morals. A person is called a *Ḥakīm* (one who possesses *Ḥikmah*) when he is wise and cultured. In this respect the name of Luqmān is specifically mentioned in the Qur'ān (Luqmān 31: 12). *Ḥakīm* Luqmān was known in Arabia for his wisdom and sagacity. Very little is known about him but he epitomizes perfect wisdom.

The prime recipients of *Ḥikmah* were Allah's messengers and prophets as well as those on whom Allah wished to bestow this blessing. The Prophet Dāwūd (peace be upon him) is specifically mentioned in the Qur'ān as one who was blessed with this virtue. Allah "*gave him wisdom and sound judgement in speech and decision*" (Ṣād 38: 20). Of course, all the other prophets were also given *Ḥikmah*. This wisdom is only acquired through revelation, and the prophets transmitted it to others. As one of their tasks was the teaching of *Ḥikmah*, "*Allah did confer a great favour on the believers when He sent among them a Messenger from among themselves, rehearsing unto them the signs of Allah, purifying them and instructing them in Scripture and wisdom, while before that they were in manifest error*" (Āl 'Imrān 3: 164; al-Baqarah 2: 129 and 151; al-Jumu'ah 62: 2). The teaching of *Ḥikmah* had two aims: giving people gems of wisdom as well as creating in them the ability to cultivate *Ḥikmah* in their thinking. The term *al-Ḥikmah* is used by many commentators to refer to the *aḥādīth* of the Prophet (peace be upon him). Of course his speech was full of pearls of wisdom.

Some Other Words from the Same Root

Ḥukm (pl. *Aḥkām*) means judgement and decision. The word is used in three different meanings in the Qur'ān.

1. Sometimes it just denotes judgement: for example "*We did witness their judgement*" (al-Anbiyā' 21: 78) and "*Do they seek after a judgement of (the Days of) Ignorance? But who for a people*

whose faith is assured, can give better judgement than Allah?" (al-Mā'idah 5: 50).

2. In certain other places it means almost what is conveyed by the word *Ḥikmah*: that is, insight and the ability to make proper decisions. For example, of the Prophet Yaḥyā (peace be upon him) it is said: "*We gave him wisdom even as a youth*" (Maryam 19: 12). Similarly about the Prophet Lūt it is written that he was endowed with wisdom and knowledge (al-Anbiyā' 21: 74).
3. Sometimes *Ḥukm* is used to mean a command or order. In Sūrah Ghāfir it is said: "*The command is with Allah, Most High, Most Great*" (40: 12). In Sūrah al-Qaṣaṣ Allah's Majesty is described thus: "*He is Allah: there is no god but He. To Him be praise at the first and the last: for Him is the command and to Him shall (you all) be returned*" (28: 70).

In summary, by *Ḥukm* three things are meant: deep insight, the ability to make good decisions, and Allah's delegated authority to judge among people. In fact, all these are constituent parts of *Ḥikmah*.

Ḥākim (pl. *Ḥukkām*) means a judge or ruler. The basic instruction to them is to decide judicial issues justly. "*Whenever you judge between people, judge with justice*" (al-Nisā' 4: 58). No one should try to bribe judges to influence their judgements (al-Baqarah 2: 188).

Muḥkam means firm, strengthened, reinforced, precise, and accurate. In Sūrah Āl 'Imrān the Qur'ānic verses are categorized into *Muḥkamāt*, meaning basic or fundamental (of established meanings), and *Mutashābihāt*, whose meanings are obscure and unclear. "*Those who are firmly grounded in knowledge say: 'We believe in the Book; the whole of it is from our Lord*" (3: 7).

References

Ḥikmah: 2: 269; 5: 110; 16: 125; 31: 12; 33: 34. *Ḥukm*: 5: 50; 12: 40 and 67; 40: 12; 60: 10. *Ḥākim*: 2: 188; 4: 35; 7: 87; 11: 45; 95: 8. *Muḥkam*: 3: 7; 47: 20.

See also *Āyah*

Hudā [هدًى] (Guidance)

Meanings

Hidāyah means to guide someone with kindness and benevolence. Thus, *Hadīyah* means a gift, and *Hudā* means guidance, one of the most important of Allah's Blessings. According to Amīn Aḥsan Iṣlāḥī, *Hudā* is used in several ways in Arabic as well as in the Qur'ān. He has identified the following meanings:

1. insight and vision
2. proof, evidence, milestone
3. a clear and straight way, hence its use as a synonym for the *Sharī'ah*
4. the act of guiding – thus not only showing the way but also leading someone to his goal.

These meanings and their implications are discussed below.

Analysis

THE PROVISION OF GUIDANCE

Guidance is given to everything in this universe. This is mentioned in several places in the Qur'ān:

> *Glorify the name of your Guardian-Lord, the Most High, Who has created, and further, given order and proportion; Who has ordained laws and granted guidance.*
>
> (al-A'lā 87: 1–3)

> *Our Lord is He Who gave to each (created) thing its form and nature, and further gave (it) guidance.*
>
> (Ṭā Hā 20: 50)

Thus, Allah brought human beings from non-being into being. Then He endowed them with form and shape and gave them faculties suited to what is expected of them and the environment in which they live, and gave them everything in due proportion. This Guidance is given to all of His creation whether animate or inanimate. They are all guided by Allah.

THE NATURE OF GUIDANCE

One. For the guidance of inanimate objects, there are Divine laws of nature, which regulate their movements, growth or decay:

> *And a Sign for them is the night: We withdraw therefrom the day, and behold they are plunged in darkness. And the Sun runs its course for a period determined for it: that is the decree of (Him), the Exalted in Might, the All-Knowing. And the Moon – We have measured (to traverse) till it returns like the old (and withered) lower part of a date stalk. It is not permitted to the Sun to catch up the Moon, nor can the night outstrip the day: each (just) swims along in (its own) orbit (according to law).*
>
> (Yā Sīn: 36: 37–40)

Two. For the guidance of living creatures, there is a primary guidance by instinct bestowed by Allah. Thus, for example the Qur'ān says of bees:

> *And your Lord inspired the Bee to build its cells in hills and trees and in (human beings') habitations. Then to eat all the produce (of the Earth) and find with skill the spacious paths of its Lord. There issues from within their bodies a drink of varying colours, wherein is healing for human beings. Verily there is a Sign for those who reflect.*
>
> (al-Naḥl 16: 68–69)

Although the word Guidance is not used in this passage, *Waḥy* (inspiration) refers to the bee's instinct to suck juice from flowers and make honey to build honeycombs.

Three. Human beings are guided by their faculty of reasoning and thinking and by the signs all around them that are manifested in nature:

> *Behold in the creation of the heavens and the earth, and the alternation of night and day – there are indeed signs for men of understanding.*
>
> (Āl ʿImrān 3: 190)

> *And among His Signs, He shows you the lightning, by way both of fear and hope, and He sends down rain from the sky and with it gives life to the earth after it is dead. Verily in that there are signs for those who are wise.*
>
> (al-Rūm 30: 24)

GUIDANCE THROUGH REVELATION

Guidance by *Waḥy* (Revelation) is conveyed through Allah's Messengers. This is the best form of Guidance given to mankind so that they can lead their lives in this world according to His commands. As human beings are superior to all other creations and as they have freedom of choice, they need more extensive and precise guidance. Thus, they are not left to rely solely on their basic instincts and reasoning faculty to regulate their lives, but throughout the ages Prophets have come to guide them to the right path.

> *Then Ādam learnt from his Lord words of inspiration and his Lord turned towards him: for He is Oft-Returning, Most Merciful. We said: "Get you down all from here: and if, as is sure there comes to you Guidance from Me, whosoever follows My Guidance, on them shall be no fear, nor shall they grieve."*
>
> (al-Baqarah 2: 37–38)

> *It is He Who sent down to you (step by step) in truth the Book confirming what was sent before it. And He sent down the* Tawrāt *and* Injīl *before this, as a guide to mankind.*
>
> (Āl ʿImrān 3: 3–4)

GUIDANCE AS INSIGHT

As mentioned above, one of the meanings of *Hudā* is insight, enlightenment and *Tawfīq* (Allah's Help). It is given to those who accept Allah's Guidance. The Qur'ān says:

> *But to those who receive Guidance, He increases the (light of) Guidance and bestows on them piety and restraint (from evil).*
>
> (Muḥammad 47: 17)

> *And if anyone believes in Allah, (Allah) guides his heart (aright).*
>
> (al-Taghābun 64: 11)

THE ULTIMATE ACT OF GUIDANCE

The ultimate act of guidance by Allah is to guide those who follow the Right Path towards *Jannah*. This is the final act of Guidance by Allah. Thus, believers, after attaining the final bliss, will proclaim:

> *Praise be to Allah Who has guided us to this (felicity): never could we have found Guidance, had it not been for the Guidance of Allah.*
>
> (al-Aʿrāf 7: 43)

THE LAWS OF RECEIVING GUIDANCE

1. Only Allah is the source of Guidance. It is not even in the domain of His prophets and messengers to force guidance on someone:

   > *It is true you will not be able to guide every one whom you love; but Allah guides those whom He will and He knows best who receive guidance.*
   >
   > (al-Qaṣaṣ 28: 56)

   Thus, it is only Allah who in His infinite Mercy guides whoever He likes. No one can guide others. This is explicitly stated in many places in the Qur'ān:

It is not required of you (O Messenger), to guide them to the Right Path, but Allah guides to the Right Path whom He pleases.

(al-Baqarah 2: 272)

The Prophet's (peace be upon him) duty was to convey and explain the message. As for its acceptance, that was the responsibility of the people (see 5: 92 and 29: 18).

2. Allah has given human beings the choice to follow either the path of righteousness or the path of disobedience:

And We have shown him the two highways (i.e. the path of virtue and the path of vice).

(al-Balad 90: 10)

We showed him the Way: whether he be grateful or ungrateful (rests on his will).

(al-Dahr 76: 3)

3. Thus, those who seek guidance from Allah, He guides to the right path:

And He guides them to Himself by a straight Way.

(al-Nisā' 4: 175)

And those who strive in Our (Cause) We will certainly guide them to Our Paths.

(al-'Ankabūt 29: 69)

4. Those who are unjust and ungrateful do not deserve guidance from Allah:

Verily Allah guides not a people unjust.

(al-Mā'idah 5: 51)

> *Verily Allah guides not such as are false and ungrateful.*
>
> (al-Zumar 39: 3)

Thus, in Sūrah al-Fātiḥah the only blessing we are instructed to ask from Allah is that of *Hidāyah*.

References

Hudā: 2: 2; 7: 43; 47: 17; 76: 3; 87: 3.

Ḥudūd [حدود]

see *'Adhāb*

Ḥukm [حكم]

see *Ḥikmah* and *Amr*

'Ibādah [عبادة] (Worship)

Meaning

The root of this word is *'Abd*, meaning to become subservient, to be subdued, not to resist, and to be submissive. Thus, the literal meaning of *'Ibādah* is to express utter humbleness, subservience and humility. In the Qur'ān, the word is also used for acts of worship. Thus, it also includes obedience, as it would be illogical if a person were to worship someone and then not obey his commands.

The word *'Abd*, which comes from *'Ibādah*, means a slave or a servant. This is the opposite of a free person or one who is independent. A slave has no control over his life for it is controlled by his master. The difference between a slave and a free person is portrayed by the Qur'ān thus:

> *Allah sets forth the parable (of two men: one) a slave under the dominion of another; he has no power of any sort; and (the*

other) a man on whom We have bestowed goodly favours from ourselves, and he spends thereof (freely), privately and publicly. Are the two equals?

(al-Naḥl 16: 75)

Analysis

The essence of *'Ibādah* is to perform all acts of worship and service exclusively to Allah and to obey and to follow His Commands unconditionally and always remain His slave and servant. These aspects of *'Ibādah* are explained explicitly on several occasions in the Qur'ān:

Verily it is We Who have revealed the Book to you in Truth: so serve Allah offering Him sincere devotion.

(al-Zumar 39: 2)

Your Lord has decreed that you worship none but Him.

(al-Isrā' 17: 23)

O People! Adore your Lord Who created you and those who came before you, that you may become righteous.

(al-Baqarah 2: 21)

For We assuredly sent amongst every people a messenger, (with the command) "Serve Allah and eschew evil".

(al-Naḥl 16: 36)

In addition to the command to worship, obey and serve Allah alone, the instruction is also not to worship, obey or serve Satan or anyone else.

Those who eschew Ṭāghūt *(Evil) and fall not into its worship and turn to Allah for them is good news.*

(al-Zumar 39: 17)

"Did I not enjoin on you, O children of Adam that you should not worship Satan; for that he was to you an enemy avowed?"

(Yā Sīn 36: 60)

Worship of Satan or *Ṭāghūt* (Evil) may be confined to only very tiny groups throughout the ages. Thus, *'Ibādah* of Satan and *Ṭāghūt* here really means to obey and to accept the overlordship and sovereignty of others instead of Allah. These others can be a person or an institution or even one's own desires.

Popular usage of the term *'Ibādah* is now restricted to acts of worship only; obedience to the laws and regulations of Allah are not usually considered as *'Ibādah*. When a person is referred to as an *'Ābid* (that is one who is diligent in *'Ibādah*), it is meant that he regularly performs prayers, fasting and other acts of worship. The whole purpose of our creation, however, is *'Ibādah*:

> *I have not created* jinns *and human beings except that they serve Me.*
>
> (al-Dhāriyāt 51: 56)

If the purpose of our creation is *'Ibādah* then it cannot be restricted to the few rites and rituals of worship we perform. Rather it is the totality of our whole life that should be spent in obedience to and in the service of Allah. As we cannot spend all our life praying and fasting, earning a lawful livelihood and performing our duties in society and living a pious and chaste life are also acts of *'Ibādāt*. Sayyid Quṭb pointed out that the *Fuqahā'* (jurists) later on divided various human activities into *'Ibādah* and *Mu'āmalāt* (social affairs). When the Prophet (peace be upon him) started his mission in Makkah the daily prayers, fasting, *Zakāh* and *Ḥajj* were not enjoined upon Muslims. Thus, *'Ibādah* at that time was to accept Allah as the Sovereign and to obey His Commands and that of His Messenger in all affairs.

Usage of the Word *'Abd*

Often *'Abd* is used as a term of endearment by Allah for His chosen or sincere servants. Similarly *'Ibādī* (My servant) or *'Ibādunā* (Our servants) indicates the closeness of Allah's relation.

Glory to (Allah) Who did take His Servant for a journey by night.

(al-Isrā' 17: 1)

And commemorate Our Servants Ibrāhīm, Isḥāq and Ya'qūb.

(Ṣād 38: 45)

And the servants of (Allah) Most Gracious are those who walk on the earth in humility.

(al-Furqān 25: 63)

The word *'Abd* has two plurals. One is *'Ibād* as in the last quotation, where it means those who are devoted to Allah's service; thus, it can be translated as devotees. The other plural, *'Abīd,* embraces all His creatures. This is the meaning in the following verse:

I do not do the least injustice to My servants.

(Qāf 50: 29)

References

'Ibādah: 4: 172; 7: 206; 18: 110; 19: 65; 46: 6. *'Abd*: 17: 1; 18: 1; 19: 2; 25: 1; 34: 9.

Iblīs [إبليس]

see *Shayṭān*

Iḍṭirār [إضطرار] (Necessity)

Meaning

Ḍarra means to harm, impair, damage, or hurt, and *Ḍarar* (pl. *Aḍrār*) is the noun meaning harm and damage. *Iḍṭirār* from this root means compulsion, exigency, predicament or emergency.

Usage

Idṭirār means to be compelled to do something by someone or circumstances against one's wishes. There could be different contexts for this compulsion. One may be compelled by external circumstances, such as being threatened by physical force or by intimidation to do an act.

Analysis

In the *Sharī'ah*, under the law of necessity, it is permissible to eat unlawful food to save one's life. However this concession requires that certain conditions must be observed.

1. This must be a situation where one's life is threatened.
2. There is no intention of breaking the law.
3. One should not consume more than what is necessary for survival.

After fulfilling these conditions, if one is really compelled by necessity to eat forbidden food, this will not be considered sinful. This ruling is based on several verses in which it is stated: "*But if one is forced by necessity without wilful disobedience, nor transgressing due limits – then one is guiltless*" (al-Baqarah 2: 173; al-Mā'idah 5: 3; al-An'ām 6: 145; al-Naḥl 16: 115).

Concession and Resoluteness

All concessions given to us by Allah result from His Mercy and Benefaction. Human beings suffer from sickness or have to go through difficult circumstances like the ordeal of travelling, so Allah has given concessions in the performance of certain obligations. Prayers can be reduced, fasting can be postponed, and if water is not available then *Tayammum* (dry ablution) can be done instead of *Wuḍū'*. In such cases it is recommended that one should not show resoluteness and refuse to take advantage of the concessions. A *ḥadīth* narrates that if there were two options the Prophet (peace be upon him) always chose the easier one. It is not piety to suffer unnecessary hardship.

However, there could be many cases when one should have enough courage to remain firm in one's *Dīn*. For example it is permissible to utter some blasphemous words to save one's life. However, the path of resoluteness is to refrain from doing so. This is the example of the courage displayed by many Companions during their persecution in Makkah.

Word from the Same Root

Ḍarar (pl. *Aḍrār*) means harm, hurt, infliction or injury. Islam does not allow harming others. Many injunctions in the Qur'ān prohibit harming others. "*And let neither scribe nor witness suffer harm. If you do such harm, it would be wickedness*" (al-Baqarah 2: 233 and 282; al-Ṭalāq 65: 6). There is a clear statement enunciating the principle that the *Dīn* is straightforward. "*He has chosen you and has imposed no difficulties on you*" (al-Ḥajj 22: 78). Allah knows the abilities and limitations of His creatures and takes these abilities and limitations into consideration when imposing any duty.

The legal maxim stated in a *ḥadīth* that "There is not to be any causing of harm nor is there to be any reciprocating of harm" (Ibn Mājah and Dāraquṭnī), is one of the most important principles of Islamic law. It touches virtually all aspects of law. According to Imām Abū Dāwūd it is one of the *aḥādīth* around which all *Fiqh* revolves.

References

Iḍṭirār: 2: 173; 5: 3; 6: 145; 16: 115. *Ḍarar*: 2: 282; 5: 76; 7: 188; 10: 49; 65: 6.

Iḥsān [إحسان] (Good Acts)

Meaning

The root of the word *iḥsān* is *ḤSN* which means good, an agreeable or desirable thing. According to Imām al-Rāghib al-Iṣfahānī this desirability may be due to its appeal to the intellect or to the carnal self or just its outward beauty. *Iḥsān* refers to those qualities in human beings that beautify their character. Such qualities are benevolence, good acts, politeness, sympathy, generosity, tolerance and consideration. This word and its derivatives are used extensively in the Qur'ān and the *aḥādīth* of the Prophet (peace be upon him), praising it as a desirable quality of the believers. In brief, *Iḥsān* is to do an act, or treat others, in the best possible way.

The Difference between *'Adl* and *Iḥsān*

Whereas justice (*'Adl*) requires one to deal with others fairly, *Iḥsān* requires that one should deal with them generously as well. One should not try to extract one's rights from others; on the contrary, one should forgo them so as to create better relations. Similarly, one should try to give others more than their due so as to create harmonious relationships in society. Such an attitude of generosity, politeness and benevolence will perhaps win the hearts of others.

Iḥsān as defined by the Prophet (peace be upon him)

Iḥsān is a very comprehensive term. It covers all types of good behaviour and concern for fellow human beings. It means that one uses one's wealth and capabilities for the good and welfare of the society in which one lives. The best explanation of *Iḥsān* is given by the Prophet (peace be upon him) in a very important *ḥadīth* known as *Ḥadīth Jibrīl*. Once Archangel Jibrīl came in human form and asked several questions about the tenets of Islam in order to teach the Companions about the *Dīn*. One of his questions to the Prophet (peace be upon him) was:

> "Tell me about *al-Iḥsān*." The Prophet (peace be upon him) explained: "It is that you worship Allah as if you see Him, but if you are unable to visualize seeing Him then (at least) visualize that He sees you."
>
> (Muslim)

In this *ḥadīth* the Prophet (peace be upon him) did not give a dictionary-type meaning of *Iḥsān*. Instead, he explained the real motivation behind the performance of one's duty. One should always be conscious that Allah is watching over all one's actions, and one's real motive should be to attain Allah's pleasure and avoid His disapproval. This brings about purity of heart. It ensures that a person is concerned with the quality of his deeds and not with mere performance of his obligations. Feeling that one sees Allah results in the performance of acts of worship in the best possible way. Such a person will be filled with awe and admiration for his Lord and he will be fully absorbed in his devotion. However, this is a difficult level for everyone to reach. The lower level is to realize that our Lord is watching us and that we are in His august presence. Thus, the presence of either level of *Iḥsān* results in worship of Allah in an excellent manner.

The Comprehensive Nature of *Iḥsān*

Iḥsān is not confined to acts of worship only: it requires that everything should be done to the best of one's ability. Attaining the status of *Iḥsān* requires excellence in the performance of all deeds. The Prophet (peace be upon him) even advised us to use a very sharp knife for slaughter so as not to inflict more pain than is necessary on the slaughtered animal. The same excellence should be observed in all other actions.

As *iḥsān* deals with purification of the inner self, it is the essence of the Islamic *tazkiyah* teachings. Thus, *Iḥsān* is the basis of the Islamic *Taṣawwuf* (Sufism). However, the purity and spontaneity of the Companions and earlier followers of the path of *Iḥsān* became contaminated with Greek, Persian and Hindu mysticism and ended up as an unIslamic mixture of questionable practices.

Words from the Same Root

The word *Ḥasanatan* from the same root is extensively used both in the Qur'ān and *aḥādīth* for good deeds that give inner pleasure. Its antonym is *Sayyi'atan*, i.e. evil deed. Both words are used together in many verses to highlight their difference (al-Nisā' 4: 78–79; al-A'rāf 7: 95; Hūd 11: 114; Fuṣṣilat 41: 34).

The word *Muḥsin* and its plural *Muḥsinīn* are applied to those who practise the precept of *Iḥsān* in their lives and are praised by Allah for their behaviour and promised reward in the Hereafter (Āl 'Imrān 3: 134; al-Mā'idah 5: 85; Hūd 11: 115; al-Ḥajj 22; 37).

References

Iḥsān: 2: 83; 9: 100; 16: 90; 17: 23; 55: 60. *Ḥasanatan*: 2: 201; 4: 79; 7: 95; 11: 114; 41: 34. *Muḥsin*: 2: 112; 12: 22; 37: 113; 39: 34; 51: 16.

Ikhlāṣ [إخلاص] (Sincerity)

Meaning

Khalaṣa literally means the act of purification by separation of impurities. Thus, it means to be pure, unadulterated and unmixed. Hence, *Mukhliṣ* means sincere and devoted, the one who is pure and of undefiled faith.

Usage

The word *Ikhlāṣ* is often used in relation to the *Dīn*: "*He is the Living (One): There is no God but He; call upon Him, giving sincere devotion. Praise be to Allah, Lord of the Worlds*" (Ghāfir 40: 65); "*And they have been commanded no more than this: to worship Allah offering Him sincere devotion being true in faith*" (al-Bayyinah 98: 5). Purifying the *Dīn* means to avoid *Riyā'* (showing off) and pretence of piety, and instead having sincere faith and doing all acts exclusively for Allah's pleasure.

Ikhlāṣ is also used in its primary meaning of separation from others. When the brothers of the Prophet Yūsuf (peace be upon him) despaired of getting back their brother who was accused of theft, they separately held a meeting. The word used in the Qur'ān is *Khalaṣū* (Yūsuf 12: 80).

Analysis

The word *Ikhlāṣ* in the Qur'ān is used as an antonym of *Nifāq* (hypocrisy). The Prophet (peace be upon him) had indicated the signs of *Ikhlāṣ* as well as of *Nifāq*. The signs of *Ikhlāṣ* are listed by Shāh Walīullāh in his book *Ḥujjatullāh al-Bālighah* as follows:

1. One should love Allah and His Prophet more than anyone else.
2. One's love for others should only be for the sake of Allah.
3. One should hate *Kufr* (unbelief) as one avoids the fire.

The Prophet (peace be upon him) has said: "Allah, the Most Exalted, does not accept any act unless it is exclusively done for Him." After saying this, the Prophet (peace be upon him) recited this verse: "*Lo! For Allah is the religion with sincere devotion*" (al-Zumar 39: 3).

According to the well-known *ḥadīth* "all actions are but by intention and one will get the reward for what one has intended" (Bukhārī and Muslim). Thus *Ikhlāṣ* of *Niyyah* (intention) is of paramount importance. This is further elucidated by another *ḥadīth* of the Prophet (peace be upon him) in which he is reported to have said: "Indeed, he has achieved salvation one who has purified his heart for faith" (Aḥmad). Similarly the Prophet (peace be upon him) said: "One who said *Lā Ilāha illāl-Lāh* with *Ikhlāṣ* will enter paradise." When asked: "What does it mean to recite this *Kalimah* with *Ikhlāṣ*?" he replied: "If this *Kalimah* stops him from doing unlawful acts this is what is meant by *Ikhlāṣ*" (Tirmidhī). *Ikhlāṣ* of both *Niyyah* and *'Amal* (actions) is necessary for the acceptance of acts by Allah.

The Words from the Same Root

Mukhliṣ (pl. *Mukhliṣīn*) means one who is sincere, devoted, virtuous, and righteous. Of course Muslims are required to be *Mukhliṣīn* in their faith, but their sincerity may get dimmed by forgetfulness. It is only in times of real crisis that people call upon Allah with sincerity. Even non-believers, when stranded in tidal waves during stormy weather, having lost all hope and overwhelmed by fear, cry out for Allah's help. It is then that they sincerely offer their devotion to Him. This scene is depicted in many places in the Qur'ān (Yūnus 10: 22; al-'Ankabūt 29: 65 and Luqmān 31: 32).

Mukhlaṣ (pl. *Mukhlaṣīn*) means one who is selected for some specific task or purpose. This term is applied to all the messengers and prophets who were selected for Divine duty. It is said about them "*Verily We did choose them for a special (purpose) – proclaiming the message of the Hereafter*" (Ṣād 38: 46). However only the Prophet Mūsā (peace be upon him) was given this honorific title by name (Maryam 19: 51). According to Mawlānā Amīn Aḥsan Iṣlāḥī, the reason for this specific honour is that he was the only Messenger with whom Allah held a conversation. This specific distinction is acknowledged in several places in the Qur'ān: for example, "*And to Mūsā Allah spoke directly*" (al-Nisā' 4: 164); "*And We called upon him from the right side of Mount (Sinai) and made him draw near to Us for intimate converse*" (Maryam 19: 52). To signify this closeness and affinity the Prophet Mūsā (peace be upon him) was singled out for this honour (*Tadabbur-i-Qur'ān*, Vol. 4, pp.118–119).

References

Ikhlāṣ: 4: 146; 38: 46; 39: 3; 40: 14; 98: 5. *Mukhliṣ*: 7: 29; 10: 22; 29: 65; 31: 32; 40: 65. *Mukhlaṣ*: 12: 24; 15: 40; 37: 40 and 74; 38: 83.

Ilāh [إِلٰه]

see Allah

Ilḥād [إِلْحَاد] (Blasphemy)

Meaning

Laḥada means to dig a grave or to bury someone, and *Laḥd* means a grave. *Laḥada* also means to deviate from the right path, to digress from the straight path or to abandon one's faith. *Ilḥād* from this root means apostasy, blasphemy or heresy.

Analysis

Ilḥād is of two types: One is to blaspheme by associating someone with Allah. Referring to the practices of pagan Arabs in the Ka'bah, it is said in Sūrah al-Ḥajj: "*And any whose purpose therein is profanity or wrongdoing, We will cause them to taste of a most grievous penalty*" (22: 25). The other type of *Ilḥād* is to blaspheme the name of Allah. "*But shun such people who use profanity in His names: for what they do will soon be requited*" (al-A'rāf 7: 180). One way of profaning of Allah's name is to imply attributes to Him that are below His dignity and honour. By such an act a wrong belief is ascribed to Allah. Even to name someone using one of Allah's personal names is considered as an *Ilḥād*.

The *Ilḥād* also means to put something to perverted use or to act profanely towards something. "*Those who pervert the truth in Our* Āyāt *(signs or verses) are not hidden from Us*" (Fuṣṣilat 41: 40). The perversion of the truth either by corrupting Allah's Book by turning its verses to false and selfish use or by neglecting the signs of Allah in nature which are all around human beings – all these meanings are implied in the above verse.

References

Ilḥād: 7: 180; 22: 25; 41: 40.

'Ilm [علم] (Knowledge)

Meaning

'Alima means to know, to have knowledge or to be aware. *'Ilm*, from this root, means knowledge and learning. This knowledge is first grasping the essence of something and secondly to know its qualities. As knowledge gives certainty, *'Ilm* also means to be sure or certain about something. It is stated in the Qur'ān that Allah taught the Prophet Ādam (peace be upon him) the names of all things (al-Baqarah 2: 31). By being taught these names, the implication is that the Prophet Ādam was taught the characteristics of all things as well. This gave him superiority over all other creations including the angels. A human being was created as the *Khalīfah* (vicegerent) of Allah on Earth. Hence, it was essential that he should be given this knowledge so that he could perform his role of *Khilāfah* (vicegerency) properly.

Imām al-Rāghib has classified knowledge into two categories: theoretical and practical. Theoretical knowledge is acquired by knowing about the subject, whereas practical knowledge can only be gained by actions: for example, knowledge about *'Ibādah* can only be acquired by practice.

Analysis

In many verses of the Qur'ān, the superior status of those who possess knowledge is mentioned. Knowledge is referred to as *Nūr* (light) and

Baṣīrah (insight) whereas ignorance is termed as *Ẓulumāt* (darkness). The word *'Ilm* and its derivatives occur 778 times in the Qur'ān. This explains its importance in Islam. In several *aḥādīth* the importance of the acquisition of knowledge is mentioned. The Prophet (peace be upon him) was sent down as a teacher.

Acquisition of knowledge is essential for being a Muslim, as Islam cannot be inherited. One has to make a conscious choice after attaining the age of reason. Real knowledge in the Qur'ānic terminology is the gnosis of Allah and consciousness of the Hereafter. If one is devoid of this knowledge, one's expertise in other branches of knowledge is of no avail.

According to the Qur'ān, the *'Ulamā'* are those, who have cognizance of Allah, and who always remain God-conscious. "*Those, who truly fear Allah, among His servants, are those who have knowledge*" (Fāṭir 35: 28). According to Mawlānā Amīn Aḥsan Iṣlāḥī the word *'Ulamā'* in this verse does not mean the traditional *'Ulamā'* who have knowledge of the Qur'ān, *Ḥadīth*, *Fiqh* (Jurisprudence) and *Kalām* (theology). They can only be designated as *'Ulamā'* if they have God-consciousness (*Tadabbur-i-Qur'ān*, vol. 4, p. 232). The subsequent verse in Sūrah Fāṭir enumerates these qualities: "*Those who rehearse the Book of Allah, establish regular Prayer, and spend what We have provided...*" (35: 29). "*Allah will raise the ranks of those who have faith and knowledge*" (al-Mujādilah 58: 11). Even among the *'Ulamā'* there are degrees of wisdom granted by Allah (Yūsuf 12: 76).

All knowledge is essential which is used for the benefit of mankind. The misuse of knowledge for worldly gain or for causing discord is disapproved of. However, indulging in magic and sorcery and acquiring other evil and black arts are strictly prohibited (al-Baqarah 2: 102).

References

'Ilm: 2: 32; 3: 7; 27: 42; 31: 20; 58: 11.

Īmān [إِيمَان] (Faith)

Meanings

The roots of *Īmān* are *Āmana*, which means to believe, to have faith, and *Amina*, to be safe or to give peace and security. The word *Īmān* is used for faith or belief as *Īmān* gives an individual peace of mind and also creates a harmonious relationship between a human being and the rest of the universe.

Usage

The word *Īmān* is used in the following meanings in the Qur'ān:

1. In its primary meaning, it conveys giving peace. For example "*Who provides them with food against hunger and with security against fear of danger*" (Quraysh 106: 4).
2. When the word *Īmān* is used with the preposition "*lām*", it means to confirm something (al-'Ankabūt 29: 26).
3. When the word *Īmān* is used with the preposition "*bā*" it means reliability and trust and believing in something.

The Articles of *Īmān*

"I bear witness that there is no deity except Allah and I also bear witness that Muḥammad is His servant and Messenger", the *Shahādah*, is the condensed form in which the complete creed of the Islamic faith is enunciated in the Qur'ān. On the basis of verse 285 of Sūrah al-Baqarah and other verses of the Qur'ān and *aḥādīth*, *Fuqahā'* (Jurists of Islam) have rendered the creed into six Articles of Faith.
The formula is as follows:

> I believe in Allah, His Angels, His Books, His Messengers, the Last Day and that the Pre-destined – whether it is good or evil – is from Allah the Exalted, and in Resurrection after death.

1. Faith in the Oneness of Allah means that one believes that He is the sole Creator and the Lord of everything that exists in this

universe. Allah as one's Lord and the Master requires voluntarily submission to His commands.

2. Faith in angels is also part of our *Īmān*. Angels belong to the world that is imperceptible to human senses. They are created from light, and thus are invisible to human beings.
3. Belief in the Revealed Books means that we accept that Allah sent down many Scriptures for the guidance of mankind and to teach human beings how to lead their life in the right way.
4. Belief in the Messengers is necessary as they conveyed the Message and the commands for the guidance of humanity.
5. Belief in the Last Day makes us realize that this world is transitory and will end one day. On that day, all creation will be destroyed and people will be raised from their graves.
6. Belief in *Qadr* – destiny – means that whatever happens emanates from Almighty Allah. This belief makes one totally dependent on the Will of Allah. It provides inner strength to bear all miseries and calamities in life.

These Articles of Faith are subsumed in essentially the three fundamental beliefs of *Tawḥīd, Risālah* and *Ākhirah*, that is, belief in the Oneness of Allah, Prophethood and the Hereafter. The entire edifice of the Islamic civilization is based on these fundamental beliefs.

The Nature of *Īmān*

There is a difference of opinion among scholars about the nature of *Īmān*. Is it static or does it increase and decrease? Imām Abū Ḥanīfah holds the first view, while Imām Bukhārī believes in its ebb and flow. There is an apparent contradiction in their views. However, the explanation is that Imām Abū Ḥanīfah, being a jurist, is looking at *Īmān* from the legal point of view. A person declaring the *Shahādah* is to be considered a Muslim and he is entitled to all the rights of a Muslim. These rights cannot be varied for any reason. Imām Bukhārī, on the other hand, was considering the state of *Īmān* as manifested by its weakness or strength which, of course, varies. Looking at the issue in this way, there is no contradiction in their views.

The Parts of *Īmān*

The Prophet (peace be upon him) said: "*Īmān* has more than seventy parts, the highest is the confession that there is no god except Allah, and the lowest is removing a harmful object from the road" (Bukhārī and Muslim). There are other *aḥādīth* such as "Modesty is part of *Īmān*" (Tirmidhī) and "Simplicity in dress is part of *Īmān*" (Ibn Mājah). These *aḥādīth* indicate that *Īmān* engulfs the totality of a Muslim's life. Of course some parts of *Īmān* – like saying of the *Shahādah*, prayers, fasting, *Zakāh* and *Ḥajj* – are more important, and neglecting them would lead to the loss of *Īmān*. Others, like removing an obstacle from a path, are marginal and their omission will not impair *Īmān*. In between them there are other aspects of varying degrees of importance.

Other Words from the Same Root

Mu'min is one who declares his faith by reciting the *Shahādah* – the declaration of faith. The *'Ulamā'* say that this creed should be sincerely believed in one's heart and recited by tongue and demonstrated by action. Only then is *Īmān* as true Faith acceptable in Allah's sight. However, a person does not lose his faith by committing any major sin as believed by the *Khawārij* or he will be in a place between Hell and Paradise forever as the *Mu'tazilah* believed.

Al-Mu'min is one of the most beautiful names (*al-Asmā' al-Ḥusnā*) of *Allah Ta'ālā*. This name is used for Allah because He gives sanctuary to His creatures. They are safe from His wrath and He will not do any injustice to them. He will fulfil all His promises. *Al-Mu'min* also means the One Whose peace embraces all the universe.

References

Īmān: 2: 108; 3: 193; 30: 56; 42: 52; 49: 14. *Mu'min*: 16: 97; 17: 19; 33: 36; 40: 28; 64: 2. *Al-Mu'min*: 59: 23.

Indhār wa Tabshīr [إنذار وتبشير] (Warning and Glad Tidings)

Meaning

One of the meanings of the verb *Nadhara* is to warn, to admonish or to announce. *Indhār* means a warning or admonition.

Bashira means to rejoice, to be happy or to be delighted. *Tabshīr* means the announcement of good news or glad tidings.

Indhār wa Tabshīr: the Mission of the Prophets

The prophets were sent down by Allah for the guidance of mankind. Their message and mission was to forewarn and alert people as well as to convey the glad tidings. They are the harbingers of the good news and of eternal success and salvation for those who accept their *da'wah* and follow the path of righteousness. For them there is triumph and happiness both in this world and in the Hereafter (al-Ṣaff 61: 12–13). As for those that reject and deny the message of prophets, for them there is eternal damnation.

The purpose of *Indhār* and *Tabshīr* is to inform people about the natural consequences of their acceptance of faith (*Īmān*) or its rejection (*Kufr*). For example a physician treating a patient explains to him the benefits of the prescribed medicine and also advises abstinence from certain foods in order for him to get better. If the patient follows his doctor's advice he will get cured. Similarly a prophet explains to his people the consequences of accepting or rejecting his *da'wah.*

For this reason a prophet is called *Nadhīr* (warner) and *Bashīr* (bringer of glad tidings). "*Verily We have sent you in truth as a bearer of glad tidings and a warner*" (al-Baqarah 2: 119; Sabā' 34: 28; Fāṭir 35: 24; Fuṣṣilat 41: 4).

The Rationale for *Indhār wa Tabshīr*

Some people criticize religion for tempting people towards righteousness by promising eternal bliss and frightening them into submission by dire warnings of Hell-Fire. This is a fallacious argument. The message of the prophets is based on reason and common sense. It provides arguments from man's own psyche as well as from the universe around him. The other rationale is that the message is based on moral and virtuous principles. These values are imbued in the human consciousness and are not alien to his thinking. People are aware of the physical consequences of dangerous things such as that fire burns and that a snake-bite is often fatal. However, many people are oblivious of the repercussions of lying and deceit. As the prophets are aware of the results of misdemeanours, they both warn about the dire consequences of transgressions and sins and also encourage people to follow the righteous path by giving glad tidings.

References

Indhār: 10: 2; 14: 44; 26: 214; 71: 1; 74: 2. *Tabshīr*: 2: 155; 10: 2; 22: 37; 39: 17; 61: 13. *Bashīr wa Nadhīr*: 2: 119; 5: 19; 7: 188; 11: 2; 17: 105.

See also *Da'wah*

Infāq [إنفاق] (Spending in Allah's Way)

Meaning

Nafaqa means to sell well, to finish something, hence, *Infāq* from this root means spending. In the Qur'ān as a keyword it is used as *Infāq fī Sabīl Allāh* – spending in the way of Allah. The mandatory *Infāq* is called *Zakāh* and the voluntary *Infāq* is called *Ṣadaqah*.

Analysis

THE MOTIVES FOR THE *INFĀQ*

The prime motive of the *Infāq* should be the natural desire to be benevolent. This should not have any element of *Riyā'* (showing off) and of course the intention should be to attain the pleasure of Allah. These aspects are emphasized in several places in the Qur'ān (al-Ma'ārij 70: 24–26; al-Insān 76: 7–10). If there are other motives besides seeking Allah's pleasure, then such *infāq* will not be accepted by Him.

RECIPIENTS OF *ṢADAQAH*

Verse 177 of Sūrah al-Baqarah enumerates the following as the recipients of *Infāq*:

Kith and kin; orphans; people in need; the wayfarers; beggars; ransom to free captives.

This is not an exhaustive list, as money can be spent on other worthy causes. Muslims are encouraged to spend in charity as much as possible. The beneficiaries should not be teased or reminded of one's gifts and generosity (al-Baqarah 2: 262).

WHAT TO SPEND

The test of one's sincerity and charity is that one gives something that one values and loves most (Āl 'Imrān 3: 92). One should not give in charity those goods that one just wants to get rid of. And one should not attempt "*to give anything that is bad*" (al-Baqarah 2: 267).

HOW MUCH TO SPEND

When the Companions asked the Prophet (peace be upon him) how much they should spend in charity, they were told: It is said in Sūrah al-Baqarah: "*Spend what is beyond your needs*" (2: 219).

REWARDS OF SPENDING

There are great rewards for those who spend freely in Allah's way, day and night, both in difficulty and in ease, publicly as well as privately, seeking only His pleasure.

Synonym

Qarḍ Ḥasan, literally, a beautiful loan. Spending in Allah's way is metaphorically described as "a beautiful loan". It is beautiful as it reflects self-denial on the part of the giver and it is given with a pure intention. This means that it is given generously just to please Allah without demanding the return of the loan, and without expectation of any reward in this world. For such spending Allah promises that it will be "*double unto his credit and multiply many times*" (al-Baqarah 2: 245). Of course what is being given in Allah's way should be from lawful earnings as

Allah only accepts lawful things and it should be something that is in good condition and is a desirable object which the giver loves himself and which is not surplus to one's needs. "*By no means shall you attain righteousness unless you give (freely) of that which you love*" (Āl 'Imrān 3: 92).

This is indeed Allah's magnificent generosity: that whatever one has truly belongs to Allah, yet when He wants His servants to spend in His way He calls it a loan which He will return manifold in the Hereafter.

Antonym

Bakhila means to be miserly or stingy. *Bukhl* is miserliness or niggardliness and it also includes an element of greed and avarice. A *Bakhīl* is a person who does not fulfil his obligation of helping others. Not only that but such a person wants others to be like him. The character of a *Bakhīl* is contrasted with that of the one who spends in Allah's way in Sūrah al-Layl 92: 5–10 and Sūrah al-Mā'ūn presents a graphic picture of the *Bakhīl* (107: 2–3). The reason for *Bukhl* is that one thinks that all one's wealth is the result of one's own capabilities; such a person lacks the attitude of *Shukr* (thankfulness) to Allah (al-Nisā' 4: 37; al-Tawbah 9: 76).

References

Infāq: 3: 92; 17: 100; 57: 10; 63: 10; 64: 16. *Ṣadaqah*: 2: 196, 271 and 276; 9: 60 and 103. *Qarḍ Ḥasan*: 2: 245; 5: 12; 57: 18; 64: 17; 73: 20. *Bukhl*: 4: 37; 9: 76; 47: 38; 57: 24; 92: 8.

See also *Ṣadaqah*

Insān [إنسان] (Human Being)

Meaning

Anisa means to be sociable, to be nice, or to be friendly. *Ins* means man, mankind, and human race, and the word *Insān* is used for man or human being. It is human nature to be sociable and to live in a society. One cannot survive alone and without the company of others. Some lexicographers say that the word *Insān* is from *Nisyān* (forgetfulness). While others maintain it is from *Ma'nūs*, to be familiar and accustomed.

The Role of Human Beings

The first pair of human beings created by Allah were the Prophet Ādam and Ḥawwā' (peace be upon them). From their progeny the human race came into existence. The purpose behind man's creation consists of fulfilling the moral part of the Divine Will – a part whose fulfilment requires that the subject be free to fulfil as well as to violate it. Being alone capable of this moral action, the human race is indeed God's "best and supreme" creation, and as such is higher than the angels.

After disobeying Allah's command on the instigation of *Shayṭān*, both Ādam and Ḥawwā' (peace be upon them) repented and were pardoned by Allah. They were sent down on earth not as punishment but to fulfil the mission of vicegerency. To help them perform this duty Allah promised to send His guidance: "*Whosoever follows My guidance, on them shall be no fear, nor shall they grieve*" (al-Baqarah 2: 38). But man has been given freedom of choice. He is free to follow the divine guidance or to reject it and follow his own whims and desires, which the *Shayṭān* tempts him to do. However, he is responsible for his acts, and he is not deprived of his freedom, even if he makes mistakes and abuses it. The uniqueness of the human situation lies in man's psychosocial volition. This potential enables him to rise to the highest pinnacle or to fall into the deepest abyss.

The Moral Code of Humanity

It is not only the advanced societies that follow a moral code of law. Even primitive societies like the Pygmies of Central Africa have a body of moral law and practice and they do not deviate from it. There is an inborn sense of morality in all human beings. Throughout the ages certain qualities have been warmly approved of by society, while others have been consistently condemned. All human beings appreciate truthfulness, charity, courage, honesty, hospitality, loyalty, sympathy, fidelity, justice and many other good qualities. Equally, they disdain hypocrisy, bigotry, injustice, falsehood, betrayal, infidelity, cowardice, cruelty and rudeness. When these personal moral values become part of the collective behaviour of society, they bring about a just, compassionate and morally upright society and state.

If the distinction between good and evil is universal and clear-cut, why is there so much muddled thinking and confusion in public life? If we reflect on these issues we find that moral laws cannot be enforced in a vacuum. They cannot be upheld without sanctions. Ethical philosophy and the code of moral behaviour for individuals and society are based on the concept of the universe, man's place in it and man's purpose on earth and whether he is accountable for his actions to his Creator. These are fundamental questions that have to be settled first.

Basic Human Weaknesses and Their Cures

a. FORGETFULNESS AND LACK OF DETERMINATION

Man by nature is forgetful and irresolute. These traits he has inherited from the Prophet Ādam (peace be upon him), the first person to be created. "*We had already beforehand taken the covenant of Ādam, but he forgot and We found on his part no firm resolve*" (Ṭā Hā 20: 115). *Dhikr* (remembrance) and *Ṣalāh* are the cures for this weakness. Five-times-a-day *Ṣalāh* makes one punctual and determined.

b. LOVE OF THE WORLD AND WEALTH

Man's other weakness is love of worldly life and its glitter: "*Heaped-up hoards of gold and silver; branded horses and cattle and well-tilled land such are the possessions of this world, that sway human beings from the righteous path*" (Āl 'Imrān 3: 14). The remedy for this is *Infāq fī Sabīl Allāh* (spending in Allah's way).

c. IMPATIENCE AND LOVE OF THE CARNAL SELF

"*Man is a creature of haste*" (al-Anbiyā' 21: 37) and he wants quick results. Fasting in the month of Ramaḍān teaches him *Ṣabr* (patience). This also puts a check on love of the carnal self, of eating, drinking and sexual gratification. The patience and self-control achieved through fasting remedy these diseases.

The total remedy for all the weaknesses and diseases of one's heart and mind is the *Ḥajj*. During *Ḥajj* one is removed from one's home and familiar surroundings. This spiritual and emotional journey is undertaken to strengthen one's *Īmān* and to remind one of one's ultimate accountability before Allah on the Day of Judgement.

References

Insān: 10: 12; 14: 34; 17: 11; 53: 39; 95: 4.

ʿIqāb [عقاب]

see *ʿAdhāb*

Iqāmah [إقامة] (Establishment)

Meaning

Iqāmah is from *Qāma*, meaning to get up, to stand up or to stand erect. Hence *iqāmah* means raising, lifting up, elevation, setting up, erection or establishment (of something). The essence of *Iqāmah* is to make something stand in such a way that it is not bent or crooked. When *Iqāmah* is used of an abstract thing, it means to establish an apparatus for it to function properly. For example it is extensively used for establishing prayers. The word *Iqāmah* is also used for staying or residing somewhere.

Iqāmat al-Ṣalāh

It is instructive to note that the instruction in the Qur'ān is always *Aqīmū al-Ṣalāt* (establish prayer) not just "pray". *Iqāmah* is a comprehensive term. It does not mean that one should pray regularly and individually but there should be a collective provision established for offering prayers. There should be a definite place of worship (mosque), facilities for *wuḍū'*, organization of *Adhān*, appointment of an *Imām*, arrangement of *Jumuʿah* prayer and *Khuṭbah*. Even standing straight in rows, according to one *ḥadīth*, is part of *Iqāmat al-Ṣalāh*.

The *Iqāmah* to alert (whose wording is similar to the *Adhān* with the addition of *qad qāmat aṣ-Ṣalāh*) is said when prayer is ready to be performed and people within the mosques get ready and form rows.

Iqāmat al-Dīn

Iqāmat of *Dīn* is the other frequent usage of this term in the Qur'ān. It implies that the whole system of *Dīn* should be established in one's own life as well as collectively in society. As *al-Dīn* embraces all aspects of life, its *iqāmah* requires that it is followed diligently as much as possible in one's life and in the life of the Muslim community.

Other Words from this Root

Many words derived from the word *Qāma* occur in the Qur'ān. The *Qiyām* is the standing posture in *Ṣalāh*. The word *Qiyām* is also used in other meanings: The *Qiyām al-Layl* means standing up in prayers at night and reciting the Qur'ān. It generally means to stay up whole or part of the night performing acts of *'ibādah*. It was compulsory for the Prophet (peace be upon him) (al-Muzzammil 73: 2–4 and 20) but other Companions also joined in this *Qiyām*. *Qiyām al-Layl* in Ramaḍān is the prescribed *tarāwīḥ* prayers and performance of other acts of *'Ibādah* during the night, especially during the last ten nights of Ramaḍān.

The *Qawwām* means the provider or supporter, manager, caretaker, guardian or custodian. This word is used in Sūrah al-Nisā' verse 34 and it means that men are the guardians and protectors of their womanfolk.

Al-Qayyūm is one of the most beautiful names (*al-Asmā' al-Ḥusnā*) of Allah which means He is the One Who is Self-Subsisting, the Everlasting or the Eternal.

Qiyāmah or *Yawm al-Qiyāmah* is the day when the dead will be raised from their graves and all of them will stand up before Allah.

Istiqāmah: The meaning of *Istiqāmah* is uprightness, sincerity, integrity, steadfastness or firmness. This is a desirable quality of believers. It means that they remain steadfast in their *Īmān* (Fuṣṣilat 41: 30; al-Aḥqāf 46: 13). The key to *Istiqāmah* is to remain upright and steadfast facing all difficulties and hardship. This can only be achieved if one's heart is full of firm *Īmān* and is devoid of any doubt. Imām Ghazālī stated that the importance and need for *Istiqāmah* is so great that Allah has ordered the recitation of Sūrah al-Fātiḥah in every *Rak'ah* of prayers where there is a supplication of *Istiqāmah* or continuous guidance to the straight path.

References

Iqāmat al-Ṣalāh: 7: 170; 9: 11; 22: 41; 35: 29; 42: 38. *Iqamāt al-Dīn*: 10: 105; 42: 13. *Qiyām*: 3: 191; 25: 63. *Qawwām*: 4: 34 and 135; 5: 8. *Al-Qayyūm*: 2: 255; 3: 2; 20: 111. *Qiyāmah*: 17: 13; 20: 124; 45: 17; 68: 39; 75: 1. *Istiqāmah*: 9: 7; 41: 6 and 30; 46: 13; 72: 16.

Irādah [إرادة] (Intention)

Meaning

Rāda and *rawd* mean to walk about, to seek, to search or to wish. *Irādah* from this root means will, volition or desire. *Irādah* means to make an effort to acquire some desired thing. It is that force or power that is composed of feelings of desire and need as well as aspiration.

Usage

The word *Irādah* is used in the following meanings in the Qur'ān:

DETERMINATION AND FINAL DECISION

When this word is used in respect of Allah it means a firm judgement. When Allah decides something His wish is His command. "*Allah does not wish to place you in difficulty, but to make you clean and complete His favour to you that you may be grateful*" (al-Mā'idah 5: 6). "*When We decide to destroy a population, We (first) send a definite order to those among them who are given the good things of this life yet transgress; so that the word is proved true against them: then We destroy them utterly*" (al-Isrā' 17: 16).

COMMAND AND ORDER

"*Allah intends every facility for you; He does not want to put you in difficulties. (He wants you) to complete the prescribed period*" (al-Baqarah 2: 185). This verse is about the completion of fasting later on for those who are unable to fast during travel or illness. It emphasizes that Allah's commands take into account human needs and situations and do not put people in difficulties.

INTENTION AND WISH

"*Those who do wish for the (things of) the Hereafter, and strive thereof with all due striving, and have faith – they are the ones whose striving is acceptable*" (al-Isrā' 17: 19). In the earlier verse it is said that those who wish for earthly and transitory things sometimes Allah grants them as He pleases. But those who have fixed their goal on the Hereafter and strive towards it, their endeavours will meet with Allah's acceptance.

SEDUCTION AND ENTICEMENT

The third verb form, *rāwada*. "*But she, in whose house he was, sought to seduce him*" (Yūsuf 12: 23). This refers to the incident in which the Prophet Yūsuf (peace be upon him) was falsely implicated. He pleaded that "*It was she that sought to seduce me from my (true) self*" (Yūsuf 12: 26).

Synonyms

Niyyah also means intention, determination or will. This word is not used in the Qur'ān. However, a famous *ḥadīth* narrated by 'Umar ibn al-Khaṭṭāb states a very important principle: "Surely all actions are but according to intentions and every person shall have but that which he intended" (Muslim). Jamaal al-Din M. Zarabozo, in his commentary on this *ḥadīth* summarizes its meaning in the following terms:

> Every conscious, intentional act that a rational person performs is driven and brought into being by his intention. Without that intention behind the act, the act would not have been performed. Now this intention must fall into one of three categories: a good, pious intention, a religiously neutral intention or an evil intention. In all cases, the person shall get only what he intended.
>
> (*Commentary on the Forty Ḥadīth of al-Nawawī*, volume I, p. 137)

'Azm is another word used in the Qur'ān having the similar meaning as *Irādah*. However it is more than *Irādah* as it means determination, firm intention or decision. The Prophet (peace be upon him) was instructed: "*When you have taken a decision put your trust in Allah*" (Āl 'Imrān 3: 159).

References

Irādah: 2: 185; 17: 19; 33: 17; 39: 38; 48: 11. *'Azm*: 3: 186; 20: 115; 31: 17; 42: 43; 46: 35.

Irtidād [إرتداد] (Apostasy)

Meaning

Radda means to send back, to bring back, to take back, to throw back, to refuse or to reject. *Irtidād* from this root means desertion, denunciation or apostasy.

Causes of *Irtidād*

Irtidād means renunciation of one's religion. In the early period of Islam, *Irtidād* was used by many mischievous and disgruntled people to sabotage the rising popularity of the new faith. They pretended to accept Islam for a short period and then rejected it (Āl 'Imrān 3: 72). Some made a mockery of the faith, as described in Sūrah al-Nisā': "*Those who believe then reject faith. Then believe (again) and (again) reject faith and go on increasing in unbelief – Allah will not forgive them or guide them on the way*" (4: 137). In Sūrah Āl 'Imrān it is said: "*But those who reject faith after they accepted it, and then go on adding to their defiance of faith – never will their repentance be accepted, for they are those who have (of set purpose) gone astray*" (3: 90).

Irtidād in Islamic Law

In Islam "*There is no compulsion in religion*" (al-Baqarah 2: 256). One is free to choose what one wants to believe in. There is no punishment prescribed for unbelievers. But once one exercises the choice and becomes Muslim, one forfeits the option to choose one's beliefs and abide by Islamic rules. Thus, after the death of the Prophet (peace be upon him), some wished to remain Muslim but did not want to pay *zakāh*; this was not acceptable, and refusal to honour the financial obligations to the Islamic state was treated as an act of treason and those responsible were punished.

References

Irtidād: 2: 109 and 217; 3: 100; 5: 21 and 54.

Islam [إسلام]

Meanings

The word *Islām* is derived from the Arabic root *SLM*, and *Salāmah* is the verbal noun which means to be in the state of being safe and sound or to remain unharmed or unimpaired and the word *Salām* comes from the same root, meaning peace. In this way, a Muslim plays an important role in society. He is at peace with his Creator as well as with his fellow human beings and all creation.

The word *Islām* also means submission. Islam is the act of resignation and total surrender to Allah's will and following His commands.

Islam as *al-Dīn*

Islam as a religion means the commitment of oneself to submit to Allah's will and readiness to obey His commands which were brought by His Messenger. In *ḥadīth Jibrīl*, when the Prophet (peace be upon him) was asked about Islam, he said: "Islam is to testify that there is none worthy of worship except Allah and that Muḥammad is the Messenger of Allah, to establish prayers, to pay *Zakāh*, to fast [the month of Ramaḍān] and to make the pilgrimage to the House [of Allah] if you have the means to do so" (Muslim).

Islam is a set of beliefs as well as acts of *'Ibādah*. The acceptance of Islam requires submission to its code of conduct in all spheres of one's life. According to the Qur'ānic view, all things, including animals and inanimate objects in this universe, are *Muslim* (obedient). This means they all obey Allah's commands and follow the laws of nature that Allah has prescribed (Āl 'Imrān 3: 83). It is only human beings and *Jinns* who have the volition either to submit or to disobey.

All prophets and messengers brought the same *Dīn* and this *Dīn* was Islam. This is the only *Dīn* acceptable in the sight of Allah (Āl 'Imrān 3: 19). Any other *Dīn* besides Islam is unacceptable to Allah (Āl 'Imrān 3: 85).

Islam and *Īmān*

The words *Islām* and *Īmān* are sometimes used interchangeably to refer to the Faith. But there is some difference between these two very important words. Whereas Islam is the code of life and a system of beliefs which distinguishes itself from other religions and ways of life, *Īmān* is the creed and faith whose acceptance makes a person Muslim or *Mu'min*. To clarify this further, if these two words are not used in close proximity to each other, then Islam means both faith and outward acts of submission; similarly *Īmān* will convey the same meaning. But if *Īmān* and Islam are used in close proximity then *īmān* refers to the belief in one's heart while Islam means acts of submission. This contrast is made very clear in Sūrah al-Ḥujurāt: "*The desert Arabs say, 'We believe.' Say, 'You have no faith,' but you (only) say, 'We have submitted our wills to Allah.' For not yet has Faith entered your hearts*" (49: 14). The next verse clearly specifies what true *Īmān* is: "*Only those are believers who have believed in Allah and His Messenger, and have never doubted, but have striven with their belongings and their lives in the cause of Allah: such are the sincere ones*" (al-Ḥujurāt 49: 15). Thus, true *īmān* means submission to Allah's will with unwavering faith and readiness to struggle in His path.

Other Words from the Same Root

Salām has two meanings: to be protected from all afflictions and defects and to remain in peace and without antagonism. Allah's command to send blessings and salutations on the Prophet (peace be upon him) means that one prays for his well-being and tranquillity as well as supporting him, refraining from opposing him, and always being subservient to him (al-Aḥzāb 33: 56).

"*Al-Salām 'Alaykum*" is the form of greeting for Muslims. It means "peace be upon you". The response to this is "*Wa 'Alaykum al-Salām*" – "and peace be on you also". This mutual prayer for peace promotes love and fellow feeling among believers. One is recommended to respond to *Salām* "*with a greeting still more courteous or (at least) of equal courtesy*" (al-Nisā' 4: 86). This means one should reply *wa 'Alaykum al-Salām wa Raḥmat Allāh* – and peace be on you and Allah's mercy, or add to it *wa Barakātuh* – and His blessing.

Al-Salām is one of the beautiful names of Allah (*al-Asmā' al-Ḥusnā*). It means Allah is the One who gives peace and security

Muslim: One who recites the *Shahādah* – declaring that there is no god but Allah and Muḥammad is His Prophet – enters the fold of Islam and joins the community of believers (*Ummah*). He sincerely submits himself wholeheartedly to Allah's will, considers Him Master, Lord, Sovereign and Deity, and follows His command brought by His Messenger.

Silm means peace. It is also used in the sense of obedience to Allah and His Messenger (peace be upon him). In this way it is a synonym of Islam, as in Sūrah al-Baqarah (2: 208).

Salam also means peace used as the opposite of war and the request for surrender (al-Nisā' 4: 90–91; al-Anfāl 8: 61).

Salīm means one who is free from (some defect), unimpaired or sound or secure. It is used twice in the Qur'ān: as a quality of the heart that will save one from the torment of Hell-Fire (al-Shu'arā' 26: 89), and as an attribute of the Prophet Ibrāhīm (peace be upon him) (al-Ṣaffāt 37: 84).

References

Islam: 3: 19 and 85; 5: 3; 6: 125; 39: 22. *Salām*: 4: 94; 6: 54; 19: 15; 36: 58; 37: 181. *Al-Salām*: 59: 23. Muslim: 2: 128; 3: 52 and 102; 29: 46; 33: 35. *Silm*: 2: 208. *Salam*: 4: 90 and 91; 8: 61. *Salīm*: 26: 89; 37: 84.

Isrāf [إسراف] (Extravagance)

Meaning

According to Imām al-Rāghib al-Iṣfahānī, *al-Saraf* means exceeding the limit of moderation but usually it is applied to extravagance in spending. In *al-Qāmūs,* it is defined as the opposite of moderation. Imām Sufyān al-Thawrī has said that anything done contrary to the obedience of Allah is *Isrāf* (*Tafsīr Maẓharī*). Thus, *Isrāf* is intemperance, prodigality and wastefulness. It is a comprehensive keyword of the Qur'ān which encompasses that attitude and style of life that is contrary to Islamic norms.

Analysis

The basic instruction given in the Qur'ān is: "*Eat and drink without going to excesses, for Allah does not love those who waste*" (al-Aʿrāf 7: 31). In Sūrah al-Furqān it is said: "*(The true servants of the Merciful One are) those who are neither extravagant nor niggardly in their spending but keep the golden mean between the two*" (25: 67). Islam teaches moderation in all affairs, and whatever bounties Allah has given are a trust which should be used according to the guidance provided. Thus, extravagance is considered a disobedience and a breach of trust. The extravagant people are not guided by Allah to the right way (Ghāfir 40: 28) and will endure a severe punishment: "*Those who exceed the limit are companions of the fire*" (Ghāfir 40: 43). Elsewhere the Pharaoh and the People of Lūṭ (peace be upon him) are cited as the worst examples of extravagance (Yūnus 10: 83; al-Aʿrāf 7: 81).

Synonym

Tabdhīr has a similar meaning to *Isrāf.* It is derived from *Badhdhara,* which means to waste, to squander and to dissipate. *Tabdhīr* is a more severe form of extravagance as it is not only excess like *Isrāf* but wanton waste and squandering. There is a subtle difference: *Isrāf* means to spend more than is required whereas *Tabdhīr* means to spend where it is not required or to squander, whether in lawful or unlawful pursuits. The

Mubadhdhirūn (squanderers) are described as the brothers of Satan, who was indeed ungrateful to Allah (al-Isrā' 17: 27).

References

Isrāf: 6: 141; 7: 31; 25: 67; 40: 28; 44: 31. *Tabdhīr*: 17: 26 and 27.

Isti'ānah [إستعانة] (Help)

Meaning

The root of the word is *'Awn*, which means to help someone or to provide support to someone. Thus, *al-Isti'ānah* means to seek help. In this sense, the word is used in several places in the Qur'ān:

> *Seek (Allah's) help with patient perseverance and Prayer.*
> (al-Baqarah 2: 45)

Analysis

It is instructive to note that both *Isti'ānah* and *'Ibādah* – seeking help and worship – are restricted to Allah only. This firmly closes all doors of *Shirk* (disbelief, associating others with Allah). While worship of Allah alone is comprehensible the instruction in this Sūrah al-Fātiḥah (1: 4) is not to seek help from anyone except Allah. However, in our daily life we do seek the help of others in many ways. The help of doctors during illness and the help of teachers in learning are obvious examples. Indeed, we are asked to help others who are in need and in distress. How can this be explained?

The *'Ulamā'* have identified two different categories of *isti'ānah*. There is a kind of seeking help where someone is physically present and renders assistance and help. In this way we are all exhorted to help the poor and the needy. This is termed *Isti'ānah Mā taḥt al-Asbāb* (seeking help under physical laws). However there is another kind of help which is called *Isti'ānah Mā fawq al-Asbāb* (seeking help in a metaphysical way). Thus, when we call upon Allah to help alleviate our difficulties, this help is of a spiritual and metaphysical nature and in such circumstances only Allah can help us and only His help should be sought. To call upon others, for example saints, pious people or angels or the dead, for help is a kind of *Shirk*.

References

Isti'ānah: 1: 4; 2: 45 and 153; 7: 128.

Istighfār [إستغفار]

see *Maghfirah*

Istiqāmah [استقامة]

see *Iqāmah*

Istiwā' [استوآء] (The Ascendancy)

Meanings

Sawiya means to be equal or to be equivalent to something or to equalize. It also means to straighten or to make something smooth. *Istiwā'* means to stand straight, to be equal, to ascend, or to set oneself to do a right thing.

Analysis

The expression *Istiwā' 'alā al-'Arsh* is used in respect to Allah six times in the Qur'ān. It means that Allah sat Himself on the throne. It is difficult for us to comprehend the exact nature of this. The purpose of stating it is to emphasize that after the creation of the heavens and the earth Allah is still governing them with all His Majesty. His authority is exercised constantly by the laws that He laid down; these are enforced in all parts of the universe. Thus, to think that He is resting somewhere detached from this world is wrong. In fact He is in full control of everything happening in the universe, and everything is under His command. He is the sole Creator and His is the command to be obeyed.

In explaining the relationship between Allah and man, the Qur'ān has used certain metaphorical expressions to enable human beings to understand certain matters that are imperceptible to human senses. Words like *al-'Arsh* or *al-Kursī* (meaning throne) are used which indicate regal status. This does not mean that Allah is confined in some specific location and has to sit somewhere. Such expressions signify that as the Sovereign and Ruler of this universe the sovereignty belongs to Him alone. "*Blessed be He in Whose hands is sovereignty and He has power over all things*" (al-Mulk 67: 1). The use of the word *hands* in this verse and elsewhere is not to be taken in a literal sense. It signifies control and authority. It does not mean that Allah has physical form with hands and other body parts. Such expressions are of allegorical nature.

Istiwā' is also used in the sense of paying attention and turning towards something. "*It is He Who has created for you all things on earth; then He turned to the heaven and made them into seven firmaments*" (al-Baqarah 2: 29).

The expression *Istiwā'* is also used for the Prophet Nūḥ's Ark resting on Mount Jūdī (Hūd 11: 44).

Words from the Same Root

Taswiyah means levelling, formation or adjustment. "*Who created and further gives order and proportion*" (al-A'lā 87: 2). The act of creation is a continuous and fascinating process. The first act is called *Khalq* (creation); and then follows *Taswiyah*, endowing human beings with forms and faculties and giving due order and proportion.

Sawā' means even, equal or straight. *Sawā' al-Sabīl* means an even path as opposed to a rough one (al-Baqarah 2: 108). The Prophet (peace be upon him) was instructed about the hypocrites not to seek forgiveness for them as: "*It is equal to them whether you pray for their forgiveness or not. Allah will not forgive them*" (al-Munāfiqūn 63: 6).

References

Istiwā': 2: 29; 7: 54; 11: 44; 28: 14; 53: 6. *Taswiyah*: 2: 29; 15: 29; 82: 7; 87: 2; 91: 7. *Sawā'*: 2: 6; 3: 64; 7: 193; 22: 25; 36: 10.

Ithm [إِثْم] (Sin)

Meanings

Athima means to sin, to err or to slip, and from this noun *Ithm* (pl. *Āthām*) means sin, wickedness, guilt or iniquity. *Āthim* is one who commits sin, a sinner.

In the Qur'ān *Ithm* is used as the opposite of *Birr* (righteousness). "*Help one another in* Birr *and* Taqwā *(piety), but help you not one another in* Ithm *and* 'Udwān *(rancour)*" (al-Mā'idah 5: 2). From this verse it appears that *'Udwān* is a more serious sin than *Ithm*; the essence of *'Udwān* is aggression, hostility and enmity, whereas *Ithm* denotes meanness and usurping others' rights.

Major and Minor Sins

The Qur'ān does not list sins in different categories. However, from the context of its description and the punishment prescribed for it, one can determine how severe the sin is. The *Fuqahā'* categorized them into *Kabā'ir* (major) and *Ṣaghā'ir* (minor).

There are three ranks in the *Kabā'ir*:

1. The most heinous sin is *Shirk* (to associate someone or something with Allah).
2. To give false evidence and perjury affecting the rights and honour of other human beings, and to perform acts affecting human life like murder or suicide.
3. Those sins affecting both Allah's and other human beings' rights: for example, adultery, homosexuality, theft, consuming intoxicants, gambling, practising magic, and neglecting the rights of parents.

As in all acts, one's intention plays a crucial part. This is taken into account by Allah in determining the severity of the sin. Wilful defiance of the *Sharī'ah* and committing sins without remorse and without the feeling of guilt can turn even a minor sin into a major one.

As regards minor sins, Allah in His mercy will overlook them. "*Those who avoid major sins and shameful deeds, only (falling into) small faults, verily Your Lord is ample in forgiveness*" (al-Najm 53: 32). The same promise of divine forgiveness is mentioned in Sūrah al-Nisā' (4: 31) and Sūrah al-Shūrā (42: 37).

References

Ithm: 2: 173; 5: 2; 6: 120; 7: 33; 42: 37.

Iṭmi'nān [اطمئنان] (Satisfaction)

Meaning

Iṭmi'nān means something which has settled well in its place and will not move on either side. For example, if pots are well-placed or the lamp's flame is straight and does not flicker on either side, these convey the meaning of *iṭmi'nān*. Similarly if the heart is well set on the faith and does not waver from the right path it is called *al-Nafs al-Muṭma'innah* (*Tadabbur-i-Qur'ān*, Vol. 1, pp. 561–562). The word is derived from *ṭam'ana* and means to be quiet, to be calm or to soothe or to appease.

Al-Nafs al-Muṭma'innah

This represents the highest stage of *īmān* when one is absolutely at peace and happy (al-Fajr 89: 27–28). Bliss and inner peace are something internal; they depend on one's inner spiritual experience. By turning to Allah one is likely to achieve enlightenment. This is the meaning of the verse in Sūrah al-Ra'd: "*Those who believe, and whose hearts find satisfaction in the remembrance of Allah, for no doubt in remembrance of Allah do hearts find satisfaction*" (al-Ra'd 13: 28; al-Naḥl 16: 106 and 112).

Synonyms

SHARḤ AL-ṢADR

The satisfaction of the heart is also referred to as *Sharḥ al-Ṣadr*, which means opening of the breast (heart). "*Whom Allah wants to guide – He opens their breasts to Islam*" (al-An'ām 6: 125). When prophethood was bestowed on the Prophet Mūsā (peace be upon him) his first prayer was: "*O my Lord! Open my heart*" (Ṭā Hā 20: 25). And the Prophet (peace be upon him) was told of Allah's blessings in these words: "*Have We not opened your heart?*" (al-Sharḥ 94: 1). The righteous soul will be addressed as *al-Nafs al-Muṭma'innah* with tidings of Allah's mercy and His reward (al-Fajr 89: 27–30).

SAKĪNAH

Sakīnah is derived from *sukūn* and means God-inspired peace of mind, calm, tranquillity. "*It is He Who sent down tranquillity into the hearts of the believers...*" (al-Fatḥ 48: 4, 18 and 26). It is this *Sakīnah* which descended in the Cave of Thawr as the Prophet (peace be upon him) and Abū Bakr, his companion, were being pursued by the Quraysh. The Prophet (peace be upon him) said: "*'Have no fear, for Allah is with us.' Then Allah sent down His* Sakīnah *(peace) on him*" (al-Tawbah 9: 40). Similarly in the Battle of Ḥunayn "*Allah did send His* Sakīnah *on the Messenger and the believers*" (al-Tawbah 9: 26). This inner calm, peace and security are the result of complete reliance on Allah which strengthens the hearts and lifts up the morale.

References

Iṭmi'nān: 3: 126; 5: 113; 8: 10; 13: 28; 16: 106. *Sharḥ al-Ṣadr*: 6: 125; 16: 106; 20: 25; 39: 22; 94: 1. *Sakīnah*: 2: 248; 9: 26 and 40; 48: 4 and 26.

Jahannam [جهنّم] (Hell)

Meaning

According to Imām al-Rāghib, some people think that the word *Jahannam* came from the Persian into Arabic. Perhaps its origin is the Hebrew *Gehenna* which is a place of eternal torment. Strictly speaking, it means the "Valley of Hinnom" (*Ge-Hinnom*), where sacrifices to Baal and Moloch were offered by the pagans. It came to be regarded as a place of unquenchable fire (*Brewer's Dictionary of Phrase and Fable*).

Jahannam is translated as "Hell" which both in Jewish and Christian theology is a place the wicked will be condemned to for punishment after death. It is a fiery subterranean abyss where the wicked will endure eternal torment.

In the Qur'ān the most frequently used name for this abode is *al-Nār* (Fire). Sometimes both words, *al-Nār* and *Jahannam*, are used together. The other word used is *Ḥarīq* (fire, conflagration) which is derived from *Ḥaraqa* meaning to burn. The word *Sa'īr* (inferno, blazing flames) is used to indicate the intensity of the fire. Similarly the words *Saqar*, which means to scorch or to brand, and *Laẓā*, meaning blazing flame of *Jahannam* (al-Ma'ārij 70: 15) are used, as is the word *Talaẓẓā* (al-Layl 92: 14).

To emphasize the sheer severity of the punishment, *Jahannam* is also described by its other characteristics such as *ḥuṭamah* (the crusher) – which is from *Ḥaṭṭama*, meaning to break, shatter, and wreck or demolish – and *Hāwiyah* meaning bottomless pit, abyss, chasm and infernal depth.

Imām al-Ghazālī considers that the many names of *Jahannam* specify separate sections indicating the severity of the punishment. In *Iḥyā' 'Ulūm al-Dīn*, he arranges them top to bottom in these seven sections: "*Jahannam*, then *saqar*, then *laẓā*, then *al-Ḥuṭamah*, then *al-Sa'īr*, then *al-Jaḥīm*, then *Hāwiyah*."

Description

In both the Qur'ān and *aḥādīth* there are vivid and graphic descriptions of *Jahannam*. As this phenomenon relates to *'Ālam al-Ghayb* (the world that is not perceptible by the human senses) in which one is required to believe, it is deemed necessary to describe *Jahannam* in great detail and in very graphic terms to help strengthen the faith of the believers. To express its horror, *Jahannam* is personified with the power of speech, rage, anger and fuming. "*When they are cast therein, they will hear the (terrible) drawing in of its breath even as it blazes forth, almost bursting with fury*" (al-Mulk 67: 7–8). "*On that day We will ask* Jahannam *'Are you filled to the full?' It will say, 'Are there any more (to come)?'*" (Qāf 50: 30). This shows that its dimensions are vast, access to *Jahannam* is through its seven gates and "*for each of these gates a (special) class (of sinners) is assigned*" (al-Hijr 15:

44). Perhaps sins will be classified into seven categories as stated in Sūrah al-Zumar: "*The unbelievers will be led in companies to* Jahannam *until they arrive there. Its gates will be opened*" (39: 71). Its fuel will be its inhabitants and stones (al-Baqarah 2: 24). Perhaps the purpose of burning stones will be to heighten the intensity of the heat or to demonstrate the futility of those who worshipped idols made of stones.

To express the awfulness and horror of *Jahannam* the word *Bi'sa* is often used. *Bi'sa* means miserable, wretched and distressful. The punishment in Hell will be of constant heat and burning. When the skins of the wicked are burnt away a new skin will be supplied them to continue the torment (al-Nisā' 4: 56). The fire will engulf them from all sides and will "*mount right up to their hearts*" (al-Humazah 104: 7). Their food will be filth and the bitter thorny plant called *Zaqqūm*, and their drink will be boiling water (al-Wāqi'ah 56: 52–56). They will live in a state of animated suspension between life and death (Ṭā Hā 20: 74). Truly it is a place of great humiliation and disgrace.

In addition to the physical torment and torture, those condemned to Hell will suffer eternal deprivation of Allah's grace. Allah will not look at them, or speak to them; nor will He cleanse them (Āl 'Imrān 3: 77).

References

Jahannam: 3: 197; 4: 140; 67: 6; 78: 21; 98: 6. *Nār*: 2: 24; 3: 103; 4: 145; 32: 20; 104: 6.

Jāhiliyyah [جاهلية] (Age of Ignorance)

Meaning

The word *Jāhiliyyah* is derived from *Jahila*, meaning to be ignorant, foolish, or irrational. Thus, *Jahl* is ignorance, foolishness and stupidity; its opposite is *'Ilm* (knowledge). *Jahl* is also used for having wrong belief about something as well as for not doing something as it ought to be performed. *Jāhiliyyah* indicates the state of ignorance or the age of ignorance and is often used to refer to the paganism of the pre-Islamic period.

The word *Jāhil* is not always used in the derogatory sense (al-Baqarah 2: 273); similarly the word *Jahūlā* (al-Aḥzāb 33: 72).

Analysis

In the Qur'ān, *Jāhiliyyah* is used as the opposite of Islamic teachings and reforms. The Islamic teachings are based on knowledge and guidance from Allah. Allah is the source of all knowledge as He taught Ādam (peace be upon him), the first human being, the names of all things (al-Baqarah 2: 31). In the pre-Islamic era the way of life and laws were not based on reason or revelation but on whims and conjecture. However, the Qur'ān does not reject all good values prevalent in Arabia before the advent of Islam. Many practices were reformed, and other good values – for example, generosity and hospitality – were retained.

The term "age of ignorance" is not applied exclusively to the pre-Islamic period. Any period in history when the attitude adopted in the governance of human affairs is one of ignoring divine guidance will be termed *Jāhiliyyah*. The word denotes any system, ideology or institution that is built on values that are based on human reason alone without reference to the guidance of Allah. Today, despite the advancement of knowledge in many fields, reason is still not sufficient to guide humanity on the right path. Human knowledge is acquired sometimes by observation and experimentation, yet many fundamental matters are based on theories and hypotheses that are similar to the practices followed in the age of ignorance of bygone days. Hence, this phenomenon is termed the modern age of *Jāhiliyyah*.

The struggle between Islam and *Jāhiliyyah* will always continue. Islam wants to create a society based on the Islamic ethical and intellectual guidance received through the Qur'ān, whereas *Jāhiliyyah* represents a system of life designed by human beings on the basis of uninformed opinions. All the 'isms' developed by man lack moderation and balance. They usually fluctuate from one extreme to the other.

The Characteristics of *Jāhiliyyah*

Society based on the system of *Jāhiliyyah* discriminates on the basis of race, colour, nationality and nobility as this system is not based on divine revelation. Attachment to the prejudices creates frictions within society. The social structures are devoid of accountability and lack moral spirit. The Prophet (peace be upon him) said: "There are four things of *Jāhiliyyah* which not all of my *Ummah* will be able to get rid of. They are: taking pride in one's noble birth, taunting someone for his lineage, attributing rainfall to stellar influence and mourning loudly" (Muslim).

References

Jāhiliyyah: 3: 154; 5: 50; 33: 33; 48: 26.

Jannah [جنّة] (Heaven)

Meaning

Janna means to cover, hide, conceal. *Jannah* is called *Jannah* because it is hidden from human perception. The other reason is that *al-Jannah* is such a lush and green garden with majestic leafy trees that its ground is not visible. Heaven is called *Jannah* to portray it as a pleasure garden or a residential garden. The plural of *Jannah* is *Jannāt* or *Jinān*.

The Categories of *Jannah*

According to ʿAbdullāh ibn ʿAbbās there are seven categories of *Jannah*: *al-Firdaws* (Paradise); *Jannat ʿAdn* (the Garden of Eden); *Jannāt al-Naʿīm* (the Gardens of Comfort and Happiness); *Dār al-Khuld* or *Jannāt al-Khuld* (the Abode of infinite duration, eternity); *Jannat al-Maʾwā* (the Gardens of Abode); *Dār al-Salām* (the Abode of Peace); *ʿIlliyīn* (Dwellings on High).

All these names are mentioned in the Qur'ān, and some of them are described in greater detail. Sūrah al-Raḥmān (55: 46–61) gives a vivid sketch of two *Jannāt*. From their description it seems that they are for those nearest to Allah (*Muqarrabūn*). They were the foremost in faith (*al-Sābiqūn*) as mentioned in Sūrah al-Wāqiʿah (56: 10–11). Verses 62–76 of Sūrah al-Raḥmān gives further description of two other *Jannāt*. From their description it seems that they are for those of lesser rank. Perhaps these are for *Aṣḥāb al-Yamīn* (the Companions of the Right Hand) (al-Wāqi'ah 56: 27).

Jannat al-Ma'wā is where the believers will be stationed first and where they will be briefly entertained before being taken to their permanent abode. These gardens will serve as rest houses for them (*Tadabbur-i-Qur'ān*, Vol. 5, p. 166). The location of *Jannat al-Ma'wā* is near *Sidrat al-Muntahā* (the Lote Tree) as mentioned in Sūrah al-Najm (53: 14–15).

The Pleasures of *Jannah*

Jannah is the manifestation of Allah's *Maghfirah* (Forgiveness) and attainment of His pleasure. It is the eternal residence of those who led a life of piety in this world. Its bliss is eternal and its pleasures are everlasting, it is one area where there is life and no death; where there is pleasure and no pain; where there is happiness and no regret; where there is peace and no turmoil. Every desire will be fulfilled and every wish complied with. The houses will be palatial and the dresses will outshine royal robes and jewellery. Graphic and detailed accounts of *Jannah* are given in the Qur'ān and *aḥādīth*. The reason is that this area belongs to *'Ālam al-Ghayb* (phenomena that cannot be perceived by human senses). It is to strengthen their *Īmān* that believers are provided with such detailed descriptions.

Jannah as a Goal

According to the Qur'ān the greatest ideal of a believer should be to enter *Jannah* and win Allah's pleasure in the eternal life of the Hereafter (Āl 'Imrān 3: 133; al-Ḥadīd 57: 21). Admission into *Jannah* is regarded by the Qur'ān as the greatest success for believers. "*The successful one is he who escapes hellfire and is admitted to* Jannah" (Āl 'Imrān 3: 185). The conditions to be fulfilled for qualifying for this high status are not difficult. *Īmān* without doubt and lifelong commitment by leading a life of piety (*Taqwā*) are all that is required (al-Baqarah 2: 3–5, 25, 82; Fuṣṣilat 41: 30).

References

Jannah: 2: 35; 3: 133; 9: 111; 50: 31; 79: 41.

Jazā' [جزآء]

see *'Adhāb* and *Thawāb*

Jihād [جهاد]

Meaning

Jāhada means to endeavour, strive, struggle, exhaust. The noun *Juhd* means the making of one's utmost effort and to struggle to achieve one's object. From this root the word *Jihād* is the Qur'ānic terminology for struggle and it means investing one's capabilities and resources by the utmost striving – including fighting – in order to obey Allah's commands and to seek His pleasure and to establish His *Dīn*. The word *Jihād* is often used as a synonym for war which is not correct. When the Qur'ān specifically means fighting in the way of Allah the words *Qitāl* or *Ḥarb* are used. We will discuss the differences between these words later.

Forms of *Jihād*

a. assimilating Islamic values

The struggle one faces in assimilating Islamic values in one's life is an enormous task which takes three different forms:

JIHĀD BI AL-NAFS

One's own desires, aspirations, passions, likes and dislikes have to be subservient to the *Sharī'ah*. Hence, this is termed the most important *Jihād*. The Prophet (peace be upon him) said: "Do *Jihād* against your carnal self."

JIHĀD AGAINST SATAN

Those who want to traverse the path of piety face many promptings and whisperings from Satan who uses insidious ways from within to try to sap one's will. These evil inclinations within one will try to deviate a person from the righteous path.

JIHĀD AGAINST THE EVILS OF SOCIETY

In addition to conquering one's own desires and trying to safeguard oneself against evil thoughts and action, one sometimes faces opposition from one's own family and friends. The piety and religiosity which are reflected in one's life sometimes cause friction as one is seen to be following a different path. So the Qur'ān warns: "*O you who believe! Truly among your wives and your children are some (that are) enemies to yourself: so beware of them!*" (al-Taghābun 64: 14). The reason is that in some cases the demands of one's family may conflict with one's moral and spiritual convictions and duties.

b. To propagate Islamic ideology

If one is convinced that one is following the right path then it is incumbent upon oneself to call others to this path. Such a person is praised by Allah: "*Who is better in speech than one who calls others to Allah, works righteousness, and says: 'I am of those who bow in Islam?*" (Fuṣṣilat 41: 33). This *Da'wah* is another form of *Jihād*. It has to be undertaken with sincerity and wholeheartedness so that it can reach the heart of the recipient. Of course when inviting others to the path of righteousness one should be able to present a good model in one's own life. The Qur'ān provides many instructions in this respect (al-Naḥl 16: 125; Fuṣṣilat 41: 34–36).

c. *Jihād* to establish Allah's *Dīn*

This is the final goal for a believer. When all the above stages have been completed and there is a Muslim community faithfully observing the dictates of the *Sharī'ah*, naturally these believers would like to fashion society on Islamic values. This struggle can take the following three forms.

PASSIVE RESISTANCE

Believers have to endure hardships, opposition, oppression and persecution. One has to be patient and never resort to retaliation. The whole purpose is to win the hearts of people. It is only with mass support that one can succeed in achieving one's goal.

ACTIVE RESISTANCE

Once there is a majority of the believers then one is permitted actively to resist oppression: "*If you do chastise, then chastise with the like of what you were being chastised with...*" (al-Naḥl 16: 126).

JIHĀD FĪ SABĪL ALLĀH

This is the final form of *Jihād*. Unless all the aforementioned stages are fulfilled this last stage cannot be contemplated. For this last stage, many conditions need to be fulfilled. *Jihād* must be called by a duly constituted state authority. It must be preceded by inviting people to Islam or to enter into a treaty giving them religious and cultural freedom to follow their own religion under the protection of an Islamic state. The other fact to be noted is that *Jihād* is not just any struggle; it is "a struggle in the cause of Allah". This means that all deeds are undertaken with sincerity to gain the pleasure of Allah and not with any other motive.

Misunderstandings about *Jihād*

Jihād is the most vilified word in the Islamic vocabulary. It is commonly translated as "holy war". *Jihād*, as we have seen above, literally means to struggle to the utmost or to exert one's utmost endeavour in promoting a cause. The avoidance in the context of this struggle of other Arabic words in the Qur'ān like *Ḥarb* (war) and *Qitāl* (fighting) is deliberate, because *Jihād* is not only war but has several other dimensions, as mentioned above.

If the meaning of *Jihād* is restricted to armed conflict and war which does not affect the daily life of a believer then *Jihād* is divorced from day-to-day life. But *Jihād* is part of one's *Īmān*. The training that believers get from all *'Ibādah* is to prepare them for *Jihād* (struggle) against their own self, family, and society, and if needs be the state. This duty is emphasized in several places in the Qur'ān:

> *Only those are believers who believe in Allah and His Messenger, and have never since doubted, but have striven with their belongings and their persons in the Cause of Allah: such are the sincere ones.*
>
> (al-Ḥujurāt 49: 15)

> *O you who believe! Shall I lead you to a bargain that will save you from a grievous penalty – that you believe in Allah and His Messenger, and that you strive your utmost* (Jihād) *in the Cause of Allah with your property and your persons: that will be best for you.*
>
> (al-Ṣaff 61: 10–11)

The other misunderstanding is that whatever war Muslims wage is termed *Jihād.* Not every armed conflict is *Jihād.* A conflict cannot be *Jihād* unless all the conditions are satisfied as stated above. Unfortunately, some people either wilfully or unwittingly exploit the term *Jihād* or mislead others. They do not make sure that the foundations are solid and firm; instead they try to build and decorate the sixth floor!

References

Jihād: 9: 24; 22: 78; 25: 52; 29: 69; 60: 1.

Jinn [جنّ]

Meaning

The root meaning of *Janna, Yajunnu* is to cover or hide. Hence, *Jinn* means something hidden or invisible. In simple terms it means a spirit or genie as it is called in English. The reason for the *Jinn*'s invisibility is that whereas human beings are created from clay, *Jinns* are created from a flame of fire (al-Raḥmān 55: 14–15).

Analysis

Both in the Qur'ān and *aḥādīth, Jinns* are described as a definite species of living beings. Like human beings they may be believers or transgressors. They also have free will to accept or reject the guidance brought by Allah's Messengers (al-Jinn 72: 14). Like human beings *Jinns* are accountable for their deeds (al-Raḥmān 55: 39) and they will be judged and rewarded or punished (al-Jinn 72: 15; al-Raḥmān 55: 51).

Iblīs or Satan was one of the *Jinns* as mentioned in Sūrah al-Kahf, who disobeyed Allah by refusing to bow down to Ādam (peace be upon him) because of his pride (18: 50). He was given respite by Allah until the Day of Resurrection and he vowed to seduce Ādam (peace be upon him) and his progeny from the path of righteousness. *Iblīs* has a large army of his own followers made up of both *Jinns* and human beings who are duped by his vain promises.

References

Jinn: 6: 130; 18: 50; 46: 29; 55: 74; 72: 1.

Jizyah [جزية] (Poll Tax)

Meaning

Jazā' means to requite, to recompense, to repay, to reward. "*Then beware of a day when no soul for another shall recompense*" (al-Baqarah 2: 48). *Jizyah* from this root means compensation. But as a technical term it means the poll tax or tribute that non-Muslims are required to pay to the Islamic state.

The Purpose of *Jizyah*

The *Jizyah* is imposed to provide security to the non-Muslims who live as *Dhimmīs* (protected people) in an Islamic state. Being a tax on the able-bodied males of military age, it is in a sense a commutation of military service. Moreover, being non-Muslims, those taxed are not liable to pay *Zakāh*. As no specific amount was fixed for this tax, in a sense it is of a symbolic nature.

It should be noted that the verse in Sūrah al-Tawbah (9: 29) that mentions the imposition of the *Jizyah* indicates that it is only imposed on those conquered *Dhimmīs* who fought against the Islamic state and were defeated and agreed to live among Muslims. The *Fuqahā'* (Jurists) have dealt separately with those non-Muslims who, without engaging in war, and of their own free will, opted to stay in the Islamic state under an agreement. They will not be required to pay the *Jizyah* and they will be treated according to the agreement they have made with the Islamic state.

To the question often raised "What do non-Muslims get in return for paying *jizyah*?" Sayyid Mawdūdī has given this explanation:

> In our view, *Jizyah* is the compensation which non-Muslims pay for the freedom they are provided to adhere to their erroneous ways while living under an Islamic state. The amount so received should be spent on the administration of that righteous state which grants them freedom and protects their rights.
>
> (*Towards Understanding the Qur'ān*, Vol. III, p. 202)

It should be noted that if a *Dhimmī* opts to do military service, he will be exempted from paying *Jizyah*. A non-Muslim is not obliged to defend the Islamic state as he does not believe in the Islamic ethos of the state but he is allowed to live in peace in exchange for paying *Jizyah*.

Reference

Jizyah: 9: 29.

Kadhib [كذب]

see *Ṣidq*

Kaffārah [كفّارة]

see *Kufr*

Kalimah [كلمة] (The Word)

Meaning

Kalimah (pl. *Kalimāt*) means word, speech, address, utterance, saying and remark. The *Kalimah* is applicable to all parts of speech whether it is a noun, verb or preposition.

Usage

The word *Kalimah* is used in several meanings in the Qur'ān:

1. the words (of guidance) and names of things (and their nature) (al-Baqarah 2: 37 and 31).
2. the word "*Kun*" (Be), uttered by Allah to create anything (Yā Sīn 36: 82).
3. *al-Kalimah al-Ṭayyibah* means "a good word". This stands for the statement of truth and sound belief. Hence it is the affirmation of *Tawḥīd* and *Risālah*. These are the fundamental truths as expounded by the Qur'ān. As opposed to this there is *al-Kalimah al-Khabīthah* which means an "evil word". This refers to all varieties of falsehood, especially all the "isms" invented by human beings in opposition to the teachings of the Prophets.
4. Allah's will or decree or purpose (al-Baqarah 2: 124; al-Zumar 39: 71; Ghāfir 40: 6).
5. *Kalimah min Allāh* (A Word from Allah). This is a reference to the Prophet 'Īsā (peace be upon him) as his birth was miraculous and not according to the laws of nature. He was born by the word *kun* (Āl 'Imrān 3: 45). The usage of the word *Kalimah* as a common noun indicates that the Prophet 'Īsā (peace be upon him) was one among many *Kalimāt* of Allah. The Christians "under the misleading influence of the Greek philosophy, equated this with the '*Logos*', which was subsequently interpreted as the Divine attribute of speech" (*Towards Understanding the Qur'ān*, Vol. II, p. 116; al-Nisā' 4: 171). This led to the false doctrine of the divinity of the Prophet 'Īsā (peace be upon him).
6. *Kalimāt* (Words) of Allah are mentioned in Sūrah al-Kahf (18: 109) and Sūrah Luqmān (31: 27). In both places the vastness of them is described by the use of an analogy: "*And if all trees on earth were pens and the ocean (were ink). With seven oceans behind it to add to its (supply) yet would not the Words of Allah be exhausted (in writing): for Allah is Exalted in power, Full of Wisdom*" (al-Kahf 18: 109). As Allah is infinite so is His knowledge and we cannot set any limit to it, let alone comprehend it. Despite the

advancement of scientific knowledge and discoveries, the area that still remains unknown is so vast that it seems that man is only able to scratch the surface of knowledge.

References

Kalimah: 2: 37; 3: 64; 14: 24 and 26; 18: 109.

Kayd [كيد]

see *Makr*

Khashyah [خشي]

see *Khushū'*

Khatm [ختم] (Seal)

Meaning

Khatama means to seal, to stamp or to close. It is used for sealing something with wax or other material using a stamp. *Khatm* is used for sealing a letter or closing something so that nothing can come out of it or be inserted in it.

Al-Khatm 'alā al-Qalb

The phrase *al-Khatm 'alā al-Qalb* (sealing of the heart) is used to indicate that a person has reached a stage of no return because of his wickedness and that no amount of warning will bring him back to the path of righteousness. A divine law operates for the purification of hearts and souls. There are those who try to purify their hearts but commit mistakes or lapse back into bad habits; if as soon as they realize their errors or someone admonishes them they repent and try to improve their affairs, Allah forgives them, helps them and guides them. However, if they persist in their wickedness then their hearts as well as their faculties of sight and hearing are sealed so that they can no longer use them to attain guidance. It is punishment from Allah. Its reason is not that Allah wants them to stray from the straight path but that they made themselves deserve this fate. As mentioned in Sūrah al-Ṣaff – where the words *Zāghū* and *Azāgha* which come from *Zaygh* (crookedness) are used – "*Then when they went crooked Allah let their hearts go crooked*" (61: 5). This is also stated in several other places in the Qur'ān: "*As to those who reject faith, it is the same to them whether you warn them or do not warn them; they will not believe. Allah has set a seal on their hearts and on their hearing. And on their eyes is a veil; great is the penalty they (incur)*" (al-Baqarah 2: 6–7; al-An'ām 6: 46; al-Jāthiyah 45: 23).

The other Qur'ānic word used as a synonym of *Khatama* is *Ṭaba'a* which means to impress with a stamp or to seal. For example in Sūrah al-Naḥl it is said: "*Those are they whose hearts, ears and eyes Allah has sealed up and they take no heed*" (16: 108). There are similar verses in nine other places.

Khātam al-Nabīyīn

The Prophet (peace be upon him) is described as *Khātam al-Nabīyīn* – the Seal of the Prophets – in Sūrah al-Aḥzāb (33: 40). The words *Khātam* and *Khātim* both mean seal or stamp as well as signet or ring. *Khātim* also means end, termination or conclusion. So *Khātam al-Nabīyīn* would mean an end of the chain of Prophethood. The Holy Prophet (peace be upon him) was the last in the line of messengers and prophets and there will be no other prophet after him. Thus, after him the line of prophets was sealed and stamped. This was not an arbitrary decision: the above-cited verse concludes by saying "*Allah has full knowledge of all things.*" In Sūrah al-Mā'idah it is stated: "*This day I have perfected your* Dīn *for you and completed My favour upon you and have chosen for you Islam as your* Dīn" (5: 3). The completion of the prophethood was the logical conclusion of the completion of *al-Dīn*.

References

Khatm: 2: 7; 6: 46; 36: 65; 42: 24; 45: 23.

Khawf [خوف]

see *Khushū'*

Khayr [خير]

see *Sharr*

Khilāfah [خلافة] (Vicegerency)

Meaning

Khalafa means to be the successor of someone, to succeed someone or to follow someone. The word *Khalīfah* comes from the same root, and means vicegerent or representative.

The *Khilāfah* is used as a keyword in the Qur'ān. Its technical meaning is to enforce Allah's laws by means of the power of the state. The purpose of this is that there should be a responsible government that acts for the welfare of humanity by enforcing Allah's rule, thereby ensuring that society is free of oppression and corruption, and leading to peace and prosperity for all. The justice that is the key objective of this universe should prevail there.

The Concept of *Khilāfah*

The first recipient of this honour was the Prophet Ādam (peace be upon him). He was the vicegerent of Allah on earth and through him all human beings were endowed with this honour. Islam views society as a divinely ordained institution necessary for man's fulfilment of the purpose of his creation. According to Islamic teachings man is created as a vicegerent (*Khalīfah*) of God on earth. As narrated in Sūrah al-Baqarah (2: 30–34), Allah declared before the angels: "*I will create a vicegerent on earth.*" The angels were surprised and questioned why He would place on earth a creature which is capable of doing evil. God answered that He had indeed a purpose unknown to the angels who cannot but obey God. The purpose behind man's creation consists of fulfilling the moral part of the divine will – a part whose fulfilment requires that the subject be free to fulfil as well as to violate it. Being alone capable of moral action, man is indeed God's "Best and Supreme" creation and is higher than angels.

Several Implications

The story of the Prophet Ādam (peace be upon him) and man's vicegerency (*Khilāfah*) has:

First, Man was created for the purpose of acting as vicegerent on earth and to fulfil his mission. This is an honour bestowed by the Creator and represents the "rise of man" to a new assignment.

Second, the role and status of vicegerency are conferred upon the human race. As such both man and woman share this honour. This lays the foundation for their essential equality as human beings, as vicegerents of God on earth, whatever different roles they perform in society.

Third, human nature is pure and good. Man is created in the best of forms. Both man and woman are made of the same substance. Everyone is born in a state of purity and innocence. Success and failure depends entirely on one's own belief and behaviour. No one is responsible for the shortcomings of others.

Fourth, man has been given freedom of choice. He is free to accept or deny reality. He is responsible for his acts, but he is not deprived of his freedom, even if he makes mistakes and abuses it. The uniqueness of the human situation lies in man's psychosocial volition. This potential enables him to rise to the highest pinnacle or to fall into the deepest abyss.

Fifth, the dangers of misuse of freedom continue to confront man throughout his life on earth. The challenge from Satan is unceasing. To safeguard man against this, Divine Guidance is provided.

Sixth, man has not been totally protected against error. This would have involved negation of freedom of choice. He may commit errors, but his redemption lies in his realization of those errors, in seeking repentance and turning back to the right path.

References

Khilāfah: 2: 30; 7: 129; 24: 55; 27: 62; 38: 26.

Khushū' [خشوع] (Humility)

Meaning

Khasha'a means to be submissive or to be humble. *Khushū'* is a noun from this root meaning submissiveness, humility, lowliness, meekness or servility. This word is also used for a whispery and quiet voice and for downcast eyes.

Analysis

The *Khushū'* is a bowing down before someone to show humility and submissiveness. As such it affects both inner feelings of the heart as well as the outward expression of the body. The *Khushū'* of the heart means a state of being overpowered by the glory and grandeur that create awe, reverence and fear. The manifestation of this *Khushū'* on the body results in bowing down one's head with downcast eyes, with the body in the state of humility and the voice very quiet, all expressing a state of fright and timidity. This is the state of someone who is in the presence of an impressive and regal personality.

The *Khushū'* is the soul of the prayer. This fact is emphasized on several occasions in the Qur'ān. Thus, what is required in the *Ṣalāh* is humility of the heart and a submissive posture of the body. There are glad tidings of *Falāḥ* (success) for those believers whose prayers are full of *Khushū'* (al-Mu'minūn 23: 1–2).

Synonyms

KHASHYAH

Other words used in the Qur'ān convey a similar meaning. One of the words closely related to *Khushū'* is *Khashyah* meaning fear, apprehension or anxiety. This feeling of awe and fear is generated by someone's greatness and powerfulness. *Khashyah* is presented as an admirable quality of the prophets and *'Ulamā'* – those possessing knowledge of truth and who live their lives in constant awe of Allah (al-Aḥzāb 33: 39; Fāṭir 35: 28).

KHAWF

Khawf is derived from *Khāfa* meaning to be frightened, scared or afraid. It is the attribute of the believers that they remain ever vigilant about their deeds and are apprehensive about their accountability before Allah on the Day of Judgement. "*And for such as had entertained the fear of standing before their Lord and restrained (their) souls from lower desires; their abode will be the Garden*" (al-Nāzi'āt (79: 40–41). "*Even those who are nearest (to Allah) they hope for His mercy and fear His wrath*" (al-Isrā' 17: 57).

Imām al-Rāzī has explained the difference between *Khashyah* and *Khawf*. He says that *Khawf* is related to one's vulnerability when facing physical danger; whereas *Khashyah* is the mental attitude creating feelings of awe and fear when one thinks about the greatness and power of someone.

RAHBAH

Rahiba means to be frightened, to be afraid or to dread something. *Rahbah* from this root means fear, fright, alarm or terror. Similar to *Khashyah*, this means manifestation of fear by shivering and trembling when thinking about the power, dignity and grandeur of some person. Banū Isrā'īl were instructed by Allah to "*fulfil your Covenant with Me as I will fulfil My Covenant with you, and fear none but Me*" (al-Baqarah 2: 40).

The words *Khushū'*, *Khashyah*, *Rahbah* and *Taqwā* convey slightly different manifestations of the fear and awe of the Supreme Being. When this fear results in quavering and shivering it is *Rahbah*, and when one feels humble and submissive it is *Khushū'* and *Khashyah*. If *Khashyah* leads one to refrain from unlawful things and makes one careful about one's actions and deeds it is called *Taqwā*.

The words *Rahbānīyah* (monasticism) and *Rāhib* (monk) come from the same root. It was excessive fear of Allah that led the Christian Church to start monasticism.

References

Khushū': 17: 109; 20: 108; 33: 35; 57: 16; 59: 21. *Khashyah*: 9: 13; 33: 37; 35: 28; 50: 33; 67: 12. *Khawf*: 2: 38; 3: 170; 10: 62; 46: 13; 106: 4. *Rahbah*: 2: 40; 8: 60; 16: 51; 21: 90; 59: 13.

Khusrān [خسران]

see *Falāḥ*

Kitāb [كتاب] (Book)

Meanings

Kitāb is derived from the root *KTB* which means to write, to record or to inscribe. Hence, the word *Kitāb* (pl. *Kutub*) means book or a piece of writing. The word *Kitāb* is used in the following five different meanings in the Qur'ān:

1. revelation of the words of Allah. In this sense it is used for the Book of Allah or Scriptures. This could be the whole Book or part of it (al-Baqarah 2: 285; Āl 'Imrān 3: 79; al-Nisā' 4: 136).
2. laws and ordinances (al-Bayyinah 98: 3).
3. letter or message (al-Naml 27: 29).
4. a record book or register in which there is a complete record (Qāf 50: 4). This is also called *al-Lawḥ al-Maḥfūẓ*, meaning "the preserved tablet" (al-Burūj 85: 22).
5. written destiny (al-Anfāl 8: 68).

Al-Kitāb (The Book of Allah) and *Ahl al-Kitāb*

Although *Kitāb* is a common noun for a book, it has acquired a specific meaning and is used for the Book of Allah. It is similar to the use by Christians of the word *scripture* for the Holy Book as well as the word *Bible*. The word *Kitāb* is used for both the Qur'ān and the *Tawrāt* as both contain the *Sharī'ah* – Allah's laws. Both the Jews and Christians are given a special status and are called *Ahl al-Kitāb* (People of the Book). Thus they are distinguished from the pagan Arabs who were idolaters (*Mushrikīn*). Muslim men are allowed to marry Jewish and Christian women and it is permissible for Muslims to eat their food (al-Mā'idah 5: 5). The other concession given to *Ahl al-Kitāb* is permission to live in an Islamic state and practise their religion by paying the *Jizyah* (al-Tawbah 9: 29). The root meaning of *Jizyah* is compensation, and this is a form of poll tax, taken in lieu of for their protection as they are not required to defend the state from outside aggression. (**See also *Jizyah***)

The Qur'ān criticizes both the Jews and Christians for their misdeeds but also invites them to reach a common meeting ground to discuss the issues of mutual interest (Āl ʿImrān 3: 64). It also distinguishes between those who are pious, God-fearing and righteous and others who are rebellious and transgressors (Āl ʿImrān 3: 112–115). Muslims are instructed to engage with them in good argument about the faith (al-ʿAnkabūt 29: 46).

Umm al-Kitāb

Āyāt al-Muḥkamāt (the basic and fundamental verses) are termed *Umm al-Kitāb* – the foundation of the Book (literally "the mother of the Book") (Āl ʿImrān 3: 7). This phrase means that these verses are the basis, the real core of the Book; all arguments emanate from them as they are the basis of all guidance. If there were to be any disagreement about any issue these are the criteria on which judgement has to be made. These verses lay down the principles and from them all problems can be solved.

Umm al-Kitāb is also used to mean the "original *Kitāb*" to which no one has access and which cannot be corrupted by man or *Jinn*. It is called *Kitāb Maknūn* (a Book Well-guarded) (al-Wāqiʿah 56: 78) and *al-Lawḥ Maḥfūẓ* (the Preserved Tablet) in Sūrah al-Burūj (85: 22). These different expressions mean that the Qur'ān is well protected and that its writ is bound to come. The source of the Qur'ān's *Nūr* (Light) is that Eternal *Nūr* that illuminates the entire universe.

References

Kitāb: 2: 285; 8: 68; 27: 29; 50: 4; 98: 3. *Ahl al-Kitāb*: 3: 64 and 71; 4: 171; 5: 19; 29: 46. *Umm al-Kitāb*: 2: 7; 13: 39; 43: 4.

See also *Āyah*

Kufr [كفر] (Unbelief)

Meanings

The root of *Kufr* is *KFR* which means to cover or hide. Hence, it also contains the meaning of denial of something, which has the underlying meaning of unbelief that is hiding the truth or denying its recognition.

Thus, *Kufr* is used as the opposite of *Īmān* which means affirmation and belief, it means unbelief and rejection. *Kufr* is also used as the opposite of *Shukr* (gratitude). In this case it means ungratefulness and ungraciousness (Ibrāhīm 14: 7).

The Forms of *Kufr*

Kufr may take different forms. One, a person may completely deny the existence of God and reject that God is the Supreme Being and the Lord of the Universe: this is atheism. Two, a person who does not believe that God is the only true deity (object of worship) and is to be worshipped exclusively is a polytheist. Three, one may believe in God but refuse to accept His Guidance and laws and reject that these are sources of knowledge and guidance. Four, one may accept that one should follow God's guidance but refuse to believe in His Messengers. Five, while believing in some of the Messengers, a person may discriminate against others. Six, despite believing in Allah, His Messengers and His Books a person may refuse to follow their teachings. They all represent different forms of *Kufr*.

Kāfir

Kāfir (pl. *Kuffār, Kāfirūn*) means one who is an unbeliever. This word was used primarily for the infidels of Arabia. As *Ahl al-Kitāb* (People of the Book) were also involved in one of the forms of *Kufr*, sometimes the word was applied to them as well (al-Bayyinah 98: 1 and 6). Despite the flagrant *Kufr* of the idolaters they were rarely addressed as *Kāfirūn*. It is to be noted that the word *Kuffār* is not a derogatory term. It is an appellation for those who reject faith.

Some *Mufassirūn* have translated the word *Kuffār* in Sūrah al-Ḥadīd (57: 20) in its literal meaning for tillers or farmers – because they sow the seed and cover it up with soil.

Kaffārah

The word *Kaffārah* means penance and atonement because these conceal and remove sins. Usually good acts atone for sinful deeds as mentioned in Sūrah Hūd: "*For those things that are good remove those that are evil*"

(11: 114). But for serious misdemeanours *Kaffārah* or *Fidyah* (meaning ransom or redemption) are necessary. Technically there is a difference between these two terms, although their meaning is the same (see al-Baqarah 2: 184, 196; 57: 15). Atonement is for making amends for the shortcomings and wrongs one has committed. This is acceptable provided there is sincerity in repentance. For different acts of commission and omission there are different forms of *Kaffārah*. Atonement may take the form of fasting, clothing and feeding the poor, or acts of charity, sacrifice of an animal or freeing of slaves. Following the abolition of slavery this last option, of course, is no longer available.

References

Kufr: 2: 108; 3: 52; 5: 41; 16: 106; 49: 7. *Kaffārah*: 5: 45, 89 and 95.

Laghw wa Lahw [لغو ولهو]
(Frivolity and Diversion)

Meaning

Laghā means to talk nonsense and the word *laghw* is applied for talk or activity that is useless, meaningless and frivolous. Such actions are unproductive and neither bring any benefit nor fulfil any real need.

Lahw means diversion, pastime, fun, and play. It is used for activities one gets so involved in that one becomes oblivious and neglectful of more important affairs.

Analysis

The guidance of the Qur'ān to believers is that they are accountable for the time they spend in this world. One should spend one's time in fruitful activities and not just try to kill time by engaging in frivolous tasks that are useless. Time is a precious commodity and one should not waste it in foolish and pointless pursuits.

While enumerating the characteristics of the true servants of Allah, the Qur'ān states: "*When they pass by the frivolity, pass by it in dignity*" (al-Furqān 25: 72) "*and when they hear any vain talk, they turn away from it, saying 'We have our deeds and you have your deeds. Peace be to you. We do not desire to be like the ignorant'*" (al-Qaṣaṣ 28: 55). Thus, the Qur'ānic guidance is that one should avoid indulging in *laghw* and should also be on one's guard and shun such activities with dignity and grace. One of the blessings of *Jannah* is that one will be spared from hearing *Laghw*. "*They will not hear any vain discourse, but only salutation of peace*" (Maryam 19: 62; al-Wāqi'ah 56: 25; al-Naba' 78: 35).

The attitude of those who do not take this life seriously and remain neglectful of its true realities is termed *Lahw*. The Qur'ān repeatedly uses the word *Lahw* with *La'ib* which means amusement, fun and play, indicating that such allurements distract worldly people from serious things like the Hereafter which requires their attention. Although play and amusement are part of worldly life, they should prepare our minds for serious things; one often, however, gives more importance to ephemeral pleasures which seduce one to forget the eternal life (al-An'ām 6: 32 and 70; al-'Ankabūt 29: 64; Muḥammad 47: 36; al-Ḥadīd 57: 20).

References

Laghw: 5: 89; 23: 3; 25: 72; 28: 55; 52: 23. *Lahw*: 6: 70; 31: 6; 47: 36; 57: 20; 62: 11.

Al-Lawḥ al-Maḥfūẓ [اللوح ٱلمحفوظ]

see *Kitāb*

Laylat al-Qadr [ليلة ٱلقدر]

see *Qadar*

Libās [لباس] (Dress)

Meaning

Labisa means to wear, to dress or to clothe. *Libās* means clothing, garment, robe or costume.

The Necessity of Dress

Libās is a human necessity as no other species needs covering up. During their stay in *Jannah*, the Prophet Ādam and his wife (peace be upon them) were unaware of those bodily parts that should remain covered. After their disobedience of Allah's command they realized that they were naked. In desperation they gathered leaves from the trees and patched them together to cover their nakedness (al-A'rāf 7: 22). This episode indicates that the covering of private parts is the natural human instinct. Modesty and the feeling of shame are imbibed in human nature. This is called *Ḥayā'* and it is a part of *Īmān*. Those who say that the covering of the private parts is the product of custom and civilization are wrong. On the contrary, modesty and bashfulness have been an integral part of human nature right from the first human beings. The first target of *Shayṭān* is to undermine man's sense of modesty, as his sexual instincts are the most vulnerable aspects of his nature. Hence, human beings should be careful not to succumb to Satan's temptations as he was responsible for pulling off their parents' clothing to reveal to them their shame. But according to the Qur'ān, it is not enough to cover up private parts and dress to protect one from climatic conditions or for adornment. A person's dress should be the dress of piety (*Libās al-Taqwā*). This means it should be modest and serve the purpose of clothing oneself respectfully neither too extravagantly nor too shabily (al-A'rāf 7: 26).

It is Allah's mercy and blessing that He has created appropriate materials to enable human beings to make garments to cover up and to protect themselves from heat and cold (al-Naḥl 16: 81). It is indeed one of the signs of Allah which is visible everywhere in this world. Nakedness and nudity are not the norm, and each nation has developed its own national costume.

Islam has not prescribed any specific dress for Muslims. The basic guidance is that it should fulfil the moral as well as aesthetic function. People are free to choose whatever dress they prefer. Fashions and designs and the use of different materials will be dictated by climate and individual taste.

Intimate Relations between Spouses

In Sūrah al-Baqarah a metaphor of dress is used to describe the intimate relationship between husband and wife. Allah says: "*They are a garment for you and you are a garment for them*" (2: 187).

This emphasizes the closeness and attachment of spouses to each other. The husband and wife both are described as each other's raiment. A garment is something nearest to the human body; it is that part of the external world that becomes a part of our being. Such is the closeness of the relationship between spouses. Dress not only covers the body but also protects it. The spouses are protectors and guardians of each other. Like dress that beautifies the wearer and enriches his personality, spouses complement each other. This relationship also protects morals: without this shield one is exposed to the temptations of illicit liaisons.

References

Libās: 2: 187; 7: 26; 22: 23; 35: 33; 78: 10.

See also *Nikāḥ*

Maghfirah [مغفرة] (Forgiveness)

Meaning

Ghafara literally means to conceal something, to erase or cover something. A helmet is called *Mighfar* as it covers the head. With respect to sins, it implies concealing a sin, thus removing its evil consequences. Hence, *Ghafara* means to forgive and to pardon and *Maghfirah* which is a noun from this root means forgiveness, remission and pardon.

Attaining *Maghfirah*

Allah is the Most Merciful, the Most Forgiving and He is ever ready to forgive. Seeking Allah's forgiveness is not difficult for the following reasons: One, it is a great blessing from Allah that He does not punish for every sin committed by an individual. The door of repentance is always open, but repentance should be done with sincerity. Two, it is simply recognizing one's shortcoming and seeking Allah's forgiveness and mercy. Three, one's good deeds erase evil deeds (Hūd 11: 114). The Prophet (peace be upon him) said: "Follow up a bad deed with a good deed and it will wipe it out" (Tirmidhī). However, one should realize that mercy and forgiveness from Allah are not due to one's actions but simply the result of Allah's overwhelming compassion and grace.

Maghfirah and *Jannah*

Attaining *Maghfirah* from Allah is the highest achievement for a believer. The physical manifestation of this supreme forgiveness is one's admission into *Jannah*. The words *maghfirah* and *Jannah* are used together in many places in the Qur'ān to emphasize this aspect (al-Baqarah 2: 221; Āl 'Imrān 3: 133; al-Ḥadīd 57: 21). No one will be admitted into *Jannah* until Allah forgives his sins. When the Companions heard this, they asked: "Even you, O Allah's Messenger?" The Prophet (peace be upon him) replied: "Yes, even me until Allah engulfs me in His mercy."

Words from the Same Root

Istighfār means to seek forgiveness. *Astaghfirullāh* means "I seek Allah's forgiveness". This is the common supplication. However, it implies both verbal pronouncement and actions to be followed. *Istighfār* is the sure way of receiving Allah's mercy and safeguarding oneself from His wrath (al-Anfāl 8: 33). All the Prophets called humanity towards worshipping of Allah and seeking His Forgiveness (*Istighfār*) (Hūd 11: 3, 52 and 90; Nūḥ 71: 10). The reward of this *Istighfār* in this world is the blessings of Allah in the form of rain and abundance in produce and wealth (Nūḥ 71: 11–12). Seeking forgiveness essentially means admission on the part of a Muslim that Allah is the Forgiver (*Ghāfir*) and thus the act of *Istighfār* is a sign of humbleness on his part.

al-Ghafūr, al-Ghaffār, al-Ghāfir: These are among *al-Asmā' al-Ḥusnā* – the most beautiful names of Allah – mentioned in the Qur'ān. They all indicate Allah's overwhelming attribute of forgiveness. *Al-Ghafūr* means one who is readily inclined to pardon and much forgiving. *Al-Ghaffār* is the superlative of *al-Ghafūr* and thus indicates an extreme inclination for forgiving. *Al-Ghāfir* is one who forgives sins (Ghāfir 40: 3). It is repeatedly emphasized that it is only Allah who can forgive (Āl 'Imrān 3: 135).

Synonym

'Afw also means forgiveness, pardon or a waiver of punishment. It is derived from *'Afā* meaning to obliterate or wipe out. However, whereas the word *Maghfirah* is used exclusively for the forgiveness which Allah bestows, the word *'Afw* and its derivatives are used for both human and Divine forgiveness. Pardon given by Allah for the shortcomings of Muslims is termed *'Afw* in Sūrah al-Baqarah (2: 187) as well as in other places. Muslims are encouraged to pardon by exhorting them: "*if you forgive it is closer to* Taqwā" (2: 237).

The word *al-'Afw* is also used to mean whatever is in excess of one's need. Hence, when the Companions asked: "*What should we spend in the Way of Allah?*" they were told: "*Whatever you can spare*" (al-Baqarah 2: 219).

The word *'Afuwwun* is used to describe one of the attributes of Allah, meaning He is All-Relenting (al-Nisā' 4: 43).

References

Maghfirah: 2: 268; 3: 133; 4: 96; 33: 35; 35: 7. *Istighfār*: 3: 17; 4: 64; 9: 114; 38: 24; 51: 18. *al-Ghafūr*: 20: 82; 38: 66; 39: 5; 40: 42. *al-Ghaffār*: 2: 235; 3: 129; 7: 167; 15: 49; 39: 53. *al-Ghāfir*: 7: 155; 40: 3. *'Afw*: 2: 187; 3: 159; 5: 13; 24: 22; 42: 40.

Maḥrūm [محروم]

see *Faqr*

Makr [مكر] (Deception)

Meaning

Makara means to deceive, to delude, to cheat or to dupe. *Makr* means deception, craftiness, slyness or trickery. It is also used for harming someone by secret planning. The person against whom such a scheme is being hatched remains in the dark and does not realize what is going to happen to him.

Thus, the nature of *makr* makes it a detestable and despicable act. It is a sign of the weakness and wickedness of those who engage in such secret planning. Hence, *Makr* gets associated with its bad meaning. However, at times it may be necessary to use *Makr* to outwit those who are trying to sabotage someone. When *Makr* is related to Allah it means that Allah is using a scheme or plan to thwart the plan of the wrongdoers and His tactics are to defeat the plots and conspiracies of the enemies of the righteous cause. "*And (the unbelievers) plotted and planned, and Allah too planned and the best of planners is Allah*" (Āl ʿImrān 3: 54; al-Anfāl 8: 30; al-Naml 27: 50).

Synonym

The word *Kayd*, which comes from *Kāda*, also means slyness, deceit, deception or artful plot or trick. It is usually used in the bad sense but when it is related to Allah its meaning is the same as *Makr*. "*As for them they are plotting a scheme, and I am planning a scheme (as well)*" (al-Ṭāriq 86: 16). Often Allah gives the wrongdoers time to reform and get back to the straight path. When they do not reform themselves then Allah says: "*Those who reject Our signs We shall gradually visit with punishment, in ways they perceive not. Respite will I grant unto them: for My scheme is strong (and unfailing)*" (al-Aʿrāf 7: 182–183).

References

Makr: 3: 54; 7: 99; 13: 42; 27: 50; 71: 22. *Kayd*: 4: 76; 20: 69; 40: 25; 52: 42; 86: 15.

Malak [مَلَك] (Angel)

Meaning

Alūkah in Arabic means message. From this comes the word *Malak* (pl. *Malā'ikah*) which means a messenger or courier. This word is exclusively used for the celestial and spiritual messengers who are commonly referred to as angels.

Nature and Functions

Faith in the angels is part of *Īmān*. The angels belong to *'Ālam al-Ghayb* (the World that cannot be perceived by human senses). They are created from light and are invisible to human beings, yet they do have forms and bodies. The Qur'ān mentions their having a set of wings (Fāṭir 35: 1). They are in total submission to Allah and are incapable of committing any sin. They are continuously engaged in Allah's praise. Each one of them has been assigned a specific task to perform in the governance of the universe. The number of angels is known only to Allah Himself. Four of them, however, are well known, being nearest to Allah:

First and foremost is Archangel Jibrīl (also called *al-Rūḥ al-Amīn*). He performed the most important task of bringing the Message of Allah to His Messengers. He no longer performs this duty as the institution of Prophethood came to an end with the Holy Prophet Muḥammad (peace be upon him). The second is Angel Isrāfīl, who by Allah's command will blow the Trumpet on the Day of Resurrection and bring the present system and order of the world to an end. The third is Angel Mīkā'īl whose duty is to arrange for rainfall and the supply of provisions to the creations of Allah by His command. And finally 'Izrā'īl is the Angel of Death. He has been appointed to take people's souls.

Other angels mentioned in the Qur'ān are *Kirāman Kātibīn* – two kind and honourable scribes – and Hārūt and Mārūt. The former are attached to every human being, and as their names imply they record good and bad deeds. The latter were sent to the Jews of Babylon as a test. In *aḥādīth* there is a mention of two other angels called Munkar and Nakīr. They visit the graves of newly buried persons and question them about their faith.

The fact that angels were asked to bow down to the Prophet Ādam (peace be upon him) indicates that man is superior to them. This superiority is due to the special knowledge given to the Prophet Ādam (peace be upon him) which is not shared by the angels (al-Baqarah 2: 31) and also because the angels do not posses volition.

The angels are a credible link between Allah and His creatures. Being of spirit in essence they are close to Allah. Being a creation of Allah, however, they share a common link with other creatures. The Qur'ān refutes the belief of the pagan Arabs that the angels are daughters of Allah (al-Isrā' 17: 40) and thus have the power of intercession (al-Naba' 78: 38).

Though invisible, the angels approach with messages of strength and encouragement to the believers. They pray to Allah on behalf of them and ask Him for their forgiveness. They support them in both this life and the Hereafter (Fuṣṣilat 41: 30–31). If a believer realizes that it is not only Allah who is seeing what he does but there are also a couple of angels recording his deeds, this should act as a deterrent restraining him from committing sins even when he is alone (al-Infiṭār 82: 11–12).

References

Malak: 2: 30; 11: 12; 53: 26; 69: 17; 89: 22.

Malakūt [ملكوت]

see *Malik, Mālik*

Malik, Mālik [مَلِك، مالك]

(Sovereign, Owner)

Meaning

There is a variant reading of this word in Sūrah al-Fātiḥah. According to some *Qurrā'* (reciters), it is *Mālik* while some others read it as *Malik*. Both come from the same root *Malaka*, meaning to own; *Mālik* means owner and *Malik* means king or a person in authority and power. The abstract noun from this is *Mulk*, meaning authority, power or kingship. Both words describe Allah's attributes as the Master and the Sovereign of the Day of Judgement. Thus, the two variant readings make the meaning of the verse all the more clear. Allah is the Master, the Lord, the Ruler and the Sovereign who has complete power and authority.

In Sūrah al-Nās Allah is referred to as *Malik al-Nās* and in Sūrah al-Mu'min Allah's absolute authority on the Day of Judgement is forcefully reiterated:

> *The Day whereon they will (all) come forth: not a single thing concerning them is hidden from Allah. Whose will be the Dominion* (mulk) *that Day? That of Allah, the One, the Irresistible!*
>
> (al-Mu'min 40: 16)

Analysis

In the Qur'ān the word *Malik* is also applied to human beings. It is used both commending and contemptuously. Thus, there is a mention of Ṭālūt being appointed as *Malik* followed by the Prophets Dāwūd and Sulaymān (peace be upon them) who were Prophets of Allah as well as having vast kingdoms. Dhū'l-Qarnayn is also referred to as a pious general and, presumably, king as well. They were all noble and praiseworthy Kings. Nimrūd, who argued with the Prophet Ibrāhīm (peace be upon him), however, and who claimed power over life and death, was a tyrant and a despot. He was condemned by the Qur'ān for his arrogance and his rejection of faith (al-Baqarah 2: 258).

When the Queen of Sabā' said: "*Kings, when they enter a country, despoil it, and make the noblest of its people its meanest. Thus they do behave*" (al-Naml 27: 34), she was reflecting on the common characteristics of kings in history.

It is significant to note that in Sūrah al-Fātiḥah, after mentioning Allah's attribute of *Raḥmah* by using two words that highlight His quality of Mercy, He is proclaimed as the "Master of the Day of Judgement". This is to explain that Allah is extremely Kind and Merciful but at the same time He is also Just and Equitable. Human beings are accountable to Him in the Hereafter for their deeds. There the righteous will be rewarded and the wrongdoers punished. This belief in accountability in the *Ākhirah* (Hereafter) is the central part of *Īmān* (Faith). This belief gives courage and sustenance to those who suffer untold miseries in this life yet who do not deviate from the path of righteousness and remain hopeful of receiving their reward in the Hereafter. Conversely, it is a dire warning for the wrongdoers that they may escape justice in this world but Allah is aware of their misdeeds and they will not escape His Retribution on the Day of Judgement.

MALAKŪT

Malakūt also comes from the root *MLK*, combining the meaning of kingship as well as that of ownership. This word is used exclusively for the vast Kingdom of Allah which is spread over everything in this universe. In Sūrah al-An'ām, Allah refers to this:

> *So We were showing Ibrāhīm the kingdom of the heavens and earth, that he might be of those having sure faith.*
>
> (al-An'ām 6: 75)

Similarly, in Sūrah al-A'rāf, mention is made of Allah's Kingdom:

> *Do they see nothing in the Dominion of the heavens and the earth and all that Allah has created?*
>
> (al-A'rāf 7: 185)

References

Malik: 2: 247; 5: 20; 12: 54; 18: 79; 27: 34. *Mālik*: 1: 3; 3: 26; 36: 71; 43: 77. *Malakūt*: 6: 75; 7: 185; 36: 83.

Ma'rūf [معروف]

see *Amr*

Mawlā, Mawlānā [مولى، مولانا]

see *Walī*

Mawt [موت] (Death)

Meaning

Māta means to die, to perish, to lose life. *Mawt* from this root means death or demise. This is the opposite of life. The word *Mawt* is used for absence of life in living creatures as well as plants and metaphorically for inanimate objects like stone where there is an absence of greenery (Qāf 50: 11).

When a person dies he loses all sensation and consciousness whereas during sleep one only suffers loss of consciousness; even this is described figuratively as death (al-Zumar 39: 42; al-An'ām 6: 60).

Death is something that is inevitable: it is the most predictable event. In the Qur'ān it is referred to as *Yaqīn* (certainty) (al-Ḥijr 15: 99; al-Muddaththir 74: 47). It is stated that "*every soul shall taste death*" (Āl 'Imrān 3: 185).

Analysis

No one can escape death. It can come about at any time and any place. It can be sudden. It can be in a crowd or it can be in seclusion. It can be on the battlefield or it may be on a hospital bed where all the sophisticated life-saving apparatus and world-renowned doctors and physicians are available to save life. "*Wherever you are death will find you out, even if you are in towers built up strong and high*" (al-Nisā' 4: 78).

When someone dies suddenly, people say it is an untimely death. But the time of everyone's death is ordained and thus it will come neither early nor late. "*Nor can a soul die except by Allah's leave, the term being fixed as by writing*" (Āl 'Imrān 3: 145). "*To every people is a term appointed: when their term is reached, not an hour can they cause delay, nor (an hour) can they advance (it in anticipation)*" (al-A'rāf: 7: 34).

Furthermore, the place of death is also ordained. "*Nor does anyone know in what land he is to die. Verily with Allah is full knowledge and He is acquainted (with all things)*" (Luqmān 31: 34).

The purpose of life and death is to test who is best in deeds (al-Mulk 67: 2). Death is not the end of the journey, as there is life after death. Death is only a stage of transition before one rises up again on the Day of Resurrection to face the final judgement.

Death is just like sleep when a person for a short time loses consciousness. In sleep souls are temporarily released from the bondage of the flesh as Allah takes them for this time. If Allah wills, the soul is not returned and the person dies peacefully in his sleep. Otherwise the soul is returned for the appointed time (al-Zumar 39: 42). This explains that death only affects the body; for the soul there is no death.

References

Mawt: 2: 94; 4: 15; 6: 61; 44: 56; 50: 19.

See also *Ajal*

Millah [ملّة]

see *Ummah*

Miskīn [مسكين]

see *Faqr*

Mithāl [مثال] (Parable)

Meaning

Mathala means to resemble, to look alike or to compare. *Mithāl* (pl. *Amthāl* or *Amthilah*) comes from this root and means similitude, parable or allegory.

Analysis

In order to explain and help people understand and make them fully aware of many metaphysical and higher spiritual facts, it is helpful to give examples. Otherwise it is very difficult for people to grasp the latent meanings of these facts. The similes may be taken from the natural environment or historical events. By the use of parables it becomes easy to explain and guide people. The prime purpose of parables is mentioned in Sūrah al-Ḥashr: "*Such are the similitudes which We propound to people that they may reflect*" (59: 21). When the similes of a spider, a fly or a donkey were used in the Qur'ān, the unbelievers objected, saying: "*What means Allah by this parable?*" not realizing the purpose of them. Even the things used as an illustration instead of providing guidance led them astray (al-Baqarah 2: 26).

As the task of Allah's messenger is to convey the message and call his people to the righteous path, he often uses parables and similes. The Prophet 'Īsā's (peace be upon him) preaching was full of parables. His many appropriate and expressive parables can be seen in the New Testament, for example the parables of the Prodigal Son and the Good Samaritan. So also in *aḥādīth* there are innumerable parables. The Qur'ānic use of similitudes and parables is impressive, appealing and apposite. For example: "*The parable of those who take protectors other than Allah is that of the spider who builds (to himself) a house; but truly the flimsiest of houses is the spider's house – if they but knew*" (al-'Ankabūt 29: 41). This is a very appropriate parable conveying the message of the helplessness of others whom people believe to be their protectors. In Sūrah al-Jumu'ah those who were given the *Tawrāt* but who subsequently failed to fulfil their obligations are compared to a donkey which carries a huge burden of books and of course does not understand their value (62: 5).

Sometimes a simile is used as a sarcastic and mocking remark. For example in Sūrah Yā Sīn: "*And he makes comparisons for Us, and forgets his own (origin and) creation*" (36: 78).

References

Mithāl: 13: 17; 14: 25; 17: 48; 24: 35; 29: 43.

Mīthāq [ميثاق]
see *'Ahd*

Mīzān [ميزان]
see *'Adl*

Mubārak [مبارك]
see *Barakah*

Muḥkamāt [محكمات]
see *Āyah*

Mu'jizah [معجزة] (Miracle)

Meaning

'Ajaza and *'Ajiza* both mean to be weak, to lack strength, to be incapable of something or be unable to do something. From this root comes *'Ājiz* meaning weak and powerless. *I'jāz* means inimitability and unsurpassable nature. *Mu'jizah* means a miracle performed by the prophets which cannot be imitated: people are incapable of performing such acts.

However, the word *Mu'jizah* is not used for the miracles in the Qur'ān and *aḥādīth*. Instead, the words *Āyah* (sign) and *Burhān* (proof) are used as they convey the proper purpose of these occurrences. The *Muḥaddithūn* have used the term *Dalā'il* (proofs) and *'Alāmāt* (signs) instead of the word *Mu'jizah*, which are nearer in meaning to the Qur'ānic terms. As *Mu'jizah* has become a more common and popular term inevitably it is used here.

The Nature of *Mu'jizah*

Mu'jizah is an act or event that is contrary to the natural and physical laws. In the earlier scriptures as well as in the Qur'ān, many such events are related from the lives of the prophets; for example, the Flood during the time of the Prophet Nūḥ (peace be upon him) when he was saved together with the believers; the inability of the fire to burn the Prophet Ibrāhīm (peace be upon him); the staff of the Prophet Mūsā (peace be upon him) turning into a serpent; and the breathing of life into the dead by the Prophet 'Īsā (peace be upon him).

The Purpose of *Mu'jizah*

The personalities of the messengers and prophets should be sufficient proof of the authenticity of their message and its revelation from Allah. Many people accepted Islam and testified that what the Prophet (peace be upon him) brought was revelation from Allah as for them his personality was a clear proof. They did not demand supernatural manifestations.

Miracles testify that Allah Almighty is in command of all the events happening in this universe. He can intervene and change the routine laws of nature. He can save His Messengers if need be. He can bestow power on them to disrupt natural and physical laws. Those who believe in Allah and His Messengers do not find any difficulty in accepting miracles. For example, Abū Bakr al-Ṣiddīq instantaneously acknowledged the authenticity of the *Isrā'* and *Mi'rāj*. For those who are obstinate and whose hearts are sealed even seeing the miracles will not be convincing. One such was the Pharaoh who disbelieved the Prophet Mūsā's (peace be upon him) staff turning into a serpent and devouring the snakes of the magicians.

Mu'jizah and *Siḥr* (Magic)

There is always a debate on how to differentiate between a *Mu'jizah* and *Siḥr*. The decisive difference between the two is that a *Mu'jizah* is an act of Allah. He empowers His Messengers to perform such acts for convincing the unbelievers. Magic, by contrast, is an art which can be acquired by those who want to learn it. Magicians earn their living by performing these acts. Unlike magicians the whole life of a prophet is based on truth and sincerity. His only mission is to invite humanity towards Allah.

The miracles given to the messengers are related to the general environment of the society into which they were sent. As magic and sorcery were prevalent in Egyptian society, the miracles given to the Prophet Mūsā (peace be upon him) were such as to challenge their art of magic. The Arabs were very proud of their literary output. Hence the Qur'ān challenged them to produce a single *sūrah* to match its eloquence.

Reference

The word *Mu'jizah* is not used for the miracles in the Qur'ān.

Munkar [منكر]

see *Amr*

Muslim [مسلم]

see Islam

Mutashābihāt [متشابهات]

see *Āyah*

Nabī [نبيّ] (Prophet)

Meaning

Naba' (pl. *Anbā'*) means news, tidings and information. *Nabī* from this root means one who gives news. Some believe its root is *Naba'a* which means to be high, elevated, prominent or raised. This suggests that the status of a *Nabī* is noble and dignified. The word *Nabī* is translated as prophet, the one who brings Allah's message to mankind. The other word conveying the same meaning is *Rasūl*, which means a messenger, envoy or emissary. The word is used for Allah's Messengers bringing His guidance. In the Qur'ān, *Rasūl* is also used for angels who were sent on special tasks. (For example, in Sūrah al-An'ām 6: 61; al-A'rāf 7: 37) for angels of death; in Sūrah Hūd (11: 69); for angels bringing glad tidings to the Prophet Ibrāhīm; and in Sūrah Hūd (11: 77) for angels sent to the Prophet Lūṭ to tempt his people.

The Distinction between a *Nabī* and a *Rasūl*

Often these two words are used interchangeably, but sometimes the Qur'ān uses the two words together. The Prophet Mūsā (peace be upon him) is referred to as a *Rasūl* and a *Nabī* (Maryam 19: 51) and in Sūrah al-Ḥajj (22: 52) these two words are used to emphasize the difference between them.

Both a *nabī* and a *rasūl* receive revelation from Allah for guidance of their people. However, a *rasūl* additionally is given a Book as well. This Book of Allah remains valid until superseded by another Book. During the interval between two Messengers many prophets were sent to guide people who had forsaken the Book and gone astray. Many Prophets sent to Banū Isrā'īl after the Messenger Mūsā (peace be upon him), and they followed the teachings of the *Tawrāt*. Thus, every *rasūl* is also a *nabī*, but not every *nabī* is a *rasūl*. Usually the word *prophet* is used as a translation for both *nabī* and *rasūl* for the sake of convenience.

The Functions of a Prophet

A prophet is any human being whom Allah has chosen to receive His revelation, and his task is to convey this to his people. A person cannot train himself to acquire this status. "*Allah knows best with whom to place His message*" (al-An'ām 6: 124). All the messengers and prophets brought the same *Dīn* (Religion, way of life) for mankind. Their basic teachings were the same. They called upon mankind, saying: "*I am a Messenger worthy of all trust. So fear Allah and obey me*" (al-Shu'arā' 26: 162–163). Of course the *Sharī'ah* (laws and regulations) differ from one Messenger to the next due to changes in situations.

Some people object to the fact that the messengers and prophets were all human beings. They think such persons should have been angels or at least human beings with superhuman qualities – that they should be different from ordinary human beings. But a little reflection will show the fallacy of such an argument. As the Messengers and Prophets were models for humanity, how could people follow their examples if they were angels or superbeings? Then, people would have argued, it is all very well for angels and superbeings to follow the path of righteousness but we cannot be expected to achieve their standards.

Allah has provided for all the physical needs of human beings. What they need is moral and spiritual guidance. Thus, the first person who was created was also designated a Prophet (Ādam – peace be upon him). He was promised that: "*O you Children of Adam! Whenever there come to you Messengers from amongst you, rehearsing My Signs unto you – those who are righteous and mend (their lives) – on them shall be no fear nor shall they grieve*" (al-A'rāf 7: 35).

Thus, it is obligatory to believe in the Messengers of Allah and to obey them as well. After the Prophet Ādam (peace be upon him) a succession of Messengers and Prophets came to renew Allah's Guidance which had either been lost or had become mixed up with human intrusions. The last Messenger and Prophet was Muḥammad (peace be upon him). He completed the chain of prophets and, thus sealed the succession. The Qur'ān and his teachings are preserved for humanity until the end of time.

References

Nabī: 3: 68; 6: 112; 8: 64; 9: 73; 33: 45. *Rasūl*: 9: 128; 21: 25; 24: 54; 25: 7; 61: 6.

Nafs [نفس] (Self)

Meanings

Nafs (pl. *Nufūs, Anfus*) means soul, self, ego, spirit, psyche, life, and human being. In the Qur'ān the word is used as a general designation for the self or spiritual reality of living creatures. The word *Anfus* is used for hearts as well. "*And know that Allah knows what is in your hearts (Anfusikum)*" (al-Baqarah 2: 235). A similar usage occurs in the Prophet 'Īsā's (peace be upon him) statement, "*You know what is in my heart (Nafsī), though I know not what is in Yours (Nafsik)*" (al-Mā'idah 5: 116).

The Classification of *Nafs*

Nafs is composed of a complex mixture of opposing forces of good and evil. Man is given the choice to follow the path of righteousness or to go the other way. As Allah says: "*We showed him the way: whether he be grateful or ungrateful (rests on his will)*" (al-Insān 76: 3). Human beings are in constant struggle against divergent forces. They are always liable to be swayed by temptation and to commit sins. As the Prophet Yūsuf (peace be upon him) acknowledged when he was able to safeguard his chastity: "*Nor do I absolve my own self (of blame): the (human) soul is certainly prone to evil, unless my Lord bestows His Mercy: but surely my Lord is Oft-Forgiving, Most Merciful*" (Yūsuf 12: 53).

The *Nafs* that tempts us to evil is called *al-Nafs al-Ammārah bi'l-Sū'* (the imperious, carnal self) (Yūsuf 12: 53). To protect human beings from the treachery of this aspect of *Nafs* there is *al-Nafs al-Lawwāmah* (the reproaching self) which is called conscience. When a person commits a sin, his conscience reproaches him for doing such a shameful act. Allah presented this as a proof for the Day of Resurrection (al-Qiyāmah 75: 2). If one listens to the voice of one's conscience and whenever one commits any sin one retracts and repents, then one returns to the path of righteousness. But if one persists and suppresses the voice of one's conscience it becomes dead and one goes down the slippery slope of doom. Those who resist temptation and practise self-restraint, accepting the dictates of their conscience, attain the blessings of *al-Nafs al-Muṭma'innah* (the happy, peaceful, satisfied self). This is the highest achievement for human beings. This is the stage when one is well-pleased and happy with one's Creator and He is well-pleased with one (al-Fajr 89: 27–28).

Rūḥ (Soul)

The other word with a similar meaning that is used in the Qur'ān is *Rūḥ*. *Rūḥ* (pl. *Arwāḥ*) means soul, spirit, and breath (of life). It is the immaterial and immortal element of a human being. The creation of the first human being is described thus: "*I fashioned him (in due proportion) and breathed into him My spirit* (Rūḥ)..." (al-Ḥijr 15: 29; Ṣād 38: 72). By this act, a divine spark was breathed into a human being, which enlightened his faculties and thus made him the noblest of all creation. This elevates humans and gives them superiority over other creatures.

Whether *Nafs* and *Rūḥ* are two different things or the same thing is a difficult question to answer. Perhaps their meanings overlap, but there are also differences. *Nafs* refers to human existence and to the human personality and psyche. This is mortal as it is mentioned: "*Every* Nafs *shall taste death*" (Āl 'Imrān 3: 185). *Rūḥ* does not perish as it has been created to abide forever. It continues to live after death and feels pleasure and pain. *Wa'l-lāhu a'lam bi'l-Ṣawāb* (Allah knows the right). In Sufi literature a distinction is made between *rūḥ* as the higher plane of soul and *nafs* as the lower or animal self.

Rūḥ is also used for *waḥy* (revelation): "*They ask you concerning the* Rūḥ. *Say the* Rūḥ *(comes) by the command of my Lord: Of knowledge it is only a little that is communicated to you*" (al-Isrā' 17: 85). Here *Rūḥ* means the nature of *Waḥy* (revelation). As *Waḥy* is one of the highest spiritual experiences it cannot be explained in terms of everyday human experience. Some commentators say that *al-Rūḥ* means Archangel Jibrīl as he is referred to by this title in other places in the Qur'ān. However, other *Mufassirūn* maintain that the question was about the nature of the human soul and its relation to the body and that the answer was that *Rūḥ* works through Allah's command, of which human beings have little understanding.

As mentioned earlier, *al-Rūḥ al-Amīn* is the title of the Archangel Jibrīl, as in Sūrah al-Naba' (78: 38) and Sūrah al-Qadr (97: 3). Sometimes Jibrīl is referred to as *Rūḥ al-Qudus* – the Holy Spirit (al-Baqarah 2: 87 and 253; al-Mā'idah 5: 110; al-Naḥl 16: 102), yet elsewhere he is honoured as *al-Rūḥ al-Amīn* – the Trustworthy Spirit (al-Shu'arā' 26: 192).

The Prophet 'Īsā (peace be upon him) is also described as *rūḥ*: "*'Īsā al-Masīḥ, the son of Maryam, was (no more than) a Messenger of Allah, and His Word which He bestowed on Maryam and a Spirit* (Rūḥ) *proceeding from Him*" (al-Nisā' 4: 171).

References

Nafs: 2:48; 3: 25; 4: 1; 16: 111; 21: 35. *Rūḥ*: 4: 171; 16: 102; 17: 85; 40: 15; 97: 4.

Naḥr [نحر]

see *Nusuk*

Na'īm [نعيم]

see *Ni'mah*

Najwā [نجوى] (Whispering)

Meaning

According to *al-Qāmūs* the word *Najwā* is derived from *Nājā*, meaning to whisper to each other or to have a secret conversation. Some believe that it is derived from *Najwah* which means elevation, high ground or hillock and that from this *Najwā* means to talk to someone a long way away to maintain secrecy. Yet other lexicographers say that it comes from *Najāt* which means escape, deliverance, safety or salvation. In this way *Najwā* will mean to say something for someone's safety and rescue. Some others are of the opinion that *Najwā* means secret planning.

Usage

As *Najwā* means to talk to someone in confidence and seclusion it is not something bad in itself. People often want to consult others about important personal, social or communal affairs in privacy, and there is nothing wrong or sinful in that. But to start a whispering campaign against someone to harm him or his reputation is forbidden.

Detailed instructions are given in Sūrah al-Mujādilah (58: 7–13) about *Najwā*. The basic guidance given is: "*O you who believe! When you hold secret counsel; do it not for iniquity and hostility and disobedience to the Messenger, but do it for righteousness and self-restraint* (Taqwā) *and fear Allah to whom you shall be brought back*" (58: 9). The same instruction is given in Sūrah al-Nisā': "*In most of their secret talks there is no good; but if one exhorts to a deed of charity or justice or conciliation between people (secrecy is permissible). To him who does this, seeking the good pleasure of Allah, We shall soon give a reward of the highest (value)*" (4: 114).

Examples of acceptable *Najwā* are mentioned in the Qur'ān. When the Prophet Mūsā (peace be upon him) was on Mount Sinai and held an intimate conversation with Allah, it is described as *Najīyā* which comes from *Najwā* (Maryam 19: 52). Similarly when the brothers of the Prophet Yūsuf saw no hope of getting their youngest brother, who was detained on the charge of stealing, released they conferred in private; this too is referred to as *Najīyā* (Yūsuf 12: 80).

Examples of *Najwā* used in the negative sense are many. Such *najwā* is attributed to *Shayṭān*: "*Secret counsels are only (inspired) by Shayṭān in order that he may cause grief to believers*" (al-Mujādilah 58: 10). The plotting of wrongdoers to oppose Allah's message, which is open and clear, is described as *Najwā* (secret counsel) (al-Isrā' 17: 47; al-Anbiyā' 21: 3). When Pharaoh and his courtiers realized that they were not dealing with an ordinary person (the Prophet Mūsā) they conferred in private and plotted to invite the magicians to confront him (Ṭā Hā 20: 62).

References

Najwā: 4: 114; 17: 47; 20: 62; 21: 3; 58: 7.

Nakāl [نكال]

see *'Adhāb*

Nār [نار]

see *Jahannam*

Naṣīḥah [نصيحة] (Advice)

Meaning

Naṣīḥah is difficult to translate into English. It embraces sincerity, good advice and well wishing. The word has two basic linguistic meanings.

One meaning is to clean, to purify or to improve something; for example to purify honey from impurities (hence, pure honey is called *Naṣīḥat al-ʿAsal*). The other meaning is to unite or to join something together such as when sewing a garment. The word *Naṣīḥah* is usually translated as giving sincere advice or friendly reminder.

Analysis

In the Qur'ān this word is used to describe the task the Prophets have performed in respect of their *Ummah*. "*So Ṣāliḥ left them, saying: 'O my people! I did indeed convey to you the message for which I was sent by my Lord. I gave you good counsel, but you love not good counsellors*" (al-Aʿrāf 7: 79). The Prophets Nūḥ and Hūd (peace be upon them) gave the same message (al-Aʿrāf 7: 62 and 68). Here *Naṣīḥah* signifies the sincere relationship which the prophets have with their people. It is a heartfelt desire to reform and to build relationships on the right lines as well as a wishing for the well-being of the whole community. So *Naṣīḥah* is a dynamic and purposeful activity.

The Prophet (peace be upon him) enunciated the guiding principle about *Naṣīḥah* as follows: "*Al-Dīn* is *Naṣīḥah*." The people asked: "To whom?" The Prophet replied, "To Allah and His Book and to His Messenger and the leaders of the Muslims and their common folk" (Muslim). In this *ḥadīth*, *naṣīḥah* in respect of Allah means absolute sincerity and devotion to Him and that a person establishes correct relations with Him. *Naṣīḥah* in respect of the Prophet is to accept him as the supreme guide and leader. And *Naṣīḥah* in respect of the leaders of Muslim society and common folk is basically to give them good advice, that is, enjoining what is good and forbidding what is wrong. Thus, a Muslim's life is to be sincere to oneself and to the rest of society.

The word *Naṣūḥ* is used with *Tawbah* (repentance) in Sūrah al-Taḥrīm: "*O you who believe! Turn to Allah with sincere repentance*" (66: 8). Here both aspects of the word *Naṣīḥah* (sincerity and purity) are fused together. It means that a person should repent with purity of intention, that there should be no hypocrisy or showing off in it. Or a person by repentance should be sincere to his own self and stop sinning and try to mend his ways and improve his life so that others may follow his example.

References

Naṣīḥah: 7: 79 and 93; 11: 34; 12: 11; 28: 12.

Nifāq [نفاق] (Hypocrisy)

Meaning

Nafaq means an underground passageway or a tunnel that opens both ways. *Nafaqā'* means a hole or burrow of a wild rat having two openings so that the rat can enter from one side and escape from the other. From this root comes the word *Nifāq* which means hypocrisy, dissembling and duplicity. Hence, *Munāfiq* (hypocrite) is one who enters from one side of the *Dīn* and departs from the other.

The Nature of *Nifāq*

The purpose of *Nifāq* is to safeguard one's interest. Lacking true conviction a *Munāfiq* can switch loyalties from one camp to another. When the tide of Islam swept through Madīnah it was seen as advantageous to accept Islam. However, when believers were required to sacrifice their wealth and to march towards the enemy, the hypocrites turned their back on Islam (al-Tawbah 9: 56–58; Āl 'Imrān 3: 167–168). Their duplicity is vividly described in the Qur'ān: *"(These are) the ones who wait and watch about you. If you do gain a victory from Allah, they say: 'Were we not with you?' But if the unbelievers gain a success, they say (to them): 'Did we not gain an advantage over you, and did we not guard you from the believers?"* (al-Nisā' 4: 141).

There are many ways of preventing the people from gaining access to the truth. When People of the Book (mainly the Jews of Madīnah) could not stop Islam gaining ground, they became jealous. In order to create doubts among the newly converted, they played a trick by accepting Islam for a short while and then renounced the faith afterwards. Innocent

Muslims, who regarded the Jews with respect, had their faith shaken (Āl 'Imrān 3: 72).

The Signs of *Nifāq*

The Prophet (peace be upon him) in sound *Aḥādīth* has described the qualities found in hypocrites. These are four: lying, betrayal of trust, not fulfilling one's promise and use of abusive language during dispute (Bukhārī and Muslim). When the hypocrites prayed they wanted to show off and they used to pray without earnestness and hardly remembering Allah. By these actions they thought that they could deceive Allah but in fact they deceived themselves (al-Nisā' 4: 142).

Thus, there are two types of *Nifāq*: one, where there is hypocrisy in one's belief, and the other where there is a resistance to fulfilling the demands of the faith. This type of *Nifāq* has to be distinguished from the weakness of *Īmān* when even true believers may lapse into negligence and disregard demands of the faith.

The Punishment of the *Munāfiqūn*

In the early Madīnan period the Prophet took no punitive action against the hypocrites as it was not prudent to stir up resistance on the home front. After the Battle of *Aḥzāb* (5 AH) the Prophet (peace be upon him) was asked to fight not only against the unbelievers but also against the hypocrites (al-Tawbah 9: 73), as the Qur'ān equates *Nifāq* with *Kufr*. Their punishment in the Hereafter is the worst. "*The hypocrites will be in the lowest depths of the Fire*" (al-Nisā' 4: 145).

References

Nifāq: 4: 145; 9: 97 and 101; 48: 6; 63: 8.

Nikāḥ [نكاح] (Marriage)

Meaning

Nakaḥa means to marry or to get married. *Nikāḥ* means marriage or matrimony. *Iḥṣān* is the other word used in the Qur'ān for marriage. The word *Iḥṣān* comes from *Ḥaṣuna* which means to be inaccessible, or to be well fortified. Hence, *Muḥṣinah* (pl. *Muḥṣināt*) means married women as they are well protected. It is also used for women who are chaste and of unblemished character (al-Taḥrīm 66: 12).

Analysis

The institution of marriage is held in high esteem in all cultures and religions. According to Islamic teachings, the family is a divinely inspired institution. In Sūrah al-Nisā' Allah says that He has created human beings from a single soul and that from the first couple the human race multiplied and progressed (4: 1). In a verse in Sūrah al-Rūm the creation of human beings and marriage ties are described as Allah's Signs on which one is asked to reflect. "*And among His Signs is this, that He created for you mates from among yourselves, you may dwell in tranquillity with them, and He has put love and mercy between your (hearts): verily in that are Signs for those who reflect*" (al-Rūm 30: 21).

Sexual attraction between males and females is natural. This is regulated by the institution of marriage that is bonded by love and affection. The couple has to bear sacrifices to bring up their children and thus help perpetuate the human race. To keep their marriage ties firm the couple solemnly enters into a binding contract. To indicate the solemnity of the marriage contract, it is referred to as *'Aqd al-Nikāḥ*, the tie or knot of marriage (al-Baqarah 2: 235). In Sūrah al-Nisā' (4: 21), this is referred to as *Mīthāqan Ghalīẓan* (a strong covenant). Thus, in Islam marriage is a social contract but it is also a sacred contract. Faith constitutes the firm foundation for the institution of marriage. As this relationship is close, an intimate sharing of faith is essential. Thus Muslims are not allowed to marry people of other faiths. The only exception is that a Muslim man can marry a Jewish or Christian woman as their religions are based on revealed books. A Muslim woman, however, is not permitted to marry a Jew or Christian or anyone who is not a Muslim. Thus, faith plays an important role in family relations. If one spouse changes his or her faith the marriage has to be dissolved.

In Sūrah al-Baqarah a metaphor of dress is used to describe the intimate relationship between husband and wife. Allah says: "*They are a garment for you and you are a garment for them*" (2: 187). This emphasizes the closeness of the relationship between the spouses. Dress is something that covers the body and protects it. The spouses are protectors and guardians of each other. The dress beautifies the wearer.

In Islam, sexual relations outside marriage are considered a criminal act and are punishable under Islamic law. Islam also reformed the practice of polygyny (having an unlimited number of wives). The Qur'ān limited the number of wives a man may marry simultaneously to four (al-Nisā' 4: 3).

References

Nikāḥ: 2: 235 and 237; 4: 6; 24: 33 and 60.

Ni'mah [نعمة] (Bounty)

Meaning

Ni'mah is derived from the root *N'M* meaning to be prosperous, to be affluent or to flourish, to bloom or to be luxuriant, to be lush. Thus, it signifies the grace, the blessings, the favours that Allah has bestowed on His obedient servants. These are listed in Sūrah al-Nisā':

> *All who obey Allah and the Messenger are in the company of those on whom is the Grace of Allah – of the Prophets (who teach), the Sincere (lovers of Truth), the Witnesses (who testify) and the Righteous (who do good); Ah! what a beautiful fellowship.*
>
> (al-Nisā' 4: 69)

This is one of the most comforting passages for believers who are engaged in their ordinary business of this world. If they have Faith and conduct their lives in accordance with Divine Guidance they will be in the company of the most august assembly. They will ascend to the top and will achieve glory of the highest rank!

The *Ni'mah* that is mentioned here is neither wealth nor material prosperity, for these favours can be enjoyed by non-believers and tyrants as well. *Ni'mah* instead refers to the real happiness and contentment of hearts. Allah has endowed this *Ni'mah* in two ways: one by the provision of *'Ilm* (knowledge) and the other by *Tawfīq* of *al-A'māl al-Ṣāliḥah* (righteous deeds). All four categories of people mentioned in the *Āyah* are the embodiment of *'Ilm* and *A'māl*. Thus, they are the ones who are on the path of righteousness.

Analysis

The most precious favour given by Allah to any nation is the role of guiding humanity to the path of righteousness. This is the responsibility granted with honour, and was accorded to *Banū Isrā'īl*:

> *O Children of Isrā'īl! Call to mind the (special) favour, which I bestowed upon you, and that I preferred you to all others (for My Message).*
>
> (al-Baqarah 2: 47)

When *Banū Isrā'īl* failed to fulfil their obligations – their indictment is recorded in Sūrah al-Baqarah (2: 40–123) – this honour was given to the Muslim *Ummah*. This change was expressed symbolically by the change of the *Qiblah* from Jerusalem to Makkah:

> *Thus have We made you an* Ummah *justly balanced that you might be witnesses over the nations and the Messenger a witness over yourselves.*
>
> (al-Baqarah 2: 143)

Words from the Same Root

Na'īm means the abundance of *ni'mah* and signifies extreme felicity and bliss:

> *As for the Righteous, they will be in Bliss.*
>
> (al-Infiṭār 82: 13)

The word is also used as a descriptive adjective for *Jannah*:

> *And those Foremost (in Faith) will be Foremost (in the Hereafter). These will be those nearest to Allah: in the Gardens of Bliss.*
> (al-Wāqi'ah 56: 10–12)

> *Make me one of the inheritors of the Garden of Bliss.*
> (al-Shu'arā' 26: 85)

Ni'ma is used to express praise and appreciation, such as "what a perfect…! wonderful…!"

> *For such the reward is forgiveness from their Lord, and gardens with rivers flowing underneath – an eternal dwelling: How excellent a recompense for those who work and (strive)!*
> (Āl 'Imrān 3: 136)

> *He is your Protector – the Best to protect and the Best to help.*
> (al-Ḥajj 22: 78)

References

Ni'mah: 2: 231; 3: 171; 16: 18; 44: 27; 93: 11. *Na'īm*: 22: 56; 56: 12; 82: 13; 83: 22; 102: 8.

Niyyah [نـيّة]

see *Irādah*

Nusuk [نسك] (Sacrifice)

Meaning

Nasaka means to lead a life of devotion, and *Nask* means piety and worship. *Nāsik* is one who is pious and devout. However, *Manāsik* relates to the ceremonies of the *Ḥajj*, and of which is *Nusuk* (sacrifice). This commemorates the supreme trial of both the Prophet Ibrāhīm and his son Ismāʿīl (peace be upon them). The father was ready to sacrifice his son following the Divine command conveyed to him in a vision. When both readily proceeded to fulfil this command it was proclaimed; "*We called out to him 'O Ibrāhīm! You have already fulfilled the Vision'*" (al-Ṣāffāt 37: 104–105). Thus, sacrifice has become an obligatory part of the *Ḥajj*, as has an optional slaughter of animals on *ʿĪd al-Aḍḥā* (the Feast of the Sacrifice) by Muslims all over the world (al-Ṣāffāt 37: 108).

The Purpose of Sacrifice

The sacrifice of a goat, sheep or camel is just symbolic. One can see that the innocent animal is firmly in one's control and is prepared to die for the Will of its Creator. This is a reminder that a believer should be ready to sacrifice his life, his possessions, his inner desires and his ego just like a helpless animal in the control of the Will of his Creator. That is the real sacrifice as: "*It is not the blood and flesh which reaches Allah, it is the* Taqwā *(God-consciousness) which reaches Him*" (al-Ḥajj 22: 37). This self-surrender is the hallmark of a true believer, who should be proclaiming: "*Truly, my prayer and my sacrifice, my life and my death are (all) for Allah, the Cherisher of the Worlds*" (al-Anʿām 6: 162).

Other, optional sacrifice is performed at the birth of a child, called *ʿAqīqah*. Sacrifice is also made in fulfilment of a vow or as compensation for acts of omission or commission during the *Ḥajj*.

Synonyms

QURBĀN

Qaruba means to be near, and *Qurbān* means anything by which nearness to Allah is sought; in this sense the word is used for sacrifice and offering that helps to gain closeness to Allah. This sacrifice could be an animal or *Ṣadaqah* or even good deeds. But nowadays the term is only used for animal sacrifice. In earlier *Sharīʿahs* people were required to place the sacrificial animal at the altar; its consumption by divine fire was the indication of its acceptance. This is narrated in the story of the two sons of the Prophet Ādam (peace be upon him): "*they each presented a sacrifice (to Allah). It was accepted from one and not from the other*" (al-Mā'idah 5: 27).

Burnt sacrifices also figured in the *Tawrāt* (Leviticus 9: 23–24). The Jews of Madīnah demanded that the Prophet show them a sacrifice consumed by fire so that they could be certain that he was a true prophet. The Prophet was asked to reply: "*There came to you Messengers before me, with clear signs and even with what you ask for: why then did you slay them, if you speak the truth?*" (Āl 'Imrān 3: 183).

HADY

Hady means a sacrificial animal. Animals are brought by pilgrims as a *Hadīyah* (gift, present, offering). They are treated as symbols of Allah. While travelling with pilgrims they wear garlands or fillets or distinguishing marks which gave them immunity from attack. They were treated as sacred symbols. This is the same immunity that was enjoyed by pilgrims (al-Mā'idah 5: 2, 95 and 97).

NAḤR

Naḥr means the upper part of the chest. It also means sacrifice, but in a restricted sense. It is used for the sacrifice of camels as they are sacrificed standing by piercing their necks with a spear (al-Kawthar 108: 2).

References

Nusuk: 2: 196; 6: 162; 22: 34. *Qurbān*: 5: 27. *Hady*: 2: 196; 5: 2, 95 and 97; 48: 25. *Naḥr*: 108: 2.

Qadar [قدر] (Destiny)

Meanings

Qadara means to decree, to ordain, to decide, to possess strength, to have power or ability, to predetermine, to estimate, to assess, to foresee, to esteem highly, to value or to cherish. The word *Qadara* (and noun *Qadar*) thus conveys a large array of meanings, and it is used in the Qur'ān in all of them. The context in which the word is used determines its exact meaning.

Usage

Īmān bi'l-Qadar means belief in the divine decree. This means that whatever happens emanates from Almighty Allah. This belief makes one totally dependent on the Will of Allah. Allah alone controls all affairs and nothing happens in this universe that is not in His prior knowledge. "*And the command of Allah is a decree determined*" (al-Aḥzāb 33: 38).

> *With Him are the keys of the non-perceptible, the treasures that none knows but He. He knows whatever there is on the earth and in the sea. Not a leaf does fall but with His knowledge. There is not a grain in the darkness (or depths) of the earth, nor anything fresh or dry (green or withered), but is (inscribed) in a record clear.*
>
> (al-An'ām 6: 59)

Qadar is used to mean having the power or ability to do things. When used of a human being it means that the person possesses the ability to perform a certain task. When it is used in respect of Allah it is not restricted to any particular task as "*Allah has power over all things*" (al-'Ankabūt 29: 20).

Qadr is also used to mean balance and proportion. "*Verily, for all things Allah has appointed a due proportion*" (al-Ṭalāq 65: 3); "*From a sperm drop He has created him and then moulded him in due proportion*" ('Abasa 80: 19); "*It is He Who created all things, and ordered them in due proportions and measures*" (al-Furqān 25: 2; al-Qamar 54: 49).

Qadr is also used to mean value and importance. "*They do not value Allah such as it is due to Him*" (al-An'ām 6: 91).

Laylat al-Qadr conveys the same meaning. It has importance and value because the Qur'ān was revealed during this night for the guidance of mankind. *Laylat al-Qadr* also means the Night of Power. It is narrated in some *aḥādīth* that it is during this night that Allah ordains all the affairs of this universe for the whole year and His decisions are conveyed to the angels. All the meanings of the word *Qadr* are infused here.

Other Words from the Same Root

Al-Qādir, al-Qadīr, al-Muqtadir. These are among *al-Asmā' al-Ḥusnā* – most beautiful names of Allah. His attributes of having power over all things are conveyed by them. *Al-Muqtadir* is translated as the Omnipotent. Yūsuf 'Alī notes that "it denotes not only complete mastery, but the further idea that the mastery arises from Allah's own nature, and depends on nothing else whatever" (al-Qamar 54: 55, p. 1395, note 5171).

Taqdīr, meaning measuring, is used in the sense of planning, management and ordering. "*And the sun and moon for the reckoning (of time); such is the planning and ordering of (Him), the Exalted in Power, the Omniscient*" (al-An'ām 6: 96; Yā Sīn 36: 38).

References

Qadar: 13: 26; 16: 75; 33: 38; 89: 16; 97: 1. *al-Qādir*: 6: 65; 17: 99; 46: 33; 75: 40; 86: 8. *al-Qadīr*: 2: 284; 3: 26; 16: 77; 42: 9; 59: 6. *al-Muqtadir*: 54: 42 and 55. *Taqdīr*: 6: 96; 36: 38; 41: 12.

Qalb [قلب] (Heart)

Meaning

The word *Qalb* (pl. *Qulūb*) is derived from *Qalaba* which means to turn around or turn about. As the heart is always in motion, turning and beating, it is called *Qalb*. In the Qur'ānic terminology *Qalb* (heart) does not mean the piece of flesh that pumps blood through the body. It is the inner self, the faculty of reason, the soul, whatever motivates a person to do something. It is the source of human reason and emotion. It is the centre of one's personality. It is the place where *Īmān* and conviction reside. It is also the place that is afflicted by disease: "*In their hearts is a disease...*" (al-Baqarah 2: 10). It is also where doubts and hypocrisy reside: "*The desert Arabs say: 'We believe.' Say: 'You have no faith'; but you should say: 'We have submitted our wills to Allah', for not yet has Faith entered your hearts*" (al-Ḥujurāt 49: 14).

The Purification of the Heart

One of the important tasks that the Prophet (peace be upon him) was entrusted with was *Tazkiyah* – the purification. One must try to purify one's heart, as it is the true key for success in the Hereafter. The Holy Qur'ān explains the reason behind this: "*It is not the eyes that go blind but it is the heart inside you that goes blind*" (al-Ḥajj 22: 46). No one will be successful "*except the one who comes to Allah with a sound heart*" (al-Shu'arā' 26: 89). The Prophet (peace be upon him) said: 'He has succeeded whose heart Allah has purified for *Īmān* and made his heart righteous and submissive' (Aḥmad and Bayhaqī in the *Shu'ab al-Īmān*). The Prophet (peace be upon him) identified the heart as a piece of flesh: if it is healthy, the whole body is healthy, and if it is corrupt the whole body is corrupted (Bukhārī and Muslim).

To keep the heart pure one should safeguard the channels that convey messages to the heart. The Prophet (peace be upon him) said: 'Ears are the filters and eyes are the conveyors of images that reach the heart' (Aḥmad and Bayhaqī). Thus, it is essential one safeguards one's eyes and ears from pornography, pop music and obscene literature.

On the Day of Judgement, people will be asked about their faculties. "*For every act of hearing or of seeing or of (feeling in) the heart, will be enquired into (on the Day of Reckoning)*" (al-Isrā' 17: 36).

Fu'ād

This comes from *Fa'ada* and *Fu'ād* (pl. *Af'idah*); it is a synonym of *Qalb* but is used only sixteen times in the Qur'ān whereas *Qalb* is used very extensively (135 times). *Tafa''ad* means to be burnt, as the heart is the centre for the acquisition of knowledge and the light of wisdom, it is called *Fu'ād*.

References

Qalb: 3: 159; 26: 89; 37: 84; 40: 35; 50: 33. *Fu'ād*: 14: 37; 17: 36; 32: 9; 67: 23; 104: 7.

See also *Khatm*

Qarḍ Ḥasan [قرض حسن]
see *Infāq*

Qasam [قسم] (Oath)

Meaning

Aqsama means to take an oath or swear. *Qasam* (pl. *Aqsām*) means oath or pledge. According to Imām al-Rāghib it is derived from *Qasāmah*. *Qasāmah* were the oaths that the heirs of a murdered person took at the time of the division (*Taqsīm*) of the deceased's assets. Nowadays it is used for every kind of oath.

The Purposes of *Qasam*

The purpose of *Qasam* is to reinforce one's claim that what is being said is true. Sometimes to make a claim more convincing one swears by using the name of Allah. As an oath is a solemn pledge it has to be fulfilled. The breaking of *Qasam* is a grave sin and requires expiation. However, this is not true of frivolous types of oath which sometimes people use mindlessly (al-Mā'idah 5: 89). If a *Qasam* is taken refraining oneself from doing good and lawful things, then it should be broken and *Kaffārah* (atonement) as prescribed should be undertaken (al-Taḥrīm 66: 2).

The oath has legal implications also. In cases where a husband or a wife alleges adultery on the part of the other spouse and is unable to produce witnesses, a decree of separation will be passed: "*If they bear witness (with oaths) by Allah that they are solemnly telling the truth and the fifth oath that they solemnly invoke the curse (or wrath) of Allah if they tell a lie*" (al-Nūr 24: 6–7).

In cases where one makes an oral will one should have two witnesses so that they can testify to its validity. The witnesses should take a solemn oath that they are reporting the truth. However, their oath can be challenged by the aggrieved heir by producing two of his own witnesses who will duly take an oath to say their account is truer than that of the earlier witnesses (al-Mā'idah 5: 106–107).

Synonyms

Ḥalf means swearing or an oath; and a similar word, *Ḥilf* (pl. *Aḥlāf*), means sworn alliance. *Ḥalīf* is the one with whom a pact or alliance is made.

Yamīn (pl. *Aymān*) means right hand or right side. Arabs while taking an oath used to strike their right hand on the right hand of the other party, so *Yamīn* came to mean *Qasam*.

The letter *Waw* and *Bā'* is also used for swearing; for example *Wa'Llāh* means that one is swearing by Allah. This form of *Qasam* is extensively used in the Qur'ān.

Aqsām al-Qur'ān

An oath is usually taken in the name of a person or thing that is held in high esteem. Hence the Prophet (peace be upon him) instructed that one should swear by Allah or remain silent. He did not approve of swearing by anything else. However, we see that there is extensive use of oaths in the Qur'ān. The purpose of the oath, as mentioned above, is to bring something as evidence for one's claim. In the Qur'ān oaths on the sky, the earth, the sun, the moon, the mountain, the sea and many other natural phenomena occur. On other occasions the same things are presented as proof as well (al-Baqarah 2: 164). By such oaths the Qur'ān invites human beings to reflect on the wonders of this universe as they all are proof of Allah's Oneness. After referring to various natural phenomena it is said: "*Is there not in these oaths (evidence) for those who understand?*" (al-Fajr 89: 5). Similarly, in Sūrah al-Wāqi'ah it is said: "*And this indeed is a mighty oath if you but knew*" (56: 76).

References

Qasam: 56: 76; 69: 38; 70: 40; 75: 1; 89: 5. *Ḥalf*: 4: 62; 5: 89; 9: 107; 58: 14; 68: 10. *Yamīn*: 2: 225; 5: 108; 9: 12; 16: 91; 68: 39. *Waw*: 68: 1; 79: 1; 85: 1; 86:1; 89: 1.

Qawwām [قوّام]

see *Iqāmah*

Qirā'ah [قرآءة]

see *Tilāwah*

Qiṣāṣ [قصاص] (Retaliation)

Meaning

The word *Qiṣāṣ* is derived from the verb *Qaṣṣa* which means to follow someone's track. *Qaṣaṣ* is used to mean story and narration because the one who narrates the incident follows the actual event, as if following it. *Qiṣāṣ* means requital, reprisal, retaliation or punishment because it follows the actual crime.

The Law of *Qiṣāṣ*

Qiṣāṣ is part of the criminal law of Islam. *Qiṣāṣ* is based on the law of equality. The punishment should fit the crime, and due process of law is observed in carrying out the sentence for murder or injuries inflicted. One who has murdered another person should also face the same penalty. "*Life for a life, eye for eye, nose for nose, ear for ear, tooth for tooth, and wounds equal to equal. But if anyone remits the retaliation by way of charity, it is an act of atonement for himself*" (al-Mā'idah 5: 45). This is the same law prescribed in the Old Testament (Exodus 21: 23–25; Leviticus 24: 18–21 and Deuteronomy 19: 21) which the Prophet Jesus (peace be upon him) also quotes, as well as modifying it in the direction of mercy (Matthew 5: 38). The Qur'ānic injunction encourages the injured to forgive and, if need be accept, reasonable compensation. However for the preservation of law and order in society, the state is empowered to deal with law breakers (al-Mā'idah 5: 32–33).

The law of equality in dealing with crimes, whether personal injuries or homicide, also means that only those who are found guilty will be punished; their relations will not be molested. This shuts the door on private vengeance or tribal retaliation, both of which were prevalent in the pre-Islamic era (al-Baqarah 2: 178).

In the case of an accidental killing by mistake or error, the penalty prescribed is to pay compensation as well as to free a slave or fast for two months by way of repentance (al-Nisā' 4: 92). The word used in this verse is *diyah* which is translated as bloodwit or blood money. It is a financial compensation payable instead of retribution to the victim or the victim's next of kin in cases of murder or wounding.

The Justification of the Death Penalty

In many Western countries the death penalty has been abolished as it was deemed to be "uncivilized". Yet from time to time when there is a murder of a policeman or policewoman or horrific murders of children or innocent people, the revival of the death penalty is often debated. There are only two alternatives: either one punishes criminals with death and safeguards society from barbarous murderers and killers or one puts them behind bars for a long period. If the death penalty is abolished, the message the criminal community receives is that they will not suffer death for their misdeeds. Hence, there is no deterrent for them to reform and refrain from their atrocious activities. The Qur'ān perceptively refers to the blessing of *Qiṣāṣ* thus: "*In the law of equality there is (saving of) life to you. O you! People of understanding, so that you may guard yourselves against violating the Law*" (al-Baqarah 2: 179).

References

Qiṣāṣ: 2: 178, 179 and 194; 5: 45.

Qisṭ [قسط]

see *'Adl*

Qiyām [قيام]

see *Iqāmah*

Qiyāmah [قيامة]

see *Ākhirah*

Qur'ān [قرآن]

Meaning

Qara'a means to read and *Qur'ān* is the verbal noun from this root meaning reading or recitation. The Qur'ān is the speech of Allah sent down upon the Prophet Muḥammad (peace be upon him) through Archangel Jibrīl. It is inimitable, unique and protected by Allah from corruption.

It is referred to as the Qur'ān itself by name in the Qur'ān. Imām Suyūṭī has enumerated fifty-three names for it that are mentioned in the Qur'ān. Some of these are as follows: *Maw'iẓah* (Exhortation), *Hudā* (Guidance), *Shifā' li mā fī al-Ṣudūr* (Healing for the Diseases of the Heart), *Raḥmah* (Mercy), *Burhān* (Convincing Proof), *Bayān* (Clear Statement), *al-Furqān* (the Criterion), *al-Muhaymin* (the Guardian), *Nūr* (Light), *Dhikr* (Remembrance), *Ghayr Dhī 'iwaj* (Not Crooked), *Mubārak* (Blessed), *Majīd* (Glorious), *Bushrā* (Glad Tidings), *al-Kitāb* (the Book, the Scripture) and of course, *al-Qur'ān*. All these attributes explain different facets of the revealed word of Allah. No other book has attempted to define itself in such a manner.

However only three names are usually used to designate the revealed Book: *al-Qur'ān*, *al-Furqān* and *al-Muṣḥaf* (Sacred Book).

History of the Revelation and Compilation

The Qur'ān was revealed piecemeal over twenty-three years during the prophethood of the Prophet Muḥammad (peace be upon him). This period comprised his stay in Makkah for thirteen years and then in Madīnah. It was memorized during the life of the Prophet (peace be upon him) and also written down on velum, parchments, bones, palm risps and other material as dictated by the Prophet. The sequence of the *Āyāt* and *Sūrahs* was learnt directly from the Prophet (peace be upon him). During the time of the first *Khalīfah*, Abū Bakr al-Ṣiddīq, all the scattered pieces were brought together. This was called *Ṣuḥuf* (pages). During the time of the third *Khalīfah*, 'Uthmān ibn 'Affān, the script was standardized and the *Muṣḥaf 'Uthmānī* became the only authentic version, which is still in existence.

The Qur'ānic Script

The script used during the lifetime of the Prophet consisted of very basic symbols expressing only the consonantal structure of a word. Later, *Tashkīl* (vowel marks) and *I'jām* (diacritical marks) were introduced. Thus, a basic system of writing developed over the ages in various types of script such as Kūfic, Maghrabī, Muḥaqqiq, Ḥijāzī, Naqsh, Nasṭ'līq and others and spread all over the world.

The Arrangement of the Qur'ān

The *Āyah* (pl. *Āyāt*) is the basic unit of the structure. It could be only one letter, such as *Qāf* or *Ṣād*, or it could be a very long sentence with clauses and subclauses. A group of *Āyāt* is collected together to form a *Sūrah*. Again, a *Sūrah* can consist of only three *Āyāt*, like Sūrah al-'Aṣr, or 286 *Āyāt* like Sūrah al-Baqarah. The usual criticism about the structure of the *Sūrah* is that the *Āyāt* are disjointed and lack coherence. This criticism is a consequence of lack of appreciation of the methodology and style of the Qur'ān. Subsequently further divisions like *Rukū'* were made for ease of reading in one *Rak'ah* and thirty *Juz'* (parts) so that reading can be completed in one month. *Ḥizb* divides the *Juz'* into two parts. The whole Qur'ān is also divided into seven *Manāzil*, so that each *Manzil* can be read in one day and the whole Qur'ān can thus be completed in a week.

The Contents

The Qur'ān is primarily a Book of Guidance. Its purpose is to provide guidelines for human beings so that they can fulfil the role of vicegerency on Earth. This Guidance was promised to the Prophet Ādam (peace be upon him) when he was sent to Earth. Thus the Qur'ān covers a vast number of subjects: moral, social, economic, political and legal, as well as matters relating to creed and metaphysics. Then there are references to natural phenomena, astronomical, botanical, medical and zoological sciences. But it should be noted that the Qur'ān is not a book of science. Those who turn to the Qur'ān for reasons other than trying to receive guidance may receive some benefit or they may be misguided. They certainly fail to get the true blessings of the Qur'ān.

Style

The Qur'ān was revealed in the form of an oration. Its style is to attract the attention of its audience. Like oratory its subjects and emphasis vary from one sentence to the next. Thus, reading it like a book reduces its effectiveness. Its metaphors and arguments bear on local scenes but its message always remains universal. It is rhymed prose differing from the poetic tradition of the time and is very soothing to the ears, all of which makes its memorization easy.

In the Makkan *Sūrahs* the style is noticeable for its brevity and very powerful diction which penetrates the hearts of the listeners. It is like a forceful mountain stream gushing down fiercely. Here there are forceful arguments on *Tawḥīd* (the Oneness of Allah), *Risālah* (Prophethood) and *Ākhirah* (the Hereafter). In contrast, the Madīnan *Sūrahs* are like the calm water of a huge river flowing smoothly through the plains. Here the topics dealt with are family law, legal and social issues as well as the laws of war and peace.

Throughout there are glimpses from the stories of the earlier prophets. It seems that they are repetitive but each time they are viewed from a different angle to support the arguments presented.

References

Qur'ān: 2: 185; 16: 98; 17: 88; 25: 30; 47: 24.

See also *Āyah* and *Kitāb*

Qurbān [قربان]

see *Nusuk*

Rabb [رَبّ] (Sustainer)

Meanings

Rabb has two meanings:

1. To be a nourisher, a sustainer and a provider. Implicit in this meaning is the fact that the nourisher trains and nourishes something or somebody to perfection. Thus, it means that it is he who gradually develops someone and leads him to the height of his perfection.
2. To be a lord and master.

From these two primary meanings, a third concept arose namely that of being a sovereign, a ruler and an administrator. Sayyid Mawdūdī mentioned two further extensions to the meaning of *Rabb*. One is where the word is applied to a person who is the central figure on whom people have unanimity and consensus and the other where he is also the protector and supervisor, responsible for the welfare of others. Thus, the array of meanings attributed to the word *Rabb* can be summed up as follows:

1. Lord and Master
2. Nourisher and Sustainer who leads to perfection
3. Ruler and Sovereign
4. The central figure on whom people rely
5. Protector and Supervisor.

Analysis

Allah is *Rabb* of this universe in all these meanings. *Rubūbīyah* entails that a person should worship Allah as his Lord. He should be a servant to Him and as such obey Him. As Allah is the One Who provides for him and He alone is his Protector he should seek His help and succour. Allah is the Lord and the Master, the servant should surrender himself to His Will and not use his own will and power to disobey Him. As He is the real Sovereign so a person should not accept the sovereignty of any other person or institution. Above all, He should be praised and thanked for all the bounties that He has provided. This is the essence of *'Ibādah.*

The first experience of God is manifested to human beings by His quality of *Rubūbīyah.* His Bounties are scattered all around us. The Qur'ān uses this as an argument that the One who nourishes and sustains should also be worshipped. In the first verse of Sūrah al-Fātiḥah we present our thankful praise to the Cherisher and Sustainer of the world. Similarly the very first revelation starts thus:

> *Recite in the name of your Lord and Cherisher Who created.*
>
> (al-'Alaq 96: 1)

Here Allah's Attribute as *Khāliq* (Creator) follows His Attribute of being *Rabb.* This primacy of *Rubūbīyah* over *Khalq* (Creation) is instructive. Just as a child clings to his mother for nourishment, protection, help and succour so human beings should turn to their Lord and Cherisher for help and protection.

The word *Rabb* is nowadays exclusively used for God. However, there are a few occasions when *Rabb* is used, as in the Qur'ān, in its literal and limited meaning of being a master and a lord. Thus, the Prophet Yūsuf (peace be upon him) reminded his co-prisoner who was about to be released:

> *Mention me to your lord* (rabb), *but Satan made him forget to mention him to his lord.*
>
> (Yūsuf 12: 42)

Here *Rabb* (lord) refers to the King of Egypt. The use of the word *Rabb* in verses 23 and 50 of the same *Sūrah* is similar.

The plural of *Rabb* is *Arbāb.* This word is also used in the Qur'ān, but its usage is confined to false gods. For example:

> *They take their priests and their monks to be their lords* (Arbāb) *in derogation to Allah.*
>
> (al-Tawbah 9: 31)

Are many lords (Arbāb) *differing among themselves better, or Allah, the One Supreme and Irresistible?*

(Yūsuf 12: 39)

The great fallacy in which human beings throughout the ages trapped themselves in was to divide the various aspects of *Rubūbīyah* across different beings. In Islam, however, all aspects of *Rubūbīyah* are concerted in One Supreme Lord and in Him alone.

References

Rabb: 2: 131; 10: 10; 21: 22; 23: 116; 56: 80.

Rahbah [رهبة]

see *Khushū'*

Raḥmah [رحمة]

see *al-Raḥmān al-Raḥīm*

Al-Raḥmān, Al-Raḥīm [الرّحمٰن ٱلرّحيم]

(The Merciful, The Beneficent)

Meanings

These are the most repeated attributes of Allah, glorified be He, and form the part of the *Bismillāh* with which all *Sūrahs* (chapters) of the Qur'ān except Sūrah al-Tawbah (Chapter 9) begin.

Both words are derived from the root *RḤM*, meaning to show mercy. The pattern of the noun formation denotes the intensity of the quality of *Raḥmah* (mercy). Thus, these attributes of Almighty Allah are often translated as the Most Merciful, Most Compassionate, Beneficent, Most Gracious or Mercy-Giving. However, these translations do not convey the full meaning of the terms nor do they distinguish between the subtle differences in meaning of *al-Raḥmān* and *al-Raḥīm*.

The difference in their meanings is explained very well by Amīn Aḥsan Iṣlāḥī in his *Tafsīr*. The following summarizes his thoughts:

> In the Arabic language words, although derived from the same root, have different shades of meaning depending on the measure of the word formation. Thus whereas *Raḥmān* denotes upsurge, overflow, outburst and passion, *Raḥīm* denotes permanence, continuity, and everlasting qualities of Mercy.

Hence, *al-Raḥmān* is the One whose Mercy is overflowing. There is an outburst of His Compassion, and there is an upsurge of His Kindness, whereas *al-Raḥīm* is the One whose Mercy is continuous, permanent and unceasing. The creation of the Universe is the result of the upsurge of His Mercy, and the continuity of His Mercy is evoked in His sustaining the entire universe.

Usage

The word *al-Raḥmān* is applicable to that person who has engulfed everything with his mercy. Thus, it is used exclusively for Allah; Sublime is He, whereas *Raḥīm* can be used for others. Thus, this attribute is also used for our most blessed Prophet in the Holy Qur'ān:

> *Now has come unto you a Messenger from amongst yourselves: it grieves him that you should perish; ardently anxious is he over you: to the Believers is he most kind and merciful.*
>
> (al-Tawbah 9: 128)

Some commentators are of the opinion that *al-Raḥmān*, like Allah, is the personal name of the Creator. This view is supported by the following verse:

> *Say: "Call upon Allah, or Call upon* al-Raḥmān: *by whatever name you call upon Him (it is well). For to Him belong the Most Beautiful Names."*
>
> (al-Isrā' 17: 110)

The word *al-Raḥmān*, unlike Allah, was not common parlance among the Quraysh before the Revelation of the Qur'ān and they were surprised and questioned its use. Perhaps they were confused, thinking Allah and *al-Raḥmān* are two different entities. Their query is mentioned in the Glorious Qur'ān:

> *When it is said to them 'Prostrate yourselves before* al-Raḥmān.' *They say, 'And what is* al-Raḥmān?'
>
> (al-Furqān 25: 60)

The Quraysh also insisted on removing the phrase *Bismillāh al-Raḥmān al-Raḥīm* from the Treaty of Ḥudaybīyah, objecting that they did not know *al-Raḥmān*. However, despite the ignorance of the Quraysh, historical and archaeological evidence proves that *al-Raḥmān* was used by Jews, Christians and believers of other religions. The article on 'Sabaeans' in the *Encyclopaedia Britannica* records the use of *al-Raḥmān* by the Sabaeans as a Jewish influence, and Christian inscriptions found in the temple of Ma'rib also begin with the words *al-Raḥmān* and *al-Raḥīm*. The Qur'ān mentions that the letter that the Prophet Sulaymān (peace be upon him) wrote to the Queen of Saba' began with *Bismillāh al-Raḥmān al-Raḥīm* (al-Naml 27: 30).

Raḥmah (Mercy)

Imām al-Ghazālī said: "The Divine Mercy is perfect, in the sense that it answers every need. It is universal in the sense that it spreads alike over those who merit it and those who do not merit it." To despair of Allah's Mercy is one of the major sins, for Mercy is one of Allah's Attributes, praise be unto Him, and to doubt whether He will show it implies disbelief in this Divine Attribute. The Qur'ān emphasized this fact in several places:

> *Say: 'O My servants who have transgressed against their souls! Despair not of the Mercy of Allah; for Allah forgives all sins: for He is Oft-Forgiving, Most Merciful.'*
>
> (al-Zumar 39: 53)

The Mercy of Allah is infinite and His Compassion unlimited. But that should not lead one to complacency and self-satisfaction. A man commits sins and says: "Allah is Merciful" and instead of repenting and reforming his life, he often continues to lead a life of disobedience. Such an attitude is dangerous. A Muslim should lead life expecting Divine Mercy and at the same time being conscious of Allah's Judgement.

The Relationship between Allah's Mercy and Justice

According to the Qur'ānic concept of Allah, there is no conflict between His Mercy and His Justice. His Mercy does not abrogate His Justice. On the contrary, His Justice means Mercy. This point is characteristically brought out in several places in the Bounteous Qur'ān. For example, Allah says:

> *He (Allah) has prescribed for Himself Mercy that He will gather you together for the Day of Judgement, there is no doubt whatever.*
>
> (al-An'ām 6: 12)

> *Tell My servants that I am indeed Oft-Forgiving, Most Merciful; and that My Penalty will be indeed the most grievous Penalty.*
>
> (al-Ḥijr 15: 49–50)

The juxtaposing of Divine Mercy and the Day of Resurrection, forgiveness, compassion and chastisement in these verses highlights the fact that in the sight of Allah, Glory be to Him, good and evil, justice and injustice, morality and immorality are not the same. To accept anything different would devalue righteousness, goodness, and morality and is tantamount to injustice. It is for this reason that Allah's Mercy demands that there should be the Day of Judgement when those who followed the path of Righteousness will be rewarded and the evildoers punished.

However, as human beings are prone to sin, it is only Allah's Mercy that can lead to their redemption and salvation. Thus, His *Maghfirah* (Forgiveness) is essential for mankind's salvation. His Mercy covers everything in this universe:

> ... *And My Mercy extends to all things.*
>
> (al-Aʿrāf 7: 156)

The Importance of Allah's Mercy for Human Sustenance and the Governance of the Universe

The importance of and emphasis on Divine Mercy are conveyed by the usage of two of Allah's attributes that denote the intensity of His *Raḥmah*. The creation of the universe and all those who dwell in it, particularly human beings, is the manifestation of Allah's Mercy. He is Self-sufficient and does not need any help or favour from His creation. He was not compelled nor was He obliged to create anything. Thus, the creation of the universe and provision for the sustenance of human beings and all other creatures are manifestations of Divine Mercy.

References

al-Raḥmān: 19: 58; 20: 5; 25: 60; 36: 11; 67: 3. *al-Raḥīm*: 2: 199; 9: 128; 22: 65; 39: 53; 57: 9.

Rasūl [رسول]

see *Nabī*

Ribā [ربوٰا] (Interest)

Meaning

Rabā means to increase, to grow, to exceed. From this verb *Ribā* means growth, increase, increment. Technically the Arabs used this word to mean the excess amount that a lender has to pay back over and above the amount of a loan. The amount used to be calculated according to an agreed rate. This surplus amount is called interest. The amount of interest was not related for the purpose of the loan. It could be for personal need or for commercial purposes.

The Legal Position

The Qur'ān categorically prohibits *Ribā*. "*O you who believe! Devour not interest doubled and multiplied. But fear Allah that you may (really) prosper*" (Āl 'Imrān 3: 130). It refutes the argument of those who maintain that *ribā* and trade are similar transactions; the Qur'ān compares this argument to madness (al-Baqarah 2: 275). Interest provides an unearned profit to the lender and imposes an unfair obligation on the borrower. In the Islamic economic system, the capital should be invested with sharing of the profit and loss between the entrepreneur and the investor. In Islamic economics this is called *Shirākah* (partnership). Thus, both lender and borrower are on an equal playing field. Or there could be an agency relationship (*Muḍārabah*) where one party provides the capital and the other brings labour and effort, with the provision of profit and loss-sharing to each on a predetermined percentage.

The Qur'ān has contrasted *Ribā* with *Ṣadaqah* (charity) as well as trade. The psychology of the money lender is to amass wealth whereas one who spends in the way of Allah is generous. Thus there is Allah's blessing in *Ṣadaqah* and His curse on *Ribā* (al-Baqarah 2: 275).

References

Ribā: 2: 275 and 276; 3: 130; 4: 161; 30: 39.

Rizq [رزق] (Provision)

Meaning

Razaqa means to provide with the means of subsistence, to bestow upon someone material or spiritual possessions, to endow someone, to bless someone. *Rizq* from this verb means provision, livelihood, nourishment, possessions, wealth, and fortune.

Analysis

The word *Rizq* in the Arabic language as well as in the Qur'ān is used both for material and spiritual endowments. It should not be restricted to only daily subsistence. The real *Rizq* is the knowledge received from Allah and the Qur'ān. This is the reason why in the Qur'ān *Waḥy* (revelation) is referred to as *Rizq*. This is the meaning of the Prophet ʿĪsā's saying "Man does not live by bread alone." The same is the implication of the prayer which the Prophet ʿĪsā (peace be upon him) taught: "Give us this day our daily bread." This is the prayer for *Rizq* meaning guidance, the same one as in Sūrah al-Fātiḥah. Whatever Allah has provided for the benefit of humanity can be termed *Rizq*. The *Rizq* that Maryam, mother of the Prophet ʿĪsā (peace be upon him), was endowed with, according to many *Mufassirūn*, is of a spiritual nature. Seeing her spirituality was what surprised the Prophet Zakarīyā (peace be upon him) (Āl ʿImrān 3: 37).

The implication of Allah's encouragement to the believers to "*spend whatever We have provided you*" (al-Baqarah 2: 3) is that they should spend their material possessions as well as invest all their capabilities and energies bestowed upon them by Him.

Al-Razzāq

One of the ninety-nine names of Allah is *al-Razzāq* meaning the Provider, the Sustainer. The believers are reminded that they should put their faith in Allah and that whatever one receives comes not from one's own efforts or from others, this is because "*Allah is the Best to provide (for all needs)*" (al-Jumuʿah 62: 11).

References

Rizq: 2: 60; 18: 19; 29: 62; 37: 41; 51: 57.

Rūḥ [روح]

see *Nafs*

Rushd [رشد] (Integrity)

Meaning

Rashada means to be on the right path, to follow the right course, to be well guided, to have the true faith, to become sensible, to become mature. *Rushd*, from this verb, means integrity, good sense, sensible conduct and maturity of mind.

This word covers all the natural instincts of goodness and basic Islamic beliefs. Unless one distorts one's natural inclinations by one's own violation, *Rushd* can lead one to the right path. Even if one is led astray, one can be guided back to the straight path by admonition and advice.

Other Words from the Same Root

Rāshid means one who is following the right path or a rightly-guided person. Thus, *al-Khulafā' al-Rāshidūn* is the appellation used for the first four *Khulafā'*: Abū Bakr al-Ṣiddīq, 'Umar ibn al-Khaṭṭāb, 'Uthmān ibn 'Affān and 'Alī ibn Abī Ṭālib (may Allah be pleased with them). A slightly varied form is *Rashīd* which also means rightly-guided, rational, intelligent and discriminating.

Al-Rashīd meaning the Guide, is one of the ninety-nine names of Allah, although it is not specifically so designated in the Qur'ān.

Murshid means a spiritual guide, a leader or an advisor. The word is used in Sufi literature for the Sufi master responsible for guiding and directing novices and disciples towards mystical knowledge. The *Murshid*'s name is the chain of transmitters going back to the founder of the order (*Silsilah*) for authenticity. It is also used by *al-Ikhwān al-Muslimūn* (The Muslim Brotherhood) for the supreme leader.

References

Rushd: 2: 256; 4: 6; 7: 146; 18: 10; 72: 2. *Rāshid*: 49: 7. *Rashīd*: 11: 78, 87 and 97. *Murshid*: 18: 17.

Al-Sā'ah [الساعة]

see *Ākhirah*

Ṣabr [صبر] (Perseverance)

Meanings

Ṣabara means to bind, to tie, to fetter or shackle. It also means to be patient, to be forbearing, to persevere. The meaning of *ṣabr* is patience, perseverance, and fortitude. Its essence is to control oneself against anxiety, despondency and dejection, and to manage to remain firm in one's standpoint. It also includes controlling oneself and refraining from all that the *Sharī'ah* has determined to be unlawful. *Ṣabr* requires one to persevere with satisfaction of heart and never swerve from the path of righteousness.

Usually people regard *Ṣabr* as submission, weakness and wretchedness. This is the attitude one adopts when one feels helpless and destitute, whereas *Ṣabr* means to override the difficulties with courage and determination.

Ṣabr is also the name of a bitter plant, aloe. This symbolically indicates that the practising of *Ṣabr* (patience) is not agreeable to human nature. Indeed it is a bitter pill to swallow.

Situations of *Ṣabr*

Ṣabr is required on many occasions as indicated in the Qur'ān: "*...And to be firm and patient, in pain (or suffering) and adversity and throughout all periods of panic...*" (al-Baqarah 2: 177). The Prophet (peace be upon him) was constantly advised to be patient with those who argued with him and rejected the message of Islam, particularly in the Makkan period (al-Muzzammil 73: 10; al-Muddaththir 74: 7; al-Naḥl 16: 127; there are 15 other references in Makkan *Sūrahs*). In the Madīnan period believers were also included in this instruction of practising *Ṣabr* (al-Baqarah 2: 153; al-Anfāl 8: 46; Āl 'Imrān 3: 200; and many other references).

Occasions for *Ṣabr* can be classified into the following three categories:

1. *Ṣabr* in adherence to the *aḥkām* (commands) of the *Sharī'ah*. Fulfilling all the obligations needs patience. For example, Ramaḍān is called the Month of *Ṣabr* as fasting requires perseverance and patience. Similarly other commandments need *Ṣabr*.
2. *Ṣabr* in safeguarding oneself from *Ḥudūd Allāh* (to remain within the boundaries set up by the *Sharī'ah*). Thus to avoid temptations of the *Nafs* (carnal self), for example the accumulation of wealth by illegal means (by cheating) and many other situations where self-control is required.
3. *Ṣabr* while conveying the message of Islam to others. One has to bear the constant ridicule and opposition. Initially it is only verbal abuse but it could be physical persecution also. Thus, in the Makkan period believers were asked to be patient against all oppression and bear this with dignity and never retaliate. This was the advice that Luqmān gave his son: "*And bear with patient constancy whatever betide you; for this is firmness (of purpose) in (the conduct of) affairs*" (Luqmān 31: 17).

The Importance of *Ṣabr*

Ṣabr is one of the greatest virtues that believers are asked to incorporate into their lives. It is praised in the Qur'ān in more than seventy places. Abū Sa'īd al-Khuḍrī relates that the Prophet (peace be upon him) said: "One who remains patient Allah gives him the patience. There is no gift better than patience given to anyone" (Muslim).

Other Words from the Same Root

Believers are required to help or assist each other in maintaining the quality of *Ṣabr* in the face of opposition from enemies, who try to exhaust one's patience. This is called *Muṣābarah* (Āl 'Imrān 3: 200).

The other word from this root used in the Qur'ān is *Iṣṭibār*. This also means patience and perseverance, but is more forceful than *Ṣabr*. In the

Arabic language additions of other letters extend the meaning of words (Maryam 19: 65).

References

Ṣabr: 2: 45; 7: 126; 42: 43; 46: 35; 103: 3. *Iṣṭibār*: 19: 65.

Ṣadaqah [صدقة] (Charity)

Ṣadaqah in Islamic terminology is used for that gift or charity that is given with purity of intention and with benevolent heart to gain Allah's pleasure. There should be no intention of showing off or of putting someone under an obligation so that they feel grateful. The essence of *Ṣadaqah* is *Ṣidq* (truth) from which this word is derived.

Ṣadaqah, *Zakāh* and *Infāq fī Sabīl Allāh* are all terms used for charitable giving. *Infāq* is a general term covering both *Ṣadaqah* (voluntary) and *Zakāh* (compulsory) alms giving. Earlier *Ṣadaqah* was used as a general term for all charity. Now the word *Zakāt* is restricted to the compulsory alms giving prescribed by the Qur'ān. Sometimes both these words were used synonymously (al-Tawbah 9: 60 and 103).

Ṣadaqah can be voluntary charity for expiation of offences (al-Baqarah 2: 217; al-Tawbah 9: 104) or for *Kaffārah* (expiation) for not having performed certain rituals during the *Ḥajj*.

Ṣadaqat al-Fiṭr is almsgiving prescribed at the end of Ramaḍān which should be given before *'Īd* prayers.

In a *ḥadīth* reported in the *Ṣaḥīḥ* of Muslim, the Prophet (peace be upon him) said: "*Ṣadaqah* is *Burhān* (a proof)." This alludes to the fact that *Ṣadaqah* is a sign of one's true belief. It is human nature to love wealth and possessions; hence to give up one's wealth for Allah's sake indicates the truthfulness of one's faith. It is a sign of the hypocrites that they act miserly and do not spend in the path of Allah.

The importance of *Ṣadaqah* is emphasized both in many Qur'ānic verses and in *aḥādīth*. It is not essential that the amount given should be large. If a person does not have much to give in charity, even a small amount given has much value in Allah's sight. Even if a person has only a desire and intention of giving *Ṣadaqah* there will be a great reward for him. The Prophet (peace be upon him) advised his Companions: "protect yourselves from the Fire, even by just half a date (given in charity)" (Bukhārī and Muslim). In another *ḥadīth* the Prophet (peace be upon him) said: "*Ṣadaqah* does not in any way decrease wealth" (Muslim).

References

Ṣadaqah: 2: 196, 271 and 276; 9: 60 and 103.

See also *Infāq* and *Zakāh*

Sā'il [سائل]

see *Faqr*

Sakīnah [سكينة]

see *Iṭmi'nān*

Ṣalāh [صلوٰة] (Prayer)

Meaning

The primary meaning of *Ṣalāh* according to Mawlānā Ḥamīd al-Dīn Farāhī is to turn towards something or to pay attention. From this meaning it was used for *Rukū'* (bowing down) and for paying respect and praying (*Mufrādāt al-Qur'ān*, pp. 52–54). Imām al-Rāghib states: "*Ṣalāh* means to pray, to praise and to pay respect." It is a Qur'ānic keyword and is fully explained in both the Qur'ān and the *Sunnah*. Its structure and timings as well as its contents are all very well recorded and preserved.

When the word *Ṣalāh* is attributed to Allah, it means that He turns towards His servants with love and affection and showers His benefaction and blessings on them (al-Baqarah 2: 157). It is in the same sense that the word *Ṣalāh* is used in Sūrah al-Aḥzāb: "*Allah and His angels send blessings on the Prophet. O you who believe! Send your blessings on him and salute him with respect*" (33: 56). *Ṣalāh* on the Prophet (peace be upon him) is said by the believers in the last part of the final *Rak'ah* after *Tashahhud* (*Salām* on him). Here it is the manifestation of the believers' praise and adoration as well as their love and affection for the Prophet (peace be upon him).

General

It is not only for this *Ummah* that *Ṣalāh* was made obligatory. The Qur'ān records that Allah enjoined the performance of *Ṣalāh* to the *Ummah* of all earlier prophets. The form of *Ṣalāh* prescribed was different from the one prescribed for this *Ummah*. However, *Qiyām*, *Rukū'* and *Sajdah* were always part of *Ṣalāh*. For example the Prophet Ibrāhīm and his offsprings (peace be upon them) (Ibrāhīm 14: 40; Maryam 19: 55); the people of the Prophet Shu'ayb (peace be upon him) (Hūd 11: 87) and the Prophet 'Īsā (peace be upon him) (Maryam 19: 31) were prescribed the offering of *Ṣalāh*.

There are strictures on the Jews for neglecting *Ṣalāh* (Maryam 19: 59) as well as on the Quraysh for reducing their *Ṣalāh* to just "*whistling and clapping of hands*" (al-Anfāl 8: 35).

The Importance of *Ṣalāh*

The purpose of *Ṣalāh* is to establish an intimate relationship between the servant and his Creator. This is renewed five times a day and it continues throughout one's life. Thus, it creates a very intimate bond with the Creator. Unlike other acts of worship such as fasting, *Ḥajj* or *Zakāh*, which are required to be performed at specific times once a year, *Ṣalāh* is to be performed in all circumstances, even when a person is ill or travelling. Again, in other acts of worship a person can do other things, for example a person can eat and drink during *Ḥajj* or buy and sell during fasting. But while praying no other task can be performed, however small it may be.

Ṣalāh is the most important obligation for a Muslim. After saying the *Shahādah*, by which one enters the fold of Islam, the very first obligation testing one's sincerity is *Ṣalāh*. Its importance can be judged by the fact that it is the only *'Ibādah* that is made compulsory by Allah while talking directly to the Prophet (peace be upon him) during the *Mi'rāj*. It is mentioned in a *ḥadīth* that on the Day of Judgement the very first question asked by Allah will be about the performance of regular *Ṣalāh*. *Ṣalāh* plays a very important role in the believers' lives as it brings them into direct communion with Allah, the Creator. Its neglect has dire consequences in the Hereafter. Its neglect will lead one into Hell-Fire. In Sūrah al-Muddaththir a conversation is narrated in which it is said the sinners will be asked: "*'What led you into Hell-Fire?' They will say: 'We were not of those who prayed'*" (74: 42–43).

It is important to note that the believers are commanded to "establish prayers" (*Iqāmah al-Ṣalāh*) and the Qur'ān very rarely refers to the performance of prayers. The difference between the two phrases can be summed up as being that one performs and executes prayer in the best possible and proper manner. This means that prayer should be performed at its proper time in congregation and in a mosque according to its *Adab* (rules and regulations). At the same time while performing the physical acts of prayer one should have the feeling of humbleness, submission and total devotion as if one is seeing Allah; if a person cannot manage that then at least he should be conscious that Allah is seeing him (Muslim).

In reality, if the *Ṣalāh* is performed as it ought to be performed it will have a lasting effect on a believer. When one's heart is rejuvenated five times a day with remembrance of Allah, then no doubt, as the Qur'ān says: "*the* Ṣalāh *restrains one from shameful and evil deeds*" (al-'Ankabūt 29: 45). *Ṣalāh* is also a source of strength and moral upliftment (al-Baqarah 2: 45 and 153).

Structure and Timings

The *Ṣalāh* must be preceded with *Wuḍū'* (ritual purification) and *Niyyah* (intention) facing *Qiblah* (the direction of Makkah). Each prayer has two, three or four *Rak'ah* (cycle), each containing *Qiyām* (standing), *Rukū'* (bowing down), two *Sajdah* (prostrations) and, in the second *Rak'ah*, sitting down and recitation of *Tashahhud* and *Ṣalāt* on the Prophet (peace be upon him). The *Ṣalāh* is started with *Takbīr* (proclaiming the greatness of Allah). In *Qiyām*, Sūrah al-Fātiḥah and some parts of the Qur'ān are recited, and in *Rukū'* and *Sujūd* phrases praising Allah are said.

The five obligatory daily prayers are at dawn before sunrise (*Ṣalāt al-Fajr*), noon (*Ṣalāt al-Ẓuhr*) after *Zawāl* (the Sun reaches its zenith), mid-afternoon (*Ṣalāt al-'Aṣr*), after sunset (*Ṣalāt al-Maghrib*) and late evening (*Ṣalāt al-'Ishā'*). *Ṣalāh* can be performed individually or communally, but the recommendation is that it should be performed in a mosque in *Jamā'ah* (congregation).

There is a general command to safeguard the sanctity and performance of the *ṣalāh* at the prescribed times. However, in Sūrah al-Baqarah a special emphasis is given on safeguarding *al-Ṣalāt al-Wusṭā* (2: 238). Literally this means the Middle Prayer. The *Mufassirūn* differ as to its exact meaning. Most maintain that it means *Ṣalāt al-'Aṣr* which is the middle prayer between the two prayers of morning and the two of evening. The reason for mentioning this particular prayer is that it can easily be missed as it is to be performed at a busy time of day.

The Friday Prayer (*Ṣalāt al-Jumu'ah*), which is performed at *Ẓuhr* time, has special significance as it is preceded by a *Khuṭbah* by an *Imām*. It has to be performed in *Jamā'ah* and is obligatory on all adult men. After the Call to Prayers (*Adhān*) for *Jumu'ah* all activities must cease until the Prayers are concluded (al-Jumu'ah 62: 9–10).

Ṣalāh of the two *'Īds* are also compulsory and they should be performed in a larger gathering for men, women and children. Two *Rak'ah Ṣalāh* are followed by a *Khuṭbah*.

Optional *Ṣalāh*

Ṣalāt al-Tahajjud (late-night prayer before dawn) was prescribed for the Prophet (peace be upon him). However, the Companions also joined in this Prayer as well. Sūrah al-Muzzammil (73: 1–6 and 20) gives clear instructions on its length (about half or more, or at least one third, of the night) in which the recitation of the Qur'ān should be in slow, measured rhythmic tones. The Prophet (peace be upon him) continued this prayer throughout his life.

Other *Nafl* (optional) prayers are *Ishrāq* (after sunrise) and *Ḍuḥā* (before noon). There are special *Ṣalāh* on occasion of eclipses of the sun and moon as well.

Ṣalawāt

The plural of *Ṣalāt* is *Ṣalawāt. Ṣalawāt* is also used in the Qur'ān for synagogues (al-Ḥajj 22: 40). Its origin is Hebrew, from *Ṣalwatā* which in fact is derived from Aramaic. It may be that it came into English through Latin as salute and salutation.

References

Ṣalāh: 5: 6; 10: 87; 24: 37; 29: 45; 62: 9.

Salām [سلام]

see Islam

Salīm [سالم]

see Islam

al-Sam' wa al-Ṭā'ah [السمع والطّاعة]

(Listening and Obeying)

Meaning

Sami'a means to hear, to listen or to pay attention. *Sam'* from this root means listening or hearing, but it conveys the meaning of not just listening but believing and accepting. It is used in this sense in many places in the Qur'ān.

Aṭā'a means to obey, to subjugate, and *Ṭā'ah* means obedience, compliance or submissiveness.

The phrase *al-Sam' wa al-Ṭā'ah* is used as a term to express the total submission of the believers to the commands of Allah and His Prophet (peace be upon him). Listening implies understanding and obeying is voluntarily without reservation.

The Importance of *al-Sam' wa al-Ṭā'ah*

This concept is part of the functioning of an Islamic society and state. Islam wants the believers to lead a disciplined and organized life. Without obedience there will be anarchy and disorder. The attitude of believers is that they totally submit to Allah and His Prophet (peace be upon him) and say: "*We hear and we obey...*" (al-Baqarah 2: 285; al-Nūr 24: 51). The believers are warned not to adopt the attitude of those who say: "*We hear, but we listen not*" (al-Anfāl 8: 21) or of the Jews who said: "*We hear but we disobey*" (al-Baqarah 2: 93; al-Nisā' 4: 46).

In many *aḥādīth* the Prophet (peace be upon him) instructed the believers that it is their duty "To listen and obey whether one likes it or not, except when one is asked to do something sinful. In that case there is no listening, no obeying" (Bukhārī and Muslim). In another *ḥadīth* the Prophet said: "I advise you to have *Taqwā* of Allah and to listen and obey even if a slave is a leader over you" (Abū Dāwūd and Tirmidhī). It is narrated by Ḥārith al-Ash'arī that the Prophet (peace be upon him) said: "I command you to perform five duties that Allah has ordered me to do. *Al-Sam'* and *al-Ṭā'ah*, and *al-Jihād* (struggling in the Way of Allah) and *al-Hijrah* (migrating from evil society to a noble society) and *al-Jamā'ah*" (Tirmidhī).

The Qur'ānic injunction with this regard is: "*O you who believe! Obey Allah and obey the Messenger and those charged with authority among you*" (al-Nisā' 4: 59). Obedience of Allah and His Messenger is to be unconditional; however, one may disagree with those in authority as the verse continues to say: "*if you differ anything among yourselves, refer it to Allah and His Messenger.*" Hence, the matter of disagreement will be resolved in the most suitable manner.

Obedience to a ruler does not depend on his piety. Even if the ruler is not the best person he should be obeyed. There is no right of rebellion or abandonment of the Muslim community. The Prophet (peace be upon him) is reported to have said: "If anyone of you finds a thing in his ruler of which he does not approve, he should bear it patiently. For one who moves a span's length from the *Jamā'ah* (Community) and dies, his death will be a period of *Jāhiliyyah* (Ignorance)" (Bukhārī and Muslim).

'Umar ibn al-Khaṭṭāb summed up the basis of Islamic social order thus: "There is no Islam without *Jamā'ah* (community). There is no *Jamā'ah* without an *Amīr* (leader) and there is no *Amīr* without *Ṭā'ah* (obedience)."

References

al-Sam' wa al-Ṭā'ah: 2: 285; 4: 46; 5: 7; 24: 51.

Sawā' [سوآء]

see *Istiwā'*

Sawā' al-Sabīl [سوآءَ ٱلسبيل]

see *al-Ṣirāt al-Mustaqīm*

Ṣawm [صوم] (Fasting)

Meaning

Ṣawm or *Ṣiyām* literally means to refrain from something or to leave something. Mawlānā Ḥamīd al-Dīn Farāhī in his research on the origin of this word states: "The Arabs used to train their horses and camels to make them accustomed to remain hungry and thirsty by depriving them of food so that they would be able to bear the periods of austerity and hardship. Similarly they used to train the animals to build up their stamina in order to withstand blustering and squally winds. This training was useful while travelling and during war" (*Tadabbur-i-Qur'ān*, vol. 1, pp. 400–401).

Injunctions relating to *Ṣawm*

In the *Sharī'ah* the word *ṣawm* means refraining from food, drink and sexual intercourse during the days of the month of Ramaḍān.

This abstinence is from dawn until sunset, and all adults are required to observe the fast. Women who are pregnant, menstruating as well as nursing mothers and those suffering ill health or travelling are exempt from this obligation. Those who are chronically ill and will not be able to fast must pay *Fidyah* (compensation) by feeding one person per day, while others are required to fast later on to make up the missed fasts.

The Importance of *Ṣawm*

The purposes for which fasting is prescribed are to teach self-control and patience (*Ṣabr*) by breaking the grip of habit and to create *Taqwā* (God-consciousness). Thus, by acquiring the qualities of *Ṣabr* and *Taqwā* a person is trained to withstand adverse situations. Fasting is of such fundamental importance that all religions have prescribed it on their followers.

Human beings are creatures of habit. The routine of one's daily work helps one to organize one's life systematically. Yet at times people became slaves of such self-imposed habits. Any change in their routine upsets them. Fasting brings about a complete change in one's daily routine. Meal times and schedules of sleep and rest are changed. Instead of being a slave to one's habits and desires one acquires control over one's life. This liberating feeling of being master of one's own destiny is achieved by fasting. Thus Ramaḍān is a month of intensive training. Not only does it cultivate qualities of *Taqwā* and piety, it also trains one to acquire self-control. This leads to spiritual development as well as self-development.

These benefits from fasting can only be acquired if one consciously sets out to achieve these goals. If fasting also becomes just another ritual, without soul and spirit, one will remain untouched by the blessings of this month. So there are very many who do not achieve anything from fasting except hunger and thirst. Similarly many spend their time in night vigils but they only have sleepless nights. They fail to reap spiritual insights and nearness to Allah.

The Prophet (peace be upon him) said: "Whoever fasts the month of Ramaḍān with *Īmān* and *Iḥtisāb* their previous sins are forgiven" (Bukhārī and Muslim). *Īmān* and *Iḥtisāb* are technical words in Islamic terminology. They mean that all good actions are done for the sake of

Allah with the hope of receiving reward from Him. Thus, there should not be any other motive. *Iḥtisāb* means scrutiny. One should take account of all one's sins and shortcomings and seek Allah's forgiveness. If one is sincere in one's repentance and prayers Allah, the Most Merciful, the Most Kind, will forgive him, *Inshā' Allāh*.

Voluntary Fasts

Many *aḥādīth* recommend fasting on the day of *'Āshūrā'* (the 10th day of the month of Muḥarram), the first six days of the month of Shawwāl, three days of each month (the 13th, 14th and 15th of the lunar month), and fasting on Mondays and Thursdays. Fasting is also recommended for those who are not in a position to marry in order to control their sexual desires.

Fasting as *Kaffārah*

Fasting is also prescribed as *Kaffārah* (expiation) of certain sins and transgression or acts of omission: for example for not fulfilling an oath (al-Mā'idah 5: 89), or accidental killing of a believer (al-Nisā' 4: 92), or clipping hair or nails during the days of *Ḥajj* (al-Baqarah 2: 196).

References

Ṣawm: 2: 183; 4: 92; 5: 89; 19: 26; 33: 35.

Sayyi'ah [سيّئة]

see *Iḥsān* and *Sū'*

Sha'ā'ir [شعآئر] (Symbols)

Meaning

Sha'īrah literally means a sign or symbol that reminds one of something important. Its plural is *Sha'ā'ir*. In *Sharī'ah* it refers to cognizance or perception (*Shu'ūr*) of the facts relating to performance of certain rites.

Thus, the word *Sha'ā'ir* is used for religious ceremony, rites and practices particularly during the *Ḥajj*.

The Importance of *Sha'ā'ir Allāh*

In themselves the symbols may not be that significant but as they are associated with religious rites they assume sacredness. For example the animals taken for slaughter during the *Ḥajj*, the *Ṣafā* and *Marwah*, the *Jamarāt* (Three Pillars in Minā) and the *Ḥajar al-Aswad* (the Black Stone in *Ka'bah*) are all *Sha'ā'ir*. Their importance is: "*Whoever holds in honour the Symbols of Allah, (in sacrifice of animals), such (honour) should come truly from piety*" (al-Ḥajj 22: 32). Believers are instructed: "*Violate not the Symbols of Allah, nor the sacred month, nor of the animals brought for sacrifice, nor garlands that mark out such animals, nor the people resorting to the Sacred House...*" (al-Mā'idah 5: 2). This directive to treat the *Sha'ā'ir Allāh* with due respect was given when there was a state of war between Muslims and the Quraysh of Makkah. The sacredness of these symbols requires that even polytheists should be allowed to proceed for Pilgrimage without molestation.

The Philosophy of *Sha'ā'ir*

While explaining the philosophy behind the importance of the *Sha'ā'ir Allāh*, Sayyid Mawdūdī has said:

> Whatever characteristically represents either a particular doctrine, creed, way of thought or conduct is recognized as its symbol. For example, official flags, uniforms of armed forces, coins, notes and stamps are symbols used by governments so that their subjects – in fact all those who live within their spheres of influence – treat them with proper respect. Cathedrals, altars and crosses are symbols of Christianity. A special bunch of hair on the head, a special kind of bead-rosary and the temple are symbols of Hinduism. A turban, bracelet and *kirpān* (a special dagger kept by the Sikhs) are symbols of the Sikh religion. The hammer and sickle are the symbols of Communism. The swastika has been the symbol of

Aryan racialism. The followers of these ideologies are required to treat these symbols with respect. (*Towards Understanding the Qur'ān*, Vol. II, pp. 128–129)

Another Word from the Same Root

Mash'ar is a place for performing sacred rites. *Al-Mash'ar al-Ḥarām* is one of the stations of *Ḥajj* between 'Arafāt and Minā which is referred to as Muzdalifah (al-Baqarah 2: 198).

References

Sha'ā'ir: 2: 158; 5: 2; 22: 32 and 36. *Al-Mash'ar al-Ḥarām*: 2: 198.

Shafā'ah [شفاعة] (Intercession)

Meaning

Shafa'a means to attach, add or subjoin with something or someone. From this root *shafā'ah* means to mediate, use one's good offices, to put in a good word, to intercede or plead on someone's behalf. *Shafā'ah* as a noun means mediation, intercession or advocacy.

Analysis

The Qur'ān generally does not accept that people should escape punishment for their deeds as this violates the concept of justice which is emphasized throughout the Qur'ān. There are many verses that reject outright the concept of *Shafā'ah* for those who believe that they can go free because of their relationship or special favour from Allah (al-Baqarah 2: 48, 123, 254; al-Zumar 39: 44).

In some verses it is mentioned that Allah may give gracious permission to someone to plead on others' behalf (Yūnus 10: 3; Ṭā Hā 20: 109; Sabā' 34: 23). Those who may be permitted to intercede on behalf of the believers are the angels (Ghāfir 40: 7; al-Najm 53: 26; al-Naba' 78: 38). Others besides angels may also be permitted to intercede as mentioned in Sūrah Maryam: "*None shall have the power of intercession, but such a one as has received permission (or promise) from (Allah) the*

Most Gracious" (19: 87). From *aḥādīth* it is clear that this high status of *Shafīʿ* (intercessor) will be given to the prophets, and martyrs. This, however, would be permissible only through Divine permission, and the final decision rests with Allah alone.

Shafāʿah could have a role within human society. Recommending a good cause is called *Shafāʿah Ḥasanah* and a person making it is entitled to its reward. There could be *Shafāʿah Sayyiʾah* – that is, someone responsible for promoting evil causes; such a person will share the burden of sin (al-Nisāʾ 4: 85).

Words from the Same Root
Al-Shafʿ means an even number as opposed to *al-Witr* an odd number (al-Fajr 89: 3).

Shafīʿ (pl. *Shāfiʿīn*) and *shāfiʿ* (pl. *Shufaʿāʾ*) means one who can intercede on someone's behalf. In a *ḥadīth* the Qurʾān is called *Shafīʿ* as well as *Mushaffaʿ*. This means that the Qurʾān will intercede for its readers and its intercession is acceptable by Allah (Ḥākim and Ṭabarānī).

References
Shafāʿah: 2: 48; 4: 85; 34: 23; 36: 23; 53: 26. *Al-Shafʿ*: 89: 3. *Shafīʿ*: 6: 51; 7: 53; 10: 3; 32: 4; 40: 18.

Shahādah [شهادة] (Witness)

Meaning
Shahida means to witness, to experience personally, to be present. From this root *Shahādah* means testimony, evidence or witness. This could be the evidence in someone's favour or against someone. Its opposite is *Ghayb*, something that cannot be perceived by human senses.

Kalimat al-Shahādah
This is the testimony of faith. By reciting "I bear witness that there is no deity except Allah and I also bear witness that Muḥammad is His servant and Messenger" one comes into the fold of Islam. Although it is a verbal

affirmation, it requires conviction in one's heart and then its manifestation by actions. This *Kalimah* (Statement) creates one's relationship with Allah and His Messenger and with other Muslims who share this faith. In the Qur'ān it is termed as *al-Kalimah al-Ṭayyibah* (A Good Word) which like a good tree is firmly based and its branches reach out to the heavens (Ibrāhīm 14: 24). This testimony is so significant and important that Allah Himself, His angels and those endowed with knowledge stand firm and make this declaration (Āl 'Imrān 3: 18).

Shāhid, Shahīd

Shāhid (pl. *Shuhadā', Shuhūd*) means a witness as he is the one who is present and thus can testify with conviction. The act of witnessing can take a number of forms as detailed below:

- *Shāhid* is used in its dictionary meaning of being a witness to certain acts or transactions. Thus, in criminal cases to determine the guilt of an accused, a witness is required to testify against him (al-Nūr 24: 4). In civil cases as well as witnessing a financial transaction or a will two or more witnesses are required (al-Baqarah 2: 282; al-Mā'idah 5: 106). There are general instructions in such cases not to be swayed by blood relationship, social status or enmity in giving evidence (al-Nisā' 4: 135; al-Mā'idah 5: 8).
- *Shāhid* is also used for the leader or spokesman who represents the views of his people (al-Baqarah 2: 23).
- *Shuhadā' 'Alā al-Nās* means to be a witness unto mankind. All the Prophets and Messengers were living witnesses in their time. With their qualities of *taqwā* (God-consciousness), truthfulness, righteousness and piety they were witnesses to Allah's existence and the veracity of receiving guidance from Him. Each Messenger was sent to his own people so that he could explain the Message to them in their own language. But the Prophethood of Muḥammad (peace be upon him) was twofold. He was sent to the people of Arabia as well as to all humankind. As he was the last Prophet and Messenger, the responsibility for conveying Allah's message to all humanity till the end of time rests on his

Ummah: "*Thus have We made you an* Ummah *justly balanced, that you might be witnesses over the nations and the Messenger a witness over yourselves*" (al-Baqarah 2: 143; al-Ḥajj 22: 78).

Thus, to protect the Message and its continuous propagation, Allah has undertaken two vital steps: first, that the Holy Qur'ān will be preserved from corruption for eternity (al-Ḥijr 15: 9). Second, there will always be at least one group in this *Ummah* that will stand firm on the *Dīn* and convey the Message of Truth and be a witness unto mankind.

- *Shahīd* (martyr) (pl. *Shuhadā'*) is one who by giving his life in the process of performing his religious obligations bears witness for what he believes (Āl 'Imrān 3: 140; al-Aḥzāb 33: 23). This in fact is the highest rank of fulfilling the duty of *Shuhadā' 'alā al-Nās*; those who sacrifice their lives in this cause, are the real *Shuhadā'* (witnesses). They do not live in the physical world but by their supreme sacrifice they attain everlasting life and the believers are instructed not to call them dead (al-Baqarah 2: 154). Indeed they are alive and provided sustenance by Allah (Āl 'Imrān 3: 169). Martyrs are considered pure and pious and thus are buried in the clothes they died in without washing before burial. Death during the *Ḥajj*, or from accidents, or from gruesome and agonizing disease or in childbirth is also considered an act of martyrdom.

References

Shahādah: 3: 18; 5: 111; 6: 19; 36: 65; 63: 1. *Shāhid*: 11: 17; 12: 26; 33: 45; 46: 10; 85: 3. *Shahīd*: 4: 41; 5: 117; 6: 19; 50: 21; 100: 7.

Sharḥ al-Ṣadr [شرح الصدر]

see *Iṭmi'nān*

Sharī'ah [شريعة]

see *Dīn*

Sharr [شر] (Evil)

Meaning

Sharr (pl. *Shurūr*) means evil, mischief, calamity, disaster, wickedness and malice. According to Imām Rāghib, *Sharr* is something that is hated by everyone as opposed to *Khayr* (good) which is liked by everyone.

Analysis

Allah is the Creator of everything and whatever He has created has a specific purpose and whatever happens good or bad is only with His knowledge and permission. All things are intrinsically good; it is the use to which they are put that determines whether they are beneficial or harmful, good or evil.

Human beings do not know what is good or bad for them so when something unpleasant happens they start complaining, but it may be that the *Ḥikmah* (wisdom) of Allah is involved. The reverse at the Battle of Uḥud was seen as a setback for the Muslims but the Qur'ānic observation on this event is: "*Allah will not leave the believers in the state in which you are now, until He separates what is evil from what is good*" (Āl 'Imrān 3: 179). Similarly when fighting was prescribed people disliked it. However, the Qur'ān says: "*It is possible you dislike a thing which is good for you, and that you love a thing which is bad for you*" (al-Baqarah 2: 216). It is Allah who knows what is best for His creation.

The last two *Sūrahs* of the Qur'ān (113 and 114) have taught the believers to seek Allah's refuge from all sorts of evil. There are different forces of evil, and different counterforces, so one should seek Allah's refuge from all the evils, especially from those that overspread in darkness, as well as from the treachery of those who practise evil arts like magic and sorcery, from those who are envious. All these evils are invisible to human beings, so one should rely on Allah's help. As *Shayṭān* is the arch enemy of mankind, along with those who follow him, one should always seek Allah's refuge from their *wasāwis* (whisperings) and evil promptings.

Antonym

Khayr is the opposite of *Sharr*. It means goodness and excellence. Hence, it is also used to mean a good thing, blessing, wealth, as well as charity. The word *Khayr* is used in all these meanings in the Qur'ān. For example inviting people to good deeds is referred to as *Khayr* (Āl 'Imrān 3: 104). So also is Allah's blessing with goodness (al-An'ām 6: 17). The word *Khayr* is commonly used for wealth (al-Baqarah 2: 180, 215; al-'Ādiyāt 100: 8).

References

Sharr: 2: 216; 5: 60; 17: 11; 70: 20; 113: 2. *Khayr*: 3: 26; 4: 149; 6: 32; 23: 118; 28: 24.

Shayṭān [شيطان] (Satan)

Meanings

Shayṭān (pl. *Shayāṭīn*) means Satan or the Devil. According to some lexicographers the word *shayṭān* is derived from *Shayṭana* which means to become distant or be far removed. Others maintained that it is derived from *Shaṭa*, meaning hasty, bad-tempered, angry, violent, and defiant. *Shayṭān*'s fiery origin indicates his violent and burning nature. *Shayṭān* is not a distinct species, as in the Qur'ān the word is used for both humans and *Jinns* (al-An'ām 6: 112). Thus, the word *Shayṭān* is applied for all those who possess violent and obnoxious qualities, defy the commands of Allah, and actively try to misguide others by alluring them and tempting them with false promises.

Iblīs

Iblīs is the other name used for *Shayṭān*. He was a *Jinn* as mentioned in the Qur'ān (al-Kahf 18: 50). In the story of the creation of the Prophet Ādam (peace be upon him) – told in several places in the Qur'ān – it is stated that it was *Iblīs* who defied Allah's command to bow down before Ādam, claiming that he was superior to Ādam as Ādam was made of clay and he was created of fire. As *Iblīs* was thrown out, he asked for respite until the Day of Judgement; his aim was to misguide the Prophet Ādam (peace be upon him) and his progeny in every possible way (al-'Arāf 7: 11–17). *Iblīs* is always used as a proper noun, while *Shayṭān* is a generic designation unless it is used with the definite article *al-Shayṭān*.

There is no verbal root of *Iblīs*. *Ablasa* means to be overcome with grief, to be desperate, struck dumb with despair. It is assumed that the word *Iblīs* is derived from this root as he lost hope and came to despair of Allah's mercy. He followed the path of defiance, whereas when Ādam and Ḥawwā' (peace be upon them) transgressed, they sought the path of repentance.

The Tricks and Treachery of *Shayṭān*

The eternal jealousy of *Shayṭān* caused him to vow to misguide and mislead mankind as he had done to their parents. He was responsible for stripping them of their raiment, to expose their shame. He outlined his plan in no uncertain terms: "*I will mislead them, and I will create in them false desires; I will order them to slit the ears of cattle, and to deface the (fair) nature created*" (al-Nisā' 4: 119). "*I will lie in wait for them on Your straight way: then will I assault them from before them and behind them, from their right and their left...*" (al-A'rāf 7: 16–17).

Shayṭān is a vindictive and treacherous enemy of mankind. Hence, there are repeated warnings in the Qur'ān to this effect so that human beings should be on their guard (al-Baqarah 2: 168, 208; al-An'ām 6: 142; al-'Arāf 7: 22). As *Shayṭān* and his tribe are invisible to mankind and can watch over them to perpetrate their acts, Allah advises human beings to be aware of this danger lest they fell prey to *Shayṭān*'s tricks (al-A'rāf 7: 27).

Shayṭān and his associates use different tricks and strategies to lure human beings as they know human weaknesses and tempt people by whispering suggestions (*Wasāwis* or *Hamazāt*) to them and presenting themselves as sincere advisors (al-Nās 114: 4; al-Mu'minūn 23: 98).

References

Shayṭān: 2: 208; 4: 76; 7: 27; 41: 36; 58: 19. *Iblīs*: 2: 34; 7: 11; 15: 31; 34: 20; 38: 74.

Shirk [شرك] (Polytheism)

Meaning

Sharika means to share with someone, to become a partner or associate. Hence *shirk* means partnership or association. In Islamic terminology it means to associate someone or something with Allah or to make someone a partner with Allah. This could be in His person, attributes, powers or rights.

The Classification of *Shirk*

- *Shirk fī al-Dhāt* means to make someone a partner with Allah or to attribute divinity to someone. For example the Christian doctrine of Trinity, or the pagan Arabs' belief that angels were Allah's daughters, or the polytheists' gods and goddesses.
- *Shirk fī al-Ṣifāt* means to associate others in Allah's exclusive attributes. For example, it is only Allah who is Omnipotent, Omnipresent and Omniscient. To believe that others also can be all-powerful, or can be present everywhere at the same time and know everything about *'Ālam al-Ghayb* (things not perceptible by human senses) is *Shirk fī al-Ṣifāt*.
- *Shirk fī al-Lawāzim* means to make others share in what are the essential corollaries of Allah's attributes, or share in His rights. For example it is Allah who controls destinies, provides sustenance, and listens to prayers. If others are considered to have these powers this will be *shirk*. Similarly it is Allah who can decree what is lawful and unlawful. If this right is attributed to others it will also be *Shirk*.

In addition to the above, in Islam certain other acts of reverence although not specifically *Shirk* are prohibited as these may lead to *Shirk*: for example, to bow down before someone or to take an oath of someone other than Allah.

Shirk of Polytheists

Shirk is not just restricted to worshipping others, which is very obvious. Some other types of *Shirk* are more subtle. The polytheists throughout the ages believed in One Supreme God. The Qur'ān gives many examples. "*If you indeed ask them who has created the heavens and the earth and subjected the sun and the moon (to His law), they will certainly say: 'Allah*" (al-'Ankabūt 29: 61). Similarly they will acknowledge that there is a Supreme Being who is the Creator. In polytheistic religions there are three types of *Shirk*. One is the worship of idols and icons. Two, these idols and icons represent some real or imaginary persons or spirits. Finally, the beliefs and dogmas that are the basis of their religion also constitute *Shirk*.

Shirk of *Ahl al-Kitāb*

Both the Jews and Christians share with Muslims the belief in the Oneness of God (*Tawḥīd*). Despite this, they indulge in *Shirk fī al-Lawāzim*. Thus, the Qur'ānic criticism is that instead of following Allah's command they obey the commands of their priests and monks. This is called by the Qur'ān "*Arbāb min dūn Allāh*" (lords in place of Allah) (al-Tawbah 9: 31).

The Christians attributed divinity to the Prophet 'Īsā (peace be upon him) by making him the son of God. Similarly the Jews considered the Prophet 'Uzayr (Ezra) (peace be upon him) to be the son of God (al-Tawbah 9: 30).

The Current Situation of Muslims Regarding *Shirk*

Despite great emphasis given to *Tawḥīd* by the Qur'ān, like the Jews and Christians some Muslims have also degenerated into *Shirk fī al-Lawāzim*. They seek the help of saints either dead or living for solving their problems and difficulties. They bestow presents and even perform acts of '*Ibādah* (such as prostration) in front of the saints' tombs. They prepare special food or make offerings and indulge in many other *Bid'ah* (innovations). All these unIslamic practices have entered into Muslim folk culture.

The Punishment for *Shirk*

Committing any kind of *shirk* mentioned above is the most grave sin. Thus, there is a dire warning in the Qur'ān to the *Mushrikīn* (polytheists). Allah will forgive all other sins but *Shirk*: as this is a direct attack on His person and integrity, it will never be forgiven (al-Nisā' 4: 116).

References

Shirk: 18: 42; 22: 26; 31: 13; 34: 22; 46: 4.

Shukr [شكر] (Gratitude)

Meaning

Shakara means to give thanks, to be thankful, to be grateful. Hence, *Shukr* from this root means thankfulness, gratefulness or gratitude. *Shukr* is the opposite of *Kufr* which means to be ungrateful and also contains the meaning of denial of something. Hence, *Kufr* is used for disbelief that is hiding the truth or denying its recognition.

Shukr has five aspects: to recognize gratitude in one's consciousness and heart, to show gratitude, to express love and respect, to thank the benefactor verbally, and to recompense this by one's actions and not misuse the favours received. One is usually polite and gives thanks for any little favour received; similarly it is incumbent upon a person that he should, as the recipient of Allah's innumerable *ni'mah* (blessings), be grateful to Him. Yet very few are thankful for Allah's bounties (Sabā' 34: 13). If one is grateful to Allah *"[one] does so to the profit of his own soul; but if any is ungrateful, verily Allah is free of all wants, Worthy of all praise"* (Luqmān 31: 12). By thanking Allah one is fulfilling one's duty, however. Allah in His infinite mercy has decreed: *"If you are grateful, I will add more (favours) unto you. But if you show ingratitude, truly My punishment is terrible indeed"* (Ibrāhīm 14: 7).

Other Words from the Same Root

Shākir and *Shakūr* are among the *al-Asmā' al-Ḥusnā* (the most beautiful names of Allah); they can also be used for people. Both words when applied to human beings have in them:

> ...the idea of appreciation, recognition, gratitude as shown in deeds of goodness and righteousness... A slight distinction in shades of meaning may be noted. *Shakūr* implies that the appreciation is even for the smallest favours and response on the other side: it is a mental attitude independent of specific facts. *Shākir* implies bigger and more specific things.
>
> (Yūsuf 'Alī – Sūrah Ibrāhīm 14: 5, Note 1877)

When Allah is described as *Shākir* and *Shakūr* it means that He recognizes and appreciates the efforts of His servants and gives suitable reward for the smallest service performed by them, however defective (al-Baqarah 2: 158; Fāṭir 35: 30; al-Taghābun 64: 17).

Synonym

The word *Ḥamd* is usually translated as praise, but gratitude is also an integral part of its meaning. The more accurate translation would be "grateful praise". *Ḥamd* is exclusively used for Allah. *Ḥamd* is more expansive than *Shukr*. *Ḥamd* is an acknowledgement that Allah embodies the excellent qualities of beneficence and radiates blessings and benedictions.

References

Shukr: 14: 7; 16: 114; 31: 12; 34: 13; 54: 35. *Shākir*: 2: 158; 4: 147; 6: 53; 16: 121; 76: 3. *Shakūr*: 14: 5; 34: 19; 35: 34; 42: 33.

See also *Ḥamd*

Shūrā [شورىٰ] (Consultation)

Meaning

The word *Shūra* is derived from *Mashwarah* or *Mushāwarah* which means consultation or deliberation. *Majlis al-Shūrā* means a consultative or advisory body.

The Role of *Shūrā* in an Islamic Social Order

Shūrā, the consultation process, occupies a pivotal role in the Islamic way of life, particularly in the political field. In Sūrah Āl ʿImrān the Prophet (peace be upon him) is instructed to consult his Companions (3: 159). Sūrah al-Shūrā, while extolling the characteristics of believers, also states: "*Their affairs are conducted by mutual consultation*" (42: 38). From these verses and many *aḥādīth* on this topic, it emerges that those who are in command should always consult the people before making decisions. In the political field while conducting the affairs of state one should follow the democratic tradition. Hence, the *Shūrā* system is contrary to the despotic regimes of dictators and kings. It is akin to the democratic process but not quite so. In a democracy, sovereignty resides in the will of the masses, but in an Islamic political system Allah is the Sole Sovereign and His Sovereignty cannot be shared by anyone.

It should be noted here that the instruction to consult is given to the Prophet (peace be upon him) who receives revelation from God and hence has no need to consult others. This does not mean that the consultation referred to was just a token process to honour his Companions. As Imām Abū Bakr al-Jaṣṣāṣ explains:

> If people knew that their views would not be considered and the consultation would not have any effect on the outcome of the affair then this cannot be considered as an honour. The fact is that although the Prophet (peace be upon him) was guided by revelation and a direction of work was set for him it was the wisdom and mercy of Allah that many matters were left to his judgement and discretion. In such matters he needed the opinions of others and in these he was directed to consult.
> (*Aḥkām al-Qur'ān*, as quoted by Muftī Muḥammad Shafīʿ in *Maʿārif al-Qur'ān*, vol. 2, p. 221)

This view is also supported by the Qur'ānic instruction: "Their affairs are conducted by mutual consultation" (al-Shūrā 42: 38). This does not mean that after the consultation the majority view can be ignored. This would be altogether contrary to this instruction.

It is also the duty of those who are consulted to give their sincere opinion without any fear or favour. They should not be swayed by any personal or other motive. Consultation is a sacred trust and it is obligatory to fulfil this duty faithfully.

The role of the *Shūrā* is applicable in all other spheres of life – social, domestic and economic. However, no specific form of consultation is prescribed. Islam being a universal and eternal way of life, the mode of consultation may vary according to time and place. This can be observed in the process of the election of the first four *Khulafā'*. Different forms of consultation were used in their appointments. There can be various forms of seeking consultation: through a direct election or through a college of representatives, or using any other suitable way. This flexibility can encompass any method that society finds acceptable.

At the microcosm level as well, it is necessary to conduct all affairs with mutual consultation, be it within a family, social organization or institution.

References

Shūrā: 2: 233; 3: 159; 42: 38.

Ṣidq [صدق] (Truth)

Meaning

Ṣadaqa means to speak the truth or to be sincere as well as to fulfil and also to make something come true, as in Sūrah al-Fatḥ (48: 27). *Ṣidq* from this root means truth or sincerity. The essence of *Ṣidq* is that a thing reflects its true nature – for example when what is being said echoes what is in one's heart. There should be harmony between the tongue and heart. Otherwise, it may be that what is being said is true, but if the speaker does not believe in it he will not be considered a truthful person. This is the reason that hypocrites were branded as liars (al-Munāfiqūn 63: 1).

Analysis

Ṣidq is considered to be a cornerstone of faith and "the mother of all virtues". *Ṣidq* as reflecting one's inner conviction and outward acts is the hallmark of a true believer. Imām al-Ghazālī, in *Iḥyā' 'Ulūm al-Dīn*, has a special chapter on *Ṣidq*. He pairs it with *Niyyah* (intention) and *Ikhlāṣ* (sincerity) and enumerates six different types of truthfulness. One, in speech: that is, safeguarding one's tongue and fulfilling one's promise. Two, in intention and volition: that is, one's *Niyyah* should always be to seek Allah's pleasure. Three, in determination: that is, one should have firm resolve. Four, in faithfulness to one's determination: that is, to do what one has promised oneself. Five, in actions or deeds: that is, one's outward behaviour should not convey an impression that does not correspond with the reality of one's inner self. This means that one should safeguard oneself from the display of outward piety. Six, in attaining the status of real *Īmān* as described in Sūrah al-Ḥujurāt: "*Only those are believers who have believed in Allah and His Messenger, and have never doubted, but have striven with their possessions and their lives in the cause of Allah: such are the truthful ones*" (49: 15).

Despite its importance, adherence to *Ṣidq* is not considered absolute. Sometimes one can use a double-meaning word or an ambiguous word to save someone's life or to protect a state secret. In judicial language this is called *Tawriyah* which means hiding the real meaning. The Prophet (peace be upon him) said: "That person is not a liar who says something good or conveys some good news to make peace between two persons" (Bukhārī).

Words from the Same Root

Ṣādiq (pl. *Ṣādiqūn*) is the one who is truthful in everything he says. Even before receiving revelation, the Prophet (peace be upon him) was known for his truthfulness. He was to be called *al-Ṣādiq* and *al-Amīn* (the Truthful and the Trustworthy). Indeed the unbelievers despite their continued refusal to accept him as a prophet still trusted him and never accused him of lying.

Ṣiddīq (pl. *Ṣiddīqūn*) means one who is strictly veracious, honest, righteous and upright. *Ṣiddīq* is one who is truthful in his speech and his beliefs; this he testifies (*Taṣdīq*) with his actions. *Ṣiddīqūn*, because of their sincerity and truth, are ranked after the prophets (al-Nisā' 4: 69). This was the rank held by the special Companions; the first among them was Abū Bakr on whom the Prophet bestowed the honour of *al-Ṣiddīq* for his unflinching love and support for him.

Muṣaddiq means credible and reliable; it also means confirming the truth. In this sense the Qur'ān is referred to as confirming the earlier Scriptures (al-Baqarah 2: 41 and 89).

Ṣadāqah means a warm and sincere bond of friendship, and *Ṣadīq* is a bosom and loyal friend.

Antonym

Kidhb/Kadhib is the antonym of *Ṣidq*. It comes from the verb *Kadhaba* which means to lie to deceive, to delude or to mislead. Thus, *Kidhb* as a noun means lie, deceit or falsehood and *Kādhib* is a liar; so also is *Kadhdhāb* which is an intensive form. The Qur'ān has portrayed the contrasting personalities of a truthful person and a liar in the following terms:

> *So he who gives (in charity) and fears (Allah) and (in all sincerity) testifies to the best – We will indeed make smooth for him the path to bliss. But he who is a greedy miser and thinks himself self-sufficient, and gives the lie to the best – We will indeed make smooth for him the path to misery.*
>
> (al-Layl 92: 5–10)

References

Ṣidq: 33: 22; 34: 20; 37: 37; 39: 33; 75: 31. *Ṣādiq*: 19: 54; 21: 38; 33: 24; 39: 33; 51: 5. *Ṣiddīq*: 4: 69; 5: 75; 12: 46; 19: 41; 57: 19. *Muṣaddiq*: 2: 89 and 101; 3: 81; 6: 92; 46: 12. *Ṣadīq*: 24: 61; 26: 101. *Kidhb*: 3: 75; 5: 41; 10: 60; 16: 116; 58: 14.

Siḥr [سحر]

see *Mu'jizah*

al-Ṣirāṭ al-Mustaqīm [الصّراط المستقيم] (The Straight Path)

Meaning

Ṣirāṭ means a way or a path that is clear. Thus, it is used for a road that is well known, prominent and clearly marked or signposted.

The word *Mustaqīm* comes from *Istiqāmah* meaning to be straight, to be in moderation, to be upright and to proceed straight without deviation.

Thus, *al-Ṣirāṭ al-Mustaqīm* means the Straight Path. Use of the definite article *al* in both words implies that it is the specific straight path that Allah has ordained for His servants so that following this path ensures their ultimate success.

Al-Ṣirāṭ al-Mustaqīm and Other Expressions

Al-Ṣirāṭ al-Mustaqīm is the only way to achieve salvation; all the Messengers guided mankind to this path. This is emphasized in several places in the Holy Qur'ān:

> *Verily, this is My Way leading straight: follow it. Follow not (other) paths: they will scatter you about from His (great) Path.*
> (al-An'ām 6: 153)

> *Verily, it is my Lord that is on a Straight Path.*
> (Hūd 11: 56)

In Sūrah al-Naḥl the same meaning is conveyed by the alternative expression *Qaṣd al-Sabīl*:

> *And unto Allah leads the Straight Way, but there are ways that turn aside. If Allah had willed, He could have guided all of you.*
> (al-Naḥl 16: 9)

Similarly in Sūrah al-Mā'idah yet another term is used to signify the same meaning. Here it is called *Sawā' al-Sabīl*:

> *Whosoever of you disbelieves thereafter has indeed gone astray from the Right Way.*
>
> (al-Mā'idah 5: 12)

A few other words such as *Ṭarīq* and *Minhāj*, meaning path, are also used in the Qur'ān. *Ṭarīq* is used nine times while *Minhāj* is used only once.

Analysis

Knowing the Right Way is necessary for human beings so that they can fashion their lives to ensure peace and tranquillity both intellectually and in their physical environment. Once the Prophet (peace be upon him) explained the Straight Path by drawing a straight line in the sand and then on either side of this some crooked lines, saying: "This straight line is the Way of Allah and the crooked lines are pathways on each of them Satan is inviting people." Then he recited this verse: "*Verily, this is My Way, leading straight: follow it: follow not (other) paths: they will scatter you about from His Path. Thus does He command you that you may be righteous*" [al-An'ām 6: 153] (Aḥmad, al-Nasā'ī, Dārimī).

This concept is explained very well by Sayyid Mawdūdī in his *Tafsīr* of *Sawā' al-Sabīl*:

> The fact that man has inherent limitations means that he is incapable of viewing in one sweep and in a balanced way the entire span of existence. Hence, man is in no position to prescribe for his kind a judicious way of life – a way of life wherein justice is done to all his powers and capacities; in which a wholesome balance is maintained between all his inherent potentialities; in which all his urges are given their due; in which his two-fold need for inner satisfaction and external self-realization is fully met; in which various aspects of human life are taken into proper consideration, giving birth to an integrated scheme with a built-in capacity to harmonize the multifarious strains and stresses of social life; in which

material resources are fully exploited in the best interests of both the individual and society and within the framework of equity, justice and righteousness.

(*Towards Understanding the Qur'ān*, Vol. II, pp. 143–144)

This is the reason that Muslims are instructed to pray for Guidance and to remain constantly on the right path.

References

al-Ṣirāṭ al-Mustaqīm: 1: 5; 2: 142; 3: 101; 5: 16; 6: 87. *Qaṣd al-Sabīl*: 16: 9. *Sawā' al-Sabīl*: 5: 12, 60 and 77; 60: 1.

Siyāḥah [سياحة] (Travel)

Meanings

Sāḥa means to flow (of water), to melt or thaw, as well as to travel on to move around. *Sā'iḥ* (pl. *Sā'iḥūn*) means traveller, itinerant or dervish. *Siyāḥah* means to move around, to travel or roam about. The word *Suyyāḥ*, also from this root, has the same meaning. *Sīḥū* (an imperative) is used in its primary meaning in Sūrah al-Tawbah: "*Move around for four months throughout the land...*" (9: 2). Later in the same *Sūrah* it is used as one of the attributes of the believers: "*Those that turn (to Allah) in repentance, that serve Him and praise Him, that wander* (Sā'iḥūn) *in devotion to the cause of Allah, that bow down and prostrate themselves in Prayer; that enjoin good and forbid evil, and observe the limits set by Allah*" (9: 112).

Interpretations

There is disagreement among the *Mufassirūn* on the exact meaning and interpretation of the word *al-Sā'iḥūn*. Both Imām Ibn Kathīr and Imām Qurṭubī interpreted it as *al-Ṣā'imūn* (those who fast). They based this meaning on a *ḥadīth* of the Prophet (peace be upon him). Other *Mufassirūn* prefer to follow its literal meaning as given in *Lisān al-'Arab* which defines *Sā'iḥ* as one who wanders around the land for the purpose of *'Ibādah*, and lives a life of austerity and abstinence. Another interpretation, given in *Ṣafwat al-Tafāsīr* (compiled by Muḥammad 'Alī al-Ṣābūnī), is that *Sāḥa* is the same in meaning as *Sayr* (to set out, to travel), as in Sūrah al-Hajj: "*Do they not travel through the land, so that their hearts (and minds) may thus learn wisdom and their ears may learn to hear...*" (22: 46). This means that by travelling around the earth they can reflect on the wonders created by Allah and gain insight and sagacity.

Mawlānā Amīn Aḥsan Iṣlāhī gives an extensive note on this word. This is the summary of what he has to say:

> It was the practice in many religions that in order to achieve complete devotion to God people used to leave their families and homes and spend all their time in seclusion and meditation, living a life of self-denial and poverty. In Christianity there are monks, in Buddhism there are *bhakshus* and in Hinduism there are *jogīs* and *sanyāsīs*. They used to go from one place to another and exist on charity and live an austere life. Islam prohibited monasticism as it is against human nature. However, it has permitted its aspects that relate to abstinence, *Tawakkul* (reliance on Allah), *Dhikr* and reflection, acquisition of knowledge, *Da'wah*, and *Jihād*; and for this purpose travelling around the world comes under the term *Sā'iḥ*.
>
> (*Tadabbur-i-Qur'ān*, vol. 2, p. 240)

Taking all these meanings and interpretations, the word *Sā'iḥ* includes all those efforts in which a person exerts oneself in the cause of Allah, be it travel for acquiring knowledge, or conveying *Da'wah*, taking part in *Jihād* as well as fasting, abstinence and self-denial.

References

Siyāḥah: 9: 2 and 112; 66: 5.

Sū' [سوء] (Evil)

Meaning

Sū' means to be or to become bad, evil or wicked. Imām al-Rāghib says: "Anything which causes grief is called *Sū'* whether it relates to worldly affairs or those of the Hereafter." The grief may be psychological or physical in origin. For example it could be due to loss of prestige or position or death of some near relations. The word *Sū'* is used in several different meanings as follows.

It is commonly used for sinful and evil acts. "*Whoever works evil, will be requited accordingly*" (al-Nisā' 4: 123). "*The evil of their actions seems pleasing to them*" (al-Tawbah 9: 37) and "*Allah accepts the repentance of those who do evil in ignorance and repent soon afterwards...*" (al-Nisā' 4: 17).

One of the miracles given to the Prophet Mūsā (peace be upon him) was that when he pressed his hand to his side it turned shining white and this was not due to any disease. The word *Sū'* is used for disease or stain (Ṭā Hā 20: 22).

Sū' is also used for physical or material loss or harm. "*And they returned with grace and bounty from Allah. No harm ever touched them*" (Āl 'Imrān 3: 174).

Other Words from the Same Root

Sā'a means to do evil, be evil or wretched. It is frequently used as an expression of abhorrence or disgust: as in Sūrah al-Nisā' (4: 22) for marrying one's widowed mother, or in Sūrah al-Isrā' (17: 32) for committing adultery. Its feminine form *Sā'at* has a similar usage: as in Sūrah al-Nisā' (4: 97) where *Jahannam* is described as an evil refuge, or in Sūrah al-Kahf (18: 29) where it is said to be a vile resort.

Sayyi'ah (pl. *Sayyi'āt*) means sin, offence or misdeed. It is the opposite of *Ḥasanah* (pl. *Ḥasanāt*) which means good deed, benefaction or merit. These two words are often used together in the Qur'ān to show the contrast in their meanings and their results. "*For those things that are good* (Ḥasanāt) *remove those that are evil* (Sayyi'āt)" (Hūd 11: 114) and "*We tried them with (both) good and evil in order that they might turn (to Us)"* (al-A'rāf 7: 168).

In addition to bad deeds and ill manners and false beliefs, the word *Sayyi'ah* encompasses misguidance as well as hardships, calamities and suffering either in this world or in the Hereafter. All the meanings of the word *Sayyi'āt* are conveyed in this verse of Sūrah Ghāfir: "*And guard them against evil. And whom You protect from evil on that Day – on them You have bestowed mercy indeed and that will be truly (for them) the highest achievement*" (40: 9).

References

Sū': 2: 169; 9: 37; 12: 24; 16: 119; 26: 156. *Sā'a*: 4: 22; 6: 31; 17: 32; 29: 4; 45: 21. *Sayyi'ah*: 4: 78; 7: 95; 13: 6; 23: 96; 28: 84.

Sunnah [سنّة] (Norm)

Meaning

Sunnah (pl. *Sunan*) literally means a clear way, well-trodden path, or a levelled path; from this it has come to mean tradition, custom, habitual practice, customary procedure or action, norm, or usage.

Allah's *Sunnah*

Allah's *Sunnah* means those principles and laws under which Allah deals with people and either rewards or punishes them according to their deeds. These laws are immutable and permanent. This is emphasized several times in the Qur'ān. "*You will never find any change in Allah's* Sunnah *and you will never find any alteration in Allah's* Sunnah" (Fāṭir 35: 43).

For the guidance of the human race, Allah in His infinite mercy has sent down prophets throughout the ages. They invited their people to obey Allah's commands and follow the path of guidance. Invariably the prophets were ridiculed and their message was rejected. This is termed *Sunnat al-Awwalīn* (the ways of the earlier nations) (al-Anfāl 8: 38; al-Ḥijr 15: 13; Fāṭir 35: 43).

After the rejection of one of His messengers, it was Allah's *Sunnah* to punish the offending nation. This punishment could be by some natural disaster, such as meted out to the People of Nūḥ, 'Ād, Thamūd and Lūṭ or it could be by inflicting defeat by the believers (al-Aḥzāb 33: 62–63; al-Fatḥ 48: 22–23).

The Qur'ān contains many laws which Allah has elucidated. They inform human beings how Allah deals with any particular situation.

The Prophet's *Sunnah*

The word *Sunnah* on its own is exclusively used to denote the practice of the Prophet (peace be upon him). Thus, *Sunnah* is the second most important source of the *Sharī'ah*. Both the Qur'ānic text and the practice of the Prophet (*Sunnah*) are continuously preserved by the *Ummah*. The Prophet (peace be upon him) said: "It is obligatory on you to follow my *Sunnah* and the *Sunnah* of my Rightly-Guided *Khulafā'* (successors)" (Abū Dāwūd and Tirmidhī).

References

Sunnah: 3: 137; 8: 38; 17: 77; 35: 43; 48: 23.

Ṭā'ah [طاعة]

see *al-Sam' wa al-Ṭā'ah*

Ṭab' [طبع]

see *Khatm*

Tabdhīr [تبذير]

see *Isrāf*

Ṭāghūt [طاغوت]

Meaning

Ṭaghā means to exceed the proper bounds, overstep the limits, be excessive. Hence, when water overflows and inundates the banks this flooding is called *Ṭughyān*; this word is used metaphorically for tyranny, oppression and repression. *Ṭāghūt* from this root means the one who transgressed from the bounds of obedience to and worship of Allah and rebelled against Him, i.e. Satan. Its meaning was further enlarged to mean anyone or anything worshipped besides Allah, be it an idol, or a false god. *Ṭāghūt*, which is the singular form, sometimes has a plural significance, and then it means idols, demons, or whatever is worshipped besides Allah.

Analysis

There are three stages of disobedience of Allah. In the first, a person, although accepting the lordship of Allah, disobeys His laws. This is called *Fisq*. In the second, one may abandon and arrogate to himself self-sufficiency or start worshipping others. This is called *Kufr*. Finally, one rebels against Allah and assumes power and compels others to obey him or worship him. This is *Ṭughyān*.

One cannot be a believer unless one repudiates the *ṭāghūt*. "*Whoever rejects* ṭāghūt *and believes in Allah has grasped the most trustworthy handhold that never breaks*" (al-Baqarah 2: 256). It is further explained that whereas Allah leads the believers from darkness unto light; "*those who reject faith are the patrons of the* ṭāghūt *who will lead them forth from light into the depths of darkness*" (2: 257).

Ṭāghiyah

This word is used in the Qur'ān to indicate the punishment that Allah metes out to those nations that transgress the limits and rebel openly against Him. Allah makes use of forces of nature that are there to serve humanity but makes them rebel: and thus storms, thunder and lightning of extreme severity are inflicted on transgressing nations. So when Thamūd rejected their Prophet Ṣāliḥ (peace be upon him), "*They were destroyed by* ṭāghiyah *(a terrible storm of thunder and lightning)*" (al-Ḥāqqah 69: 5).

References

Ṭāghūt: 2: 256; 4: 60 and 76; 5: 60; 39: 17.

Ṭahārah [طهارة] (Cleanliness)

Meaning

Ṭahara means to be clean or pure and the noun *Ṭahārah* means cleanliness or purity as well as chastity or sanctity. The word *Ṭahārah* does not appear in the Qur'ān, but, its various derivatives in verbal form are frequently used both for physical cleanliness and spiritual purification.

Physical Cleanliness

One of the most important and basic Islamic teachings is *ṭahārah* and *naẓāfah* – both mean purification and cleanliness. One has to be in the state of purity before offering prayers. There are two types of impurities that need acts of cleaning. Major impurity is caused by sexual intercourse or nocturnal emission. For the purpose of purification one needs a ritual bath (*Ghusl* – literally to wash) (al-Nisā' 4: 43). Minor impurity is caused by natural bodily functions, and for this one needs to perform *Wuḍū'* (minor ritual ablution). *Wuḍū'*, derived from the verb *Waḍā'ah*, means to be pure or to be clean, and *Wuḍū'* means purity and cleanliness. This is necessary before offering prayers (al-Mā'idah 5: 6). The word *Wuḍū'* and its verbal forms appear in *Ḥadīth* literature but do not appear in the Qur'ān.

The purpose of physical cleanliness is that one becomes fresh and ready to receive spiritual purification. In case one cannot find water or there is a shortage of water and there is not enough to perform *Ghusl* or *Wuḍū'*, one can purify oneself by *Tayammum* (dry ablution). *Tayammum* literally means to intend, to approach, or to aim at something. Thus, it means that if you do not find water then aim for clean dust with the intention of purifying yourself. *Tayammum* involves using clean dust and rubbing it lightly over one's face and both hands. Although *Tayammum* cannot purify one like water, its purpose is to keep the sense of *Ṭahārah* ingrained in one's consciousness. This is because Allah does not want to cause hardship but wants to make the believers clean and to complete His favour to them (al-Mā'idah 5: 6). Once water is available the concession of *tayammum* is finished.

Spiritual Purification

Muṭahhar (pure, immaculate) is used to indicate spiritual loftiness and exalted position. "*Behold! The angel said: 'O Maryam! Allah has chosen you and purified you – chosen you above the women of all nations*" (Āl 'Imrān 3: 42). Similarly it is said about the wives of the Prophet (peace be upon him) that Allah wants "*to make you pure and spotless*" (al-Aḥzāb 33: 32). The companions of the believers in *Jannah* are described as pure and holy (al-Baqarah 2: 25; Āl 'Imrān 3: 15; al-Nisā' 4: 57).

The Qur'ān is also called *Muṭahharah* (pure and holy) in Sūrah 'Abasa (80: 14) and in Sūrah al-Bayyinah (98: 2).

The Importance of *Ṭahārah*

In Islam there is great stress on cleanliness and purity. As one is required to pray five times during the day, a believer should try to remain in a state of purity. There is a *ḥadīth* in which the Prophet (peace be upon him) stated: "Purification is half of the faith" (Muslim). As ablution is a prerequisite of prayers, it not only removes external impurities but also prepares one to receive spiritual blessings by purification of one's heart. Imām al-Ghazālī states that when a person makes the testimony of faith, he has completed half of the faith. When he cleanses his heart, he has completed the other half.

References

Ṭahārah: 3: 42; 8: 11; 22: 26; 74: 4; 76: 21. *Muṭahhar*: 2: 25; 9: 108; 56: 79; 80: 14; 98: 2.

Taḥrīf [تحريف] (Corruption)

Meaning

Ḥarrafa means to slant, to incline, to bend off, to deflect, or to distort or corrupt. *Taḥrīf* means alteration, change, distortion, corruption or perversion. The word *Taḥrīf* is used only in its verbal form in the Qur'ān.

Analysis

The word *Taḥrīf* is used for distortion of either the words or the meanings of the Divine Scriptures. There are many ways in which *Taḥrīf* was attempted by *Ahl al-Kitāb* (the People of the Book), particularly the Jews. The Qur'ān gives examples of both types of distortion.

Distortion of the Words

After conquering a town, the Jews were commanded by Allah to enter it not with arrogance but in humility chanting '*Ḥiṭṭah*' signifying repentance. "*But the transgressors changed the word from that which had been given them*" (al-Baqarah 2: 59; al-A'rāf 7: 161).

In order to mock the Prophet (peace be upon him), the Jews of Madīnah twisted an ordinary word like *Rā'inā* meaning "please attend to us". By pronouncing it with a twist of the tongue, they suggested an insulting meaning: "O our shepherd!" Muslims were asked to avoid using this word and were instead asked to use another word of respect when addressing the Prophet (peace be upon him) (al-Baqarah 2: 104; al-Nisā' 4: 46).

Distortion of the Meanings

The Jews were indicted for distorting the Scriptures' meanings in order to misinterpret them. When they came across any word that went against their interest and belief, they distorted the meaning deliberately. "*There is among them a section who distort the Book with their tongues: (As they read), you would think it is part of the Book, but it is not part of the Book, and they say 'That is from Allah,' but it is not from Allah. It is they who tell a lie against Allah, and (well) they know it!*" (Āl 'Imrān 3: 78).

Another form of distortion attempted by *Ahl al-Kitāb* was to cover up in their Scriptures certain things which the Qur'ān has revealed (al-Mā'idah 5: 15). One such incident is the prophecy given by the Prophet 'Īsā (peace be upon him). He gave tidings of the coming of a Messenger after him named Aḥmad (al-Ṣaff 61: 6). In the Greek Bible the word used for Aḥmad (meaning the Praised One) was *Periclyots* which conveyed the same meaning. However, Christian theologians changed it to *Paracletos* which in the English version is translated as "Comforter" (John 14: 16; 15: 26 and 16: 7). (Yūsuf 'Alī, p. 1461)

The Jews corrupted the names of *Marwah* (a place in Makkah where the Prophet Ibrāhīm offered the sacrifice of his son) and *Bakkah* (another name for Makkah) into *Mowrah* or *Morya* and Valley of Buka respectively in the Old Testament, in order to obliterate all connections of the Prophet Ibrāhīm (peace be upon him) with Makkah. (*Tadabbur-i-Qur'ān*, Vol. 7, pp. 360–361)

References

Taḥrīf: 2: 75; 4: 46; 5: 13 and 41.

Ṭalāq [طلاق] (Divorce)

Meaning

Ṭalaqa means to leave, to forsake to set free or to release. *Ṭallaqa* from this root means to grant a divorce; *Ṭalāq* means divorce.

General

In Islam *Ṭalāq* is not considered to be a desirable act. The Prophet (peace be upon him) said that the most hateful thing among the permissible acts in the sight of Allah is *Ṭalāq*.

However, despite the initial existence of a close and loving relationship between spouses, disputes and friction can sometimes occur. Such is human nature. Islam tries to solve this by providing a system of reconciliation through impartial arbitrators from the two families (al-Nisā' 4: 35). Their efforts should help to resolve the problem within both families. Sometimes even this may not succeed and then the only solution is the dissolution of marriage. There is provision for divorce and for remarriage of both spouses after their separation. However, the divorced woman has to wait for three monthly periods before remarrying (al-Baqarah 2: 228). This waiting period is called *'Iddah*. The reason is to ascertain the paternity of any child born after divorce.

The Procedure for Divorce

Islam has reformed the pre-Islamic tradition of divorce where a person could pronounce *Ṭalāq* and then repudiate it any number of times. A cooling-off period is provided so that the parties if acting hastily can think again before separation. Two divorces (with the prospect of reconciliation in between) are allowed to each couple. After that, the parties should make up their minds either to stay together or to part amicably (al-Baqarah 2: 229). After the third divorce a person "*cannot…remarry (his wife) until after she (has) married another husband and he has divorced her*" (al-Baqarah 2: 230).

Khul'

Under Islamic law a woman can demand a separation: this is called *Khul'*. The wife has to agree to make some payment to the husband to release her from the marriage bond (al-Baqarah 2: 229). This procedure can only be undertaken in a court of law.

Other Forms of *Ṭalāq*

In pre-Islamic Arabia a pagan system of divorce was prevalent called *Ẓihār*. If a man told his wife, "you are to me as the back (*Ẓahr*) of my mother", by the pagan custom this amounted to divorce. By equating his wife with his mother it is implied that there cannot be any conjugal relations between them. This custom was reformed by Islam, and the husband if he wants to resume conjugal relations must make an atonement of freeing a slave or fasting for two months consecutively (al-Mujādilah 58: 2–4).

Another similar pagan system very unfair to women was called *Īlā'*. Sometimes in a fit of anger a man would take an oath that he would not have marital relations with his wife. The position of the wife was precarious as she was in such a case neither divorced nor married. The Qur'ān allowed a period of four months for the husband to reconsider the decision and see if the resumption of the marriage would be possible. If not, after that the parties would be separated by a divorce (al-Baqarah 2: 226).

References

Ṭalāq: 2: 227 and 229; 33: 49; 65: 1; 66: 5. *Ẓihār*: 58: 2 and 3. *Īlā'*: 2: 226.

Taqdīr [تقدير]

see *Qadar*

Taqwā [تقوىٰ] (God-consciousness)

Meanings

Waqā means to guard, to protect, to preserve, to shield, and to keep one safe from some harm. In Qur'ānic terminology it is that state of the heart that gives certainty of the presence of Allah at all times, thus differentiating between good and evil and disposing one towards good and creating hatred of evil. It is best translated as God-consciousness. This consciousness requires that one should constantly seek to be protected from Allah's anger and punishment and this comes from His fear. Thus, *taqwā* is often translated as fear of Allah, but God-consciousness is a better translation.

Taqwā is used in several different meanings in the Qur'ān:

1. to protect oneself from harmful things (al-Muzzammil 73 : 17).
2. to be aware of and to be on guard against disasters (al-Anfāl 8: 25).
3. to be fearful of Allah Who rewards and punishes His servants (al-Zumar 39: 73).
4. to combine all three meanings. Thus, being fearful of the result of evil deeds (Āl 'Imrān 3: 179).

The Concept of *Taqwā*

The real place of *Taqwā* is the heart, as mentioned both in the Qur'ān and *aḥādīth*. In Sūrah al-Ḥajj, it is said: "*Whoever holds in honour the symbols of Allah (in the sacrifice of animals), such (honour) should truly come from* Taqwā *of heart*" (22: 32). In a *ḥadīth* reported by Abū Hurayrah, the Prophet (peace be upon him) said: "*Taqwā* is right here" and he pointed to his chest three times (Muslim).

Deeper study of the Qur'ān shows that *Taqwā* is the purpose of all *'Ibādah* whether it is *Ṣalāh, Zakāh,* Fasting, *Ḥajj* or the sacrifice of animals. The following verses indicate this: it is Sūrah al-Baqarah, verse 177 that enumerates many righteous deeds of the Truthful (*Ṣādiqīn*) and of the God-fearing (*Muttaqīn*). In this list are "*those who establish Prayer and practise regular charity* (Zakāh)". In the same *sūrah*, verse 197 states: "*And take provision (with you) for the journey (of the* Ḥajj*), but the best provision is* Taqwā" (al-Baqarah 2: 197). In Sūrah al-Ḥajj Allah says: "*It is neither their meat nor their blood that reaches Allah: it is your* taqwā *that reaches Him*" (22: 37). Similarly, in all other aspects of our lives *taqwā* is required. In our dress, in retribution or in administering justice, in all we do, God-consciousness is required. Even Guidance from the Qur'ān is for those who are *Muttaqīn* (al-Baqarah 2: 2). Thus, the first call of all prophets was: "*I am to you a Messenger worthy of all trust. So fear Allah and obey me*" (al-Shu'arā' 26: 125–126).

Taqwā is the key resource for receiving help from Allah in this world. "*For whoever has* taqwā *of Allah, He makes matters easy for him.*" (al-Ṭalāq 65: 4) And in the Hereafter it is only those who are *Muttaqīn* (people of *Taqwā*) will attain the good end (Paradise). (Ṭā Hā 20: 132)

In Sūrah Āl 'Imrān it is said: "*O you who believe! Have* taqwā *of Allah as is His right to have* Taqwā" (3: 102). What is Allah's right of *Taqwā*? This is explained in a *ḥadīth* narrated by 'Abdullāh ibn Mas'ūd, who said that the Prophet (peace be upon him) has said: "The Right of *Taqwā* is the obedience of Allah in all affairs and nothing should be done against His obedience. One should always remember Allah and never forget Him. One should always be thankful to Allah and never be ungrateful." The other verse in Sūrah al-Taghābun states: "*Have* Taqwā *of Allah as much as you can*" (64: 16). According to 'Abdullāh ibn 'Abbās, this is the explanation of the verse in Sūrah Āl 'Imrān as narrated above. It means one should have *Taqwā* of Allah as much as humanly possible. This is what is meant by right of *Taqwā.*

References

Taqwā: 2: 197; 5: 8; 7: 26; 9: 109; 49: 3.

Tasbīḥ [تسبيح] (Glorification)

Meanings

Sabaḥa means to swim in water or to float in air quickly. In this sense it is applied metaphorically for movement of stars and planets in space. "*It is He Who created the night and the day and the sun and the moon; all (the celestial bodies) float along, each in its rounded course*" (al-Anbiyā' 21: 33).

Sabaḥa is also used to denote moving quickly or gliding along; as in Sūrah al-Nāzi'āt (79: 3) this term was used for the angels.

Sabbaḥā (a second verb form) means to praise; the word *Tasbīḥ* from this root means to declare that Allah is above all imperfections, fallibilities and deficiencies as these are below the supreme dignity of Allah. In short it is the glorification of Divine Being. When one is saying *Tasbīḥ* it also means that one is bowing down in humility before Allah. *Tasbīḥ* by action means one is surrendering oneself before the injunctions of Allah.

Tasbīḥ as a Universal Obligation

It is mentioned frequently in the Qur'ān that "*Whatever is in the heavens and on earth does declare the praise and glory* (Tasbīḥ) *of Allah*" (al-Jumu'ah 62: 1). This means that in this universe – either living or inanimate every thing is engaged in praise of the Almighty Allah. Of course this is beyond human perception and awareness. "*The seven heavens and the earth and all beings therein declare His glory. There is nothing but celebrates His praise and yet you understand not how they declare His glory!*" (al-Isrā' 17: 44).

The oral declaration of *Tasbīḥ* is to say "*Subḥān Allāh*" which means that Allah is pure and above all imperfections. This phrase is incorporated in the expressions of praise and glory in *Rukū'* and *Sujūd* (bowing down and prostrations) in the *Ṣalāh*. The declaration of *Tasbīḥ* is usually accompanied by *Ḥamd* (praise) and *Taqdīs* (sanctification) so as to include the positive aspects of Allah's virtues; this is because *Tasbīḥ* has the overwhelming aspect of negation of all imperfections. When one declares that Allah is above all shortcomings then He should also be praised and thanked for all His benefactions.

The reasons for mentioning that everything in the universe is proclaiming Allah's glory and praise are threefold:

1. If a human being also engages in praising and glorifying Allah, then he will be in harmony with the rest of the universe and will attain inner peace. This gives satisfaction of heart.
2. It helps to keep up the morale of the believers that they are not alone in performing this *Tasbīḥ* but part of the entire universe.
3. It explains to non-believers that Allah is not dependent on them. On the contrary they themselves are the losers by neglecting their obligation.

The Difference between *Sabbaḥa* and *Yusabbiḥu*

Sabbaḥa is the past tense, signifying that the act of *Tasbīḥ* has taken place and it is a statement of fact. *Yusabbiḥu* covers both present and future, explaining that the act of *Tasbīḥ* is continuously being done. In this way both terms together span the whole period of time, while space is already covered by the declaration that everything in the universe is engaged in Allah's *Tasbīḥ*.

References

Tasbīḥ: 17: 44; 24: 41; 48: 9; 57: 1; 68: 28.

Taswiyah [تسوية]

see *Istiwā'*

Tawakkul [توكّل] (Trust)

Meaning

Wakkala means to entrust to someone, to authorize, to empower or to appoint someone as representative. *Tawakkul* from this root means trust or confidence. It is used for trust in Allah.

The essence of this reliance on Allah means that one should have complete faith in Allah's guidance. It means that the *Sharīʿah* which He has ordained and all the laws which one is required to obey are for the benefit of human beings. *Tawakkul* also requires that one should not rely on one's own abilities and endeavours but exclusively put faith in Allah's help and support. One should have absolute conviction and confidence that whatever promises Allah has made to the believers will definitely be fulfilled. In this way one should leave the result with Allah and have faith in Him that the result will be favourable.

Tawakkul in Allah and Human Prudence

Although *Tawakkul* requires one to rely on Allah, this does not mean that one should not make any effort to achieve the desired result. It is incumbent upon human beings to make all possible efforts yet not to rely solely on them but instead to have *Tawakkul* in Allah that the efforts will be fruitful. This is illustrated by the advice of the Prophet (peace be upon him) which he gave to a person who asked him: "Should I tie the rope of the camel or leave it alone and have *Tawakkul* in Allah (that the camel will be safe)?" The Prophet (peace be upon him) said: "Tie the camel and have *Tawakkul* in Allah" (Tirmidhī).

The same was the case when the Prophet Yaʿqūb (peace be upon him) sent his sons to Egypt as a precautionary measure, instructing them to enter from different gates of the city. However, he realized that his own precaution would only work if that was what Allah willed. He said: "*I cannot avail you against Allah at all. In Him do I put my trust and let all that trust put their trust in Him*" (Yūsuf 12: 67).

The Qur'ānic advice in this respect is that, in all affairs, believers should have mutual consultation (*Shūrā*) and then "*when a decision has been taken, put your trust in Allah for Allah loves those who put their trust in Him*" (Āl 'Imrān 3: 159).

Wakīl (Ally)

Wakīl (pl. *Wukalā'*) means a person in whom one puts one's trust, or to put someone in charge of one's affairs. Such a person assumes full responsibility for representing the interest of his clients. One of Allah's attributes is *al-Wakīl.* It means if one relies on Allah and leaves one's affairs to Him then "*Allah suffices and He is the best* Wakīl *(disposer of affairs)*" (Āl 'Imrān 3: 173; al-Nisā' 4: 81; al-Ṭalāq 65: 3).

The word *Wakīl* is used in the Qur'ān in the three following meanings: responsible or accountable "*We made you not one to watch over their doings nor are you an overseer unto them*" (al-An'ām 6: 107); Guardian or minder "*Such is Allah, Your Lord! There is no god but He, the Creator of everything; so worship Him. And He is of everything a Guardian*" (al-An'ām 6: 102); Guarantor or surety "*So let it be between me and you, whichever of the two terms I fulfil, it shall be no injustice to me; and Allah is surety of what we say*" (al-Qaṣaṣ 28: 28).

References

Tawakkul: 3: 159; 4: 81; 25: 58; 27: 79; 33: 48. *Wakīl*: 3: 173; 6: 102; 10: 108; 28: 28; 39: 62.

Tawbah [توبة] (Repentance)

Meaning

Tāba means to return, to incline, to be attentive, and the noun *Tawbah* means the act of returning to Allah. "*Truly I turn to You and truly do I bow (to You) in Islam*" (al-Aḥqāf 46: 15).

When the word *Tāba* is used with the preposition *'Alā*, it means turning towards someone with mercy; such as restoration of Allah's grace and His forgiveness: "*Allah turned with favour to the Prophet, the* Muhājirūn, *and the* Anṣār – *who followed him in distress...*" (al-Tawbah 9: 117). When *Tāba* is used with the preposition *Ilā* it means repentance and penitence. "*Seek you the forgiveness of your Lord and turn to Him in repentance*" (Hūd 11: 3).

Acceptance of *Tawbah*

Verses 17 and 18 of Sūrah al-Nisā' provide the basic guidelines on acceptance or non-acceptance of *Tawbah*. "*Allah accepts the repentance of those who do evil in ignorance and repent soon afterwards; to them will Allah turn in mercy; for Allah is full of knowledge and wisdom. Of no effect is the repentance of those who continue to do evil until death faces one of them...*" (4: 17–18).

When one commits a mistake or a sin usually one has a feeling of guilt or shame, and one regrets having done it. If this remorse and guilt are present then there is hope that one can reform oneself. When someone persistently keeps sinning without regret and remorse, all the avenues of reform are closed. The Prophet (peace be upon him) said: "Remorse is a kind of repentance" (Ibn Mājah).

Repentance after committing a sin and promising to oneself not to do it again means that a person has reverted to piety. When a person returns to piety, Allah also returns to him with His Mercy. When one feels remorseful and guilty after committing a sin one should repent and should have the determination to avoid sinning again. There should be sincerity in one's repentance. This is termed *Tawbatan Naṣūḥā*. "*O you who believe! Turn to Allah with sincere repentance*" (al-Taḥrīm 66: 8).

It is narrated that 'Alī ibn Abī Ṭālib (may Allah be pleased with him) saw a Bedouin repenting very hastily. He remarked that this is *Tawbat al-Kādhibīn* meaning a repentance of liars. That person then asked him what is proper repentance? 'Alī replied that there are six essential requirements of repentance. First, there should be remorse for whatever wrong you have done. Second, you should fulfil the obligation that you have neglected. Third, you should restore the rights of those you have usurped. Fourth, you should seek forgiveness from those you hurt. Fifth, you should be determined not to repeat your sin, and sixth, you should make your soul subservient to Allah's obedience. The pleasure you felt from sinning should be counterbalanced by real self-denial, so that your soul should suffer the pain of anguish (*Kashshāf*).

Words from the Same Root

Al-Tawwāb is one of the attributes of Allah. It means the One who again and again or repeatedly accepts the *tawbah* of His servants. "*He (Allah) is Oft-Returning and Most Merciful*" (al-Baqarah 2: 37).

The word *al-Tawwāb* is also used for those who always repent. "*Allah loves those who turn to Him constantly and those who keep themselves pure and clean*" (al-Baqarah 2: 222).

Matāb means acceptable conversion or return. "*And whosoever repents and does good has truly turned to Allah with an (acceptable) conversion*" (al-Furqān 25: 71). "*For those who believe and work righteousness, is (every) blessedness and a beautiful place of (final) return*" (al-Ra'd 13: 29).

References

Tawbah: 4: 17; 9: 104; 42: 25; 66: 8; 110: 3. *Al-Tawwāb*: 2: 37 and 160; 9: 104; 24: 10; 49: 12. *Matāb*: 13: 30; 25: 71.

Tawḥīd [توحيد]

see Allah

Tayammum [تيمّم]

see *Ṭahārah*

Tazkiyah [تزكية] (Purification)

Meaning

Zakā means to grow, to thrive, to increase, as well as to be pure or purified. Hence, the word *Tazkiyah* from this verb carries the meanings of 'purifying' and of 'facilitating growth'. They are interrelated in that what is free of impurity, corruption and evil is bound to flourish naturally. In Qur'ānic terminology, it means purification of a person's heart and his actions. *Tazkiyah* is a comprehensive term and encompasses both the intellect and the actions as well as the physical and inner self which stimulates the spiritual instincts. Although it often refers to the purification of an individual, it also has social and communal dimensions.

The Importance of *Tazkiyah*

The purification of mankind is one of the important objectives for which the Messengers were sent. This is explicit in the Qur'ānic account of the objectives of the Prophet's (peace be upon him) mission: "*It is He Who sent among the unlettered ones a Messenger from among themselves, reciting to them His verse, purifying them, and teaching them the Book and wisdom. And they had been before in manifest error*" (al-Jumu'ah 62: 2). Similar verses, with minor variations in wording, occur in other places in the Qur'ān, highlighting the importance of self-purification (al-Baqarah 2: 129 and 151; Āl 'Imrān 3: 164). The purification accomplished by the Messengers of Allah carried both elements of *Tazkiyah*. The Messengers purged people's hearts of evil, especially their immoral acts, and also they helped their moral sense to blossom and develop.

A person's abiding success consists in his exercising self-restraint, especially control over his base desires and pursuing the way of goodness and virtue: "*Indeed he succeeds who purifies his own self. And indeed he fails who corrupts his own self*" (al-Shams 91: 9–10). Almost the same truth features in another Qur'ānic verse: "*He attains success who purifies himself*" (al-A'lā 87: 14). Thus, a person's deliverance and success are contingent upon his self-purification (*Tazkiyah*).

The attainment of *Tazkiyah* depends solely on the mercy of Allah. It is granted to those who sincerely ask for and work for its attainment. "*Have you not seen those who claim purification for themselves? Nay – but Allah does purify whom He pleases*" (al-Nisā' 4: 49). The task of *Tazkiyah* was given by Allah to His prophets as stated above.

The word *Zakāh* also comes from the same root; its purpose too is to purify: "*Of their goods take alms so that you might purify and sanctify them*" (al-Tawbah 9: 103).

The Sufi Concept of *Tazkiyah*

Tazkiyah as understood by mystics and Sufis signifies self-purification from all bad traits and habits, and devotion to the worship of Allah, as well as not immersing oneself in worldly affairs to such an extent that it makes one oblivious of one's accountability to Allah. Thus one tries to lead a pious life in order to achieve gnosis or a degree of union with God.

However, according to the Qur'ān and the *Sunnah*, it is not piety to run away from the problems of life, nor is this the attainment of union with Allah. Worldly success is also desirable but felicity in the Hereafter is the final goal. Obedience to Allah and His Messenger (peace be upon him) in all the affairs of one's life is the zenith of self-purification. It demands spiritual development but also entails that one tries to lead a balanced life, looking after one's family, reforming society and being an active and sincere citizen.

References

Tazkiyah: 2: 129; 3: 77; 53: 32; 87: 14; 91: 9.

Thawāb [ثواب] (Reward)

Meaning

Thāba means to return, to come back to its original condition; it also conveys the meaning to reward, to repay and to requite for one's good deeds. Hence, *Thawāb* means that reward, recompense or requital that one gets for one's deeds. The word, though including both recompense for good or bad deeds, is mostly used for the reward for good deeds that Allah gives to His servants. "*And admit them into* Jannah *with rivers flowing beneath – a reward from the presence of Allah and from His presence is the best reward*" (Āl 'Imrān 3: 195). However, this word is sometimes used for punishment as well: "*Have not the unbelievers been paid back for what they did?*" (al-Muṭaffifīn 83: 36).

The *Thawāb* by Allah can be given in this world as well as in the Hereafter (Āl 'Imrān 3: 148). However, from the Islamic point of view it is crucial that one's intention be focused on the reward in the Hereafter; and what one receives in this world is an added bounty from Allah.

Synonym and Antonym

The word *Jazā'* also means to recompense, to requite, to reward or to repay. Unlike *Thawāb* it is neutral in its meaning and can be used for both a good or a bad reward. Recompense for actions is the basic Qur'ānic theme which is emphasized repeatedly. This recompense can be awarded in this world. "*The recompense for an injury is an injury equal thereto (in degree)...*" (al-Shūrā 42: 40). However, the final recompense will surely be in the Hereafter. "*On that Day people will proceed in groups sorted out, to be shown the deeds that they (had done). Then shall anyone who has done an atom's weight of good, see it! And anyone who has done an atom's weight of evil, will see it*" (al-Zalzalah 99: 6–8). *'Adhāb* means Divine punishment and is the opposite of *Thawāb.*

See also *'Adhāb*

Words from the Same Root

Thawb (pl. *Thiyāb* or *Athwāb*) means garment, dress or cloth material (al-Muddaththir 74: 4). The reason for this meaning is given by Imām al-Rāghib. He says: "As the purpose of spinning cotton is to make cloth, the cotton reverts to its ultimate purpose by becoming a cloth."

Mathūbah also means requital, recompense or reward. "*If they had kept their faith and guarded themselves from evil, far better had been the reward from their Lord, if they but knew*" (al-Baqarah 2: 103).

Mathābah means a place to which one returns, or resorts, or a rendezvous. Hence, Ka'bah is referred to as a *Mathābah* so that people should assemble there (al-Baqarah 2: 125).

References

Thawāb: 3: 145; 4: 134; 18: 31; 19: 76; 28: 80. *Jazā'*: 2: 85; 5: 29; 10: 27; 18: 88; 41: 28. *Thawb*: 18: 31; 22: 19; 71: 7; 74: 4; 76: 21. *Mathūbah*: 2: 103. *Mathābah*: 2: 125.

Tilāwah [تلاوة] (Recitation)

Meaning

Talā and *Tulūw* means to follow, to succeed, to ensue, to declare, and to meditate. In this sense the word is used for the moon following the sun (al-Shams 91: 2). *Tilāwah,* from this root, means recitation or reading, as one word follows another while reading. But reading is the secondary meaning of *Tilāwah*; the primary meaning is to follow. Hence, the word is never used in the ordinary meaning of reading: for example, reading a letter or a book. It is used exclusively for reading of the Qur'ān as it implies that one is following its commands as well.

The Mode of *Tilāwah*

Often recitation of the Qur'ān is performed without any real understanding. Usually by recitation (*Tilāwah*) it is meant that one is merely reading without using the faculty of one's heart and mind. The Qur'ān emphasizes the appropriate manner of *Tilāwah* as: "*Those to whom We have given the Book, they recite it as it ought to be recited, they are the ones who believe in it*" (al-Baqarah 2: 121). Here *Tilāwah* means to follow, not just to read: to abide closely with and go in pursuit, to take it as a guide and to accept its authority. So, when one reads, one should try to understand, follow, and act upon its Guidance. Thus, *Tilāwah* involves one's whole personality – soul, heart, mind, tongue and body. This is graphically illustrated in the Qur'ān: "*For believers are those who, when Allah's name is mentioned, their hearts quake, and when His verses are recited to them their faith grows, and who put their trust in their Lord*" (al-Anfāl 8: 2). "*Allah has revealed the best discourse in the form of a Book, consistent with itself, oft-repeating whereat shiver the skins of those who fear their Lord; then their skins and hearts soften to the remembrance of Allah*" (al-Zumar 39: 23).

In summary, *Tilāwah* means the recitation of the Qur'ān with understanding and with the intention of following it. In this way one can claim to have proper faith in it. Thus, *tilāwah* has practical implications whereas the *Qirā'ah* is mere reading of something.

One of the important functions of Allah's Messengers was to recite and teach the Book of Allah. "*And recite (and teach) what has been revealed to you of the Book of Your Lord*" (al-Kahf 18: 27; al-'Ankabūt 29: 45).

Synonyms

Qirā'ah means recitation and reading. It is also used for the manner of recitation, punctuation and vocalization of the Qur'ānic text. This word comes from *Qara'a* which means to read or to recite. The first revelation to the Prophet (peace be upon him) started with the command *Iqra'* (read), and he was instructed to "*read from the Qur'ān as much as may be easy for you*" (al-Muzzammil 73: 20). The word Qur'ān also comes from the same root.

Ratila means to compose in an elegant, well-ordered and neat manner. From this root *Tartīl* means the recitation of the Qur'ān in slow, measured rhythmic tones (al-Muzzammil 73: 4; al-Furqān 25: 32). *Tartīl* is also a technical term of *'Ilm al-Tajwīd* (the science of Qur'ānic recitation) indicating slow reading and reflection.

References

Tilāwah: 2: 121; 19: 58; 31: 7; 62: 2; 98: 2. *Qirā'ah*: 7: 204; 16: 98; 17: 45; 75: 18; 96: 1. *Tartīl*: 25: 32; 73: 4.

Ukhuwwah [أُخُوَّة] (Brotherhood)

Meaning

Akh (pl. *Ikhwah*, *Ikhwān*) means brother. It is also used for a friend, companion or neighbour. *Ākhā* means to fraternize, to associate as brothers; *Ukhuwwah* means brotherhood or fraternity.

The Duties of Brotherhood

As the Declaration of Faith (*Kalimah*) creates a believer's relationship with Allah it also establishes a bond of brotherhood among those sharing this faith. Thus, Allah has decreed that "*The believers are but a single brotherhood*" (al-Ḥujurāt 49: 10). The basis of this brotherhood is mutual love, respect, sincerity, trust and mercy.

This brotherhood in faith is the greatest social ideal which Islam has achieved among the warring tribes and by unifying them. The establishment of a bond of brotherhood by the Prophet (peace be upon him) between the *Muhājirūn* (immigrants) from Makkah and *Anṣār* (helpers) of Madīnah is the best example of this *Ukhuwwah*. One *Muhājir* was made a brother of one *Anṣār*; thereby they shared the same house and lived together like real brothers. "*Those who believe and adopt exile, and fight for the faith with their property and their persons, in the cause of Allah, as well as those who gave (them) asylum and aid – these are (all) friends and protectors of one another*" (al-Anfāl 8: 72).

Of course this bond does not establish legal rights and obligations such as the right of inheritance. However, the duties of brotherhood demand sincerity, willingness to sacrifice, the giving of preference to others, and readiness to forgive. Only with such qualities can hearts be bonded with eternal love.

On occasions where there is disagreement or dispute (even war) between two Muslim groups, it is not permissible to remain neutral. It is the duty of other Muslims to arbitrate between the warring factions and support the one whose rights are denied (al-Ḥujurāt 49: 9).

The prophets are the best well-wishers of their communities, and as they grew up in their own societies they are referred to as brothers of their people. "*To the 'Ād people (We sent) Hūd, one of their (own) brothers*" (al-A'rāf 7: 65). The same is said of Ṣāliḥ and Shu'ayb (al-A'rāf 7: 73 and 85). It means that the prophets are as much concerned for the well-being and welfare of people as their real brothers.

References

Ukhuwwah: 2: 220; 3: 103; 9: 11; 49: 10; 59: 10.

Ummah [أُمَّة] (People)

Meaning

Ummah (pl. *Umam*) means nation, people or generation. It is used for a group of people who are related by a common creed or geographical or natural affinity, whether voluntarily or involuntarily. The word is not restricted to human beings but is used in relation to other species. "*There is not an animal (that lives) on the earth, nor a being that flies on its wings, but (forms part of) communities like you*" (al-An'ām 6: 38).

The word *Ummah* is also used in the Qur'ān to mean a definite period or term (Hūd 11: 8; Yūsuf 12: 45).

Analysis

The human race is descended from the progeny of one pair of male and female (the Prophet Ādam and Ḥawwā' – peace be upon them). Hence, the Qur'ān declares: "*Mankind was one single* Ummah *(nation)*" (al-Baqarah 2: 213). Later, as the population grew, people were divided "*into nations and tribes that they may know each other. Verily the most honoured of you in the sight of Allah is (one who is) the most righteous of you*" (al-Ḥujurāt 49: 13). This was Allah's plan and in His wisdom He divided people into different races, languages and different physical features. "*He would have made you a single people but (His plan is) to test you in what He has given you; so strive as in a race in all virtues*" (al-Mā'idah 5: 48). In order that Allah's message should reach all nations "*To every* ummah *(was sent) a Messenger*" (Yūnus 10: 47). All the Messengers brought the same message from Allah, and all those who accepted this message constituted the *Ummah* of the Messenger. They followed his teachings even after his death. Allah designated this *Ummah* as Muslims. This is mentioned in the Prophet Ibrāhīm's prayer (al-Baqarah 2: 128) as well as in Sūrah al-Ḥajj (22: 78).

The Muslim *Ummah*

Before the advent of the Prophet Muḥammad (peace be upon him), Banū Isrā'īl were the *Ummah* entrusted to convey Allah's message to all mankind. As they failed in this duty, the *Ummah* of the Prophet Muḥammad (peace be upon him) was given this honour. This was signified by the change of the *Qiblah* from *Bayt al-Maqdis*, Jerusalem to *Bayt Allāh* (the Ka'bah in Makkah). After mentioning this change of the *Qiblah* Allah says: "*Thus have We made of you an* Ummah *justly balanced, that you might be a witness over the nations and the Messenger a witness over yourselves; and We appointed the* Qiblah *to which you were used to*" (al-Baqarah 2: 143). The phrase 'justly balanced' (*Wasaṭ*) implies the essence of Islam as a median community, avoiding all extravagances on either side and remaining sober and moderate; establishing justice and equity, and thus leading the whole of mankind to the middle path of justice and peace.

It is on account of the leading role that Muslims are required to play that this *Ummah* is called "*Khayr Ummah*" – the best of people. "*You are the best of people evolved for mankind, enjoining what is right and forbidding what is wrong and believing in Allah*" (Āl 'Imrān 3: 110). The title of the best *Ummah* is bestowed because this *Ummah* is required to serve humanity and guide it to the path of righteousness. This is the same honour that was accorded to Banū Isrā'īl before (al-Baqarah 2: 47 and 122).

Millah

The word *Millah* (pl. *Milal*) is commonly used for religion; in this sense it is a synonym for *Dīn*. It is usually related to a specific prophet: for example, the "*Millah* of Ibrāhīm" (al-Ḥajj 22: 78). In this way it is akin to *Ummah*. However, the word *Millah* is also used for other religions as well (Yūsuf 12: 37).

References

Ummah: 2: 128; 3: 110; 4: 41; 21: 92; 42: 8. *Millah*: 2: 130; 4: 125; 6: 161; 16: 123; 22: 78.

Ummī [أمّي] (Unlettered)

Meaning

Ummī (pl. *Ummīyūn*) means one who has not acquired any education; in other words it is used for an unlettered, uneducated and illiterate person.

Usage

The word *Ummī* was in common use to denote the Arabs who were the descendants of the Prophet Ismā'īl (peace be upon him). The Arab pagans were generally unlettered and nomadic people; in contrast to

Banū Isrā'īl who were People of the Book. Generally, *Ummī* was not used as a word of contempt. It is in this sense that the word *ummīyūn* is used in Sūrah Āl 'Imrān: "*And say to the People of the Book and to those who are unlettered: 'Do you (also) submit yourselves?'*" (3: 20). For this reason *Ummī* is used as a distinct attribute of the Prophet (peace be upon him) twice in Sūrah al-A'rāf (7: 157–158) as well as in Sūrah al-Jumu'ah (62: 2).

However, the word *Ummī* is also used in other senses in the Qur'ān. For example it is used for the uneducated among the Jews who were not conversant with their own scriptures: "*And there are among them illiterates, who know not the Book but (see therein their own) desires and they do nothing but conjecture*" (al-Baqarah 2: 78).

According to Sayyid Mawdūdī, the word *Ummī* for the Jews is similar in meaning to the Hebrew term *goim*, which is translated as "gentile" in English. The term gentile refers to the non-Jewish people. At first it was used to mean races; however, later the Jews started using it for other races only and then considered all non-Jews to be uncivilized and heathen. Thus, it became a term of contempt like "Barbarians". *Ummīyūn* is used in this sense in Sūrah Āl 'Imrān: "*They say: 'there is no call on us (to keep faith) with these ignorant (Pagans)'*" (3: 75) (*Tafhīm al-Qur'ān* [Urdu], vol. 5, pp. 486–487).

References

Ummī: 2: 78; 3: 75; 7: 157 and 158; 62: 2.

Umm al-Kitāb [أم الكتاب]

see *Kitāb*

'Umrah [عمرة]

see *Ḥajj*

Waḥy [وحي] (Revelation)

Meanings

Waḥā means to inspire, to reveal, to give an idea, to give an impression or to suggest, as well as to speak quietly, or to speak to someone secretly. *Waḥy*, from this root, means inspiration or revelation. It is implicit in its meaning that the suggestion or inspiration is covert and not apparent to anyone else.

Waḥy is a technical term for revelation from Allah. It is now exclusively used for the messages conveyed to His Messengers and Prophets. However, in the Qur'ān no such distinction is made. There, *Waḥy* is used for conveying the commands of Allah to all His creation. This can assume many different forms.

1. Commands. While describing the creation of the heavens and earth, it is said: "*He revealed to each heaven His command*" (Fuṣṣilat 41: 12). Similarly *Waḥy* is sent to the Earth so that it can relate all that it is storing (al-Zalzalah 99: 5). Even angels receive their commands by *waḥy*. "*Remember Your Lord inspired the angels (with the message): 'I am with you*" (al-Anfāl 8: 12).
2. Natural Instincts. The honey bees are taught to extract juice from flowers to produce honey (al-Naḥl 16: 68–69). Similarly animals, birds and insects all receive their guidance from natural instincts placed in them by Allah.
3. Inspired Guidance. All the scientific discoveries and inventions as well as literary masterpieces happened because their authors received inspiration and they followed it. Even in everyday life, some ideas may attract one and by following them, one achieves what one is looking for.

The knowledge that Allah imparts to His creation is not given in a formal educational set-up. The method used is refined, elegant and imperceptible. To distinguish *waḥy* in the technical sense of revelation to prophets, other words are used for the above categories of inspiration.

The word *Ilhām* (from *Alhama* to inspire) is used for receiving some hidden knowledge (al-Shams 91: 8). This word is used for the inspiration received by a Muslim. The word *Ilqā'* (to put) is used for some thoughts entering a person's heart and thereby guiding him (al-Nisā' 4: 171). This word is used for guidance received by an ordinary person. Both *Ilhām* and *Ilqā'* are from Allah to a person who possesses *Īmān* but is not a prophet.

Methods of Receiving *Waḥy* by the Prophets

Four different methods were used by Allah to convey His message to His prophets.

1. Inspiration directly put into the heart of the prophets (al-Nisā' 4: 163).
2. Allah directly speaking to His Messenger. For example the Prophet Mūsā had direct conversation with Allah on Mount Sinai (Ṭā Hā 20: 12–36).
3. The Archangel Jibrīl brought *Waḥy* to the Prophet (al-Baqarah 2: 97; al-Shūrā 42: 51).
4. Sometimes inspirations can be received by the prophets through dreams or visions. Instructions thus received are binding on them. For example the Prophet Ibrāhīm (peace be upon him) was asked in a dream to sacrifice his son (al-Ṣāffāt 37: 102). Similarly the Prophet (peace be upon him) saw in his dream that he was performing the *'Umrah* (al-Fatḥ 48: 27).

References

Waḥy: 18: 110; 21: 45; 29: 45; 53: 4; 72: 1.

Wakīl [وكيل]

see *Tawakkul*

Walī [وليّ] (Friend)

Meanings

Waliya means to be near, to be close. *Walā'* and *Wilāyah* means to be a friend. *Walī* (pl. *Awliyā'*) from this root means helper, supporter, benefactor, friend, close associate, sponsor, protector, patron or guardian.

Mawlānā Amīn Aḥsan Iṣlāḥī in his *Tafsīr* has ascertained the following shades of meaning of the term *Walī*:

1. One whose instructions are followed and whose customs, practices, laws and regulations are observed (al-Nisā' 4: 118–120; al-A'rāf 7: 3, 27–30).
2. One whose guidance is trusted and who is believed to lead a person to the right path and save him from transgression (al-Baqarah 2: 257; al-Isrā' 17: 97; al-Kahf 18: 17 and 50; al-Jāthiyah 45: 19).
3. One who is believed to save a person from the punishment of the *Ākhirah* despite his wrongdoings and misdeeds in this life (al-Nisā' 4: 123 and 173; al-An'ām 6: 51; al-Ra'd 13: 37; al-'Ankabūt 29: 22; al-Aḥzāb 33: 65; al-Zumar 39: 3).
4. One who is seen as being able to help metaphorically; to protect a person from calamities and disasters and fulfil his desires and needs (Hūd 11: 20; al-Ra'd 13: 16; al-'Ankabūt 29: 41). (*Tadabbur-i-Qur'ān,* Vol. 4, p. 48)

Who is a *Walī Allāh*

In the popular belief the *Walī Allāh* is a person who is close to Allah through his pious life and obedience to Him. *Walī* is translated as a holy man or a saint and *Wilāyah* is translated as sainthood. This status is confined to a few special people chosen by Allah to interpret the inner meaning of His revelation. They are the intermediaries between Allah and human beings. In pseudo-Sufism the *Walī* is believed to be given Divine protection to save him from error.

Unfortunately these misconceptions are common among the masses, even those who are not influenced by pseudo-Sufism. In Islam the most superior *Awliyā'* are the Messengers and the prophets followed by the

Companions and the Successors. The Qur'ān defines the *Awliyā'* thus: "*Behold! Verily on the friends of Allah there is no fear; nor shall they grieve: those who believe and (constantly) guard against evil*" (Yūnus 10: 62–63). On this basis Imām Ibn Taymīyah wrote regarding the *Awliyā'*:

> The *Awliyā'* of Allah have no visible sign that distinguishes them from others. There is a saying that states that there are many pious men in plain clothing and many heretics in religious garb. The *Awliyā' Allāh* may come from any sector of the *Ummah* of Muḥammad (peace be upon him). What is required of them is that they stay away from every doctrine which is unjustified and eschew any practice which is immoral. (Quoted from *Majmū'*, Vol. 10, p. 194 by Jamaal al-Din M. Zarabozo in the *Commentary on the Forty Ḥadīth of Al-Nawawī*, vol. 3, pp. 1437–1438.)

Legal and Social Implications of *Wilāyah*

MUSLIMS LIVING IN A NON-MUSLIM STATE

There is a bond of *Wilāyah* between Muslims and they are *Awliyā'* of one another. However, when the Prophet (peace be upon him) migrated to Madīnah with many other of his Companions, a minority of Muslims were left behind in Makkah as they could not migrate due to their personal circumstances. It was decreed in Sūrah al-Anfāl that "*As to those who believed but did not migrate, you owe them no duty of protection* (Wilāyah) *until they migrate. But if they seek your help in religion it is your duty to help them*" (8: 72). The duty of *Wilāyah* applies only among the Muslims living in an Islamic state. However, the duties of brotherhood will always remain. The reason for this ruling is that there are legal implications of treaty obligations between an Islamic state and other states that cannot be violated.

THE RELATIONS WITH NON-MUSLIMS

There is a specific prohibition against making non-Muslims close associates and bosom friends in the sense of sharing secrets against the interests of Muslims (Āl 'Imrān 3: 28; al-Nisā' 4: 144; al-Mā'idah 5: 51). On the other hand, as regards social relations with non-Muslims, believers are required to treat every human being with respect. They do not discriminate on account of anyone's faith or beliefs. The verse stating that the pagans are unclean (al-Tawbah 9: 28) only refers to their beliefs and does not indicate physical impurity. Thus, if food which is not *ḥarām* is cooked by a non-Muslim and water is touched by him this does not render them unclean. Muslims can accept the invitation to share food with non-Muslims provided it is not *ḥarām*. The Qur'ān instructs Muslims to co-operate with others in activities that aim at the betterment of society (al-Mā'idah 5: 2). The exchange of gifts also helps to foster good relations. This was the established practice of the Prophet (peace be upon him). In short, Islam exhorts its adherents to have cordial relations with non-Muslims. The question arises of how this can be reconciled with guidance given in the Qur'ān about avoiding close relations with non-Muslims and confiding in them. For this purpose we have to understand the context in which such verses were revealed. It was the early Madīnan period when non-believers, Jews and Christians, despite their differences, were united in their opposition to the newly formed Islamic state. There was a constant state of war created by intrigues and conspiracies to topple or undermine Muslim rule. In this situation the Muslims were advised to remain firm in their *Dīn* and be aware of the duplicity of hypocrites as they are more dangerous than their enemies. Thus the Muslims were warned to be on their guard against their enemies. In modern times, in a state of war nationals of belligerent powers are treated with suspicion and even imprisoned. When a state of war was over, Allah instructed the Muslims to have good relations with non-Muslims. Thus in Sūrah al-Mumtaḥinah after instructing Muslims not to befriend those who were inimical to the cause of Islam, the following verse states:

> *It may be that Allah will grant love (and friendship) between you and those whom you (now) hold as enemies. For Allah has power (over all things); and Allah is Oft-Forgiving, Most Merciful. Allah forbids you not, with regard to those who fight you not for (your) Faith nor drive you out of your homes, from dealing kindly and justly with them: for Allah loves those who are just. Allah only forbids you, with regard to those who fight you for (your) Faith,*

and drive you out of your homes, and support (others) in driving you out, from turning to them (for friendship and protection). It is such as turn to them (in these circumstances), that do wrong.
(al-Mumtaḥinah 60: 7–9)

These verses give very clear instructions for cultivating friendship and good relations with those who are not involved in any subversive or undermining activity against Islam. With these people we are instructed to be kind and just.

Other Words from the Same Root

Mawlā (pl. *Mawālī*) means master, lord, protector, patron, friend or companion. "*And hold fast to Allah! He is your Protector – the best protector and the best help*" (al-Ḥajj 22: 78). The word *mawlā* is used for a client or servant as in al-Dukhān (44: 41), as well as for one related by blood (al-Nisā' 4: 33; Maryam 19: 5). The word also means a freed slave.

Mawlānā also means our master and lord. It is used as a form of address to a sovereign. It is in this sense that Allah is referred to as *Mawlānā* in Sūrah al-Baqarah (2: 286) and Sūrah al-Tawbah (9: 51).

In the Indo-Pakistan this term is used for an *'Ālim* like in Arabic the term *Sayyidī* is used to mean "my master".

References

Walī: 2: 257; 10: 62; 29: 41; 45: 19; 62: 6. *Mawlā*: 8: 40; 22: 78; 47: 11; 57: 15; 66: 2. *Mawlānā*: 2: 286; 9: 51.

Waṣiyyah wa Wirāthah [وصيّة ووراثة]
(Will and Inheritance)

Meanings

Waṣiyyah and *Wirāthah* are very closely related terms. *Waṣiya* means to entrust, to direct, to order or to appoint someone to take charge or care of some affair. *Waṣiyyah* means instruction, advice, counsel or exhortation, as well as will, testament or bequest.

Waritha means to be heir to something or to inherit. *Wirāthah* means the transfer of assets from one to another without commercial transaction or gift. In this sense inheritance or legacy that one acquires from a deceased person is called *Wirāthah.* It is also used in the sense of inheriting knowledge or to be custodian of the cultural heritage, as it is said that the *'Ulamā'* are the inheritors of the prophets.

Usage of the Word *Waṣiyyah*

Waṣiyyah is used in the sense of exhorting, guiding or instructing a younger person or persons either at the time of one's death or at any other time. The person instructed is required to perform certain tasks after one's death or in certain situations. The word is used for exhortation and giving sincere advice in many places in the Qur'ān. For example, in Sūrah al-'Aṣr it is said: "*Verily man is in loss, but not those who believe and work righteous deeds, and enjoin upon each other truth and enjoin upon each other steadfastness*" (103: 2–3). The word is also used for receiving guidance and direction from Allah. "*Verily We have directed the People of the Book before you and you (O Muslims) to fear Allah*" (al-Nisā' 4: 131).

Waṣiyyah is also used in the sense of making a will and giving important advice as well as direction for the distribution of one's assets after death. "*And this is the legacy that Ibrāhīm left to his sons, and so did Ya'qūb: 'O my sons! Allah has chosen the faith for you; then die not except in the state of submission (to Allah)*'" (al-Baqarah 2: 132).

The Qur'ān has stipulated two conditions for those making a will: it should be made near the time of death and is prescribed if one is leaving some assets (al-Baqarah 2: 180). As there are laws of inheritance as discussed below, bequests can only be made if they do not exceed one-third of the estate. Furthermore, those who are designated heirs cannot be the beneficiaries of a bequest. These rules are laid down in *aḥādīth.*

Usage of the Word *Wirāthah*

Wirāthah is used in the sense of transference of assets from the deceased to his relations. The Qur'ān has laid down detailed rules for the distribution of assets in Sūrah al-Nisā' (4: 7–13 and 176). Before the distribution of the assets all outstanding debts owed by the deceased will be paid and then the beneficiaries of bequests will receive their shares and the remainder will be paid according to their shares as laid down in the Qur'ān. It is recommended that other relatives or orphans and poor people who are present but they are not entitled to receive any share, may be given something out of the property as a gift (al-Nisā' 4: 8).

The word *Wirāthah* is also used in the sense of receiving blessings and reward from Allah. The righteous are said to be the inheritors (*Wārithūn*) of Paradise (al-Mu'minūn 23: 10–11) and of the Qur'ān: "*Then We have given the Book for inheritance to such of Our servants as We have chosen*" (Fāṭir 35: 32).

Al-Wārith (The Inheritor) is one of the beautiful names (*al-Asmā' al-Ḥusnā*) of Allah as He is the Sole Survivor and thus: "*To Allah belongs the heritage of the heavens and the earth*" (Āl 'Imrān 3: 180; al-Ḥadīd: 57: 10). In Sūrah al-Ḥijr it is said: "*And verily, it is We Who give life and Who give death; it is We Who remain Inheritors (after all else passes away)*" (15: 23). Material wealth and property belong to human beings only for a short period of time; they ultimately revert to Allah. *Al-Wārith* is also used for human beings who are inheritors from their relations.

References

Waṣiyyah: 2: 180; 4: 12; 5: 106; 31: 14; 42: 13. *Wirāthah*: 4: 19; 7: 137; 19: 6; 7: 137; 21: 105. *Al-Wārith*: 2: 233; 15: 23; 21: 89; 23: 10; 28: 5.

Waswasah [وسوسه] (Whispering)

Meanings

Waswasa means to speak under one's breath, to whisper, to prompt or to tempt. The noun *Waswasah* (pl. *Wasāwis*) means whispering, temptation or insinuation. The word is always used for the prompting of evil thoughts and wicked ideas. The method used by the tempter is imperceptible and hidden as well as persistent, and the person who is the victim of this nefarious act is unaware of its happening. The word *Waswasah* itself indicates the frequent repetition of this action, as a person is not usually deceived or misled by only one attempt.

The one who tempts is called *Waswās*, and *al-Waswās* (the Tempter) is of course *Shayṭān*. The last *sūrah* of the Qur'ān, Sūrah al-Nās, deals with his evil whisperings. The attribute of *al-Waswās* used there is *al-Khannās*. That means that after whispering he withdraws. *Al-Khannās* also means the one who withdraws or hides then reappears. It disappears when Allah's name is mentioned. These tempters could be evil persons among *Jinns* or human beings (al-Nās 114: 6).

The other word used for the promptings of *Shayṭān* is *Hamz* (pl. *Humazāt*), which means prodding, urging or pressing. "*And say 'O my Lord I seek refuge with You from the promptings of the evil ones*" (al-Mu'minūn 23: 97). As in Sūrah al-Nās, one should seek Allah's protection from all *Wasāwis*.

Safeguarding Oneself from *Wasāwis*

Wasāwis takes different forms. These include distraction of mind, doubt, temptation, and worldly thought which keep the mind wandering from one thing to the next. This often happens in the Prayers. One suddenly remembers things that have been forgotten for a long time. This is due to Satan who tries to distract one from remembering Allah properly. To overcome this, the *'Ulamā'* recommend that one should consciously say: "I take refuge of Allah from accursed Satan." One should not read the Qur'ān silently but barely aloud so that one can hear oneself. If you know what you are reading it will help to concentrate your mind. It is essential that one keep one's thoughts clean. Thus, even if one is distracted one will still be thinking about good things and not bad and evil things. If, after all these efforts, one is still distracted then one should try to counter feelings of self-doubt by positively thinking about the Prayers. And finally if one tries to understand the purpose of prayer, that it is an act of submission to the Creator, surely Allah will help.

One should always try to remember Allah consciously and recite the last two Sūrahs, al-Falaq and al-Nās, as well as *Āyat al-Kursī* (al-Baqarah 2: 255). These are effective countermeasures for safeguarding oneself from *wasāwis*.

References

Waswasah: 7: 20; 20: 120; 50: 16; 114: 4 and 5.

Wuḍū' [وضوء]

see *Ṭahārah*

Yaqīn [يقين] (Certainty)

Meanings

Yaqina means to be sure, to be certain or to be convinced. *Yaqīn* means certainty, certitude or conviction. Its opposite is *ẓann* and *rayb* (doubt, suspicion, uncertainty).

As death is the most certain event in human life, it is referred to as *yaqīn*. "*And serve your Lord until there come unto you the hour that is certain (death)*" (al-Ḥijr 15: 99; al-Muddaththir 74: 47).

Three Kinds of *Yaqīn*

There are levels of certainty of knowledge. The first is the certainty of mind. Human beings use their knowledge and experience and infer from something they know something of which they are not quite certain. For example by looking at smoke one infers that there must be fire somewhere. In the Qur'ānic terminology this is called *'Ilm al-Yaqīn* (al-Takāthur 102: 5). The Qur'ānic assertion is that if one uses one's faculty of reason one can be certain of the Day of Judgement. Otherwise, one has to believe it when one sees the retribution of one's sin and the reality of the Hell-Fire with one's own eyes. As it is said: "Seeing is believing". In the Qur'ānic terminology this is called *'Ayn al-Yaqīn*: "*You will see it with certainty of sight*" (al-Takāthur 102: 7).

Yet there is a further degree of certainty with no possibility of error of judgement or error of sight. This is the absolute truth and it is called *Ḥaqq al-Yaqīn*; "*Verily, this is the very Truth and assured certainty*" (al-Wāqi'ah 56: 95; al-Ḥāqqah 69: 51).

Going back to the example of smoke leading one to assume the existence of fire is *'Ilm al-Yaqīn*. However certainty by seeing the fire with one's own eyes is *'Ayn al-Yaqīn*. *Ḥaqq al-Yaqīn* is when one puts one's hand in fire and it burns.

The Difference between *Yaqīn* and *Īmān*

Īmān means to believe or to testify and to accept, which is the opposite of to deny or to reject; whereas *Yaqīn* is certainty of belief which is the opposite of doubt. Believing in something is not conditional on certainty. Maybe persisting in acts of submission could lead to *Īmān*. "*The desert Arabs say: 'We believe.' Say: You have no faith, but you (only) say: 'We have submitted our wills to Allah'. For not yet has faith entered your hearts. But if you obey Allah and His Messenger, He will not diminish any of your deeds: for Allah is Oft-Forgiving, Most Merciful*" (al-Ḥujurāt 49: 14).

Similarly to have certainty may not lead one to *Īmān*. The Jews were certain that the Prophet (peace be upon him) is the true Messenger of Allah yet they did not accept *īmān*. "*Those to whom We have given the Book recognize him as they recognize their own sons; yet those who have lost their own souls will not believe*" (al-An'ām 6: 20; al-Baqarah 2: 146).

References

Yaqīn: 27: 22; 56: 95; 69: 51; 102: 5 and 7.

Yawm al-Dīn [يوم ٱلدّين]

see *Ākhirah*

Zakāh [زكوٰة]

Meaning

Zakā means to grow, to thrive, to increase as well as to be pure or purified. From this root *zakāh* means purity, blessing and growth. It is significant that the Qur'ān uses this word for setting aside a portion of one's wealth for helping the needy and poor in society. A portion of one's wealth is given in alms so as to purify the rest. It is for this reason that charity is called *Zakāh*. "*Of their goods take alms, so that you might purify and sanctify them*" (al-Tawbah 9: 103).

The Importance of *Zakāh*

After prayers, the other most important commandment of Allah is *Zakāh*. Prayers are the acknowledgement of the Creator's right to be worshipped and obeyed. *Zakāh* is meeting the need of fellow human beings. It is to provide help and welfare to those who are unable to meet their needs due to poverty, illness or disability. *Ṣalāh* and *Zakāh* are twin duties that all prophets have commanded their followers to observe. "*And We made them leaders guiding (people) by Our commands, and We sent them revelation to do good deeds, to establish regular prayers, and to practise regular charity; and they constantly served Us (and Us only)*" (al-Anbiyā' 21: 73).

Their neglect is the cause of eternal damnation as this conversation in Hell illustrates: "'*What led you into Hell-Fire?' They will say: 'We were not of those who prayed; nor were we of those who fed the poor*'" (al-Muddaththir 74: 42–44). Allah urges the believers to spend from their wealth so that they can save themselves from a grievous penalty: "*O you who believe! Spend out of (the bounties) We have provided for you, before the Day comes when no bargaining (will avail), nor friendship nor intercession*" (al-Baqarah 2: 254).

There is a tendency in human beings either to save money or to spend it on their own needs. This greediness and selfishness is cured by imposing a duty to give away money to others so that those who are unable to compete in the economic arena can be looked after and no one remains destitute in society. This act of purification is accomplished by giving *Zakāh* as well as other *Ṣadaqāt* in the way of Allah. The comprehensive term for charity is *Infāq fī Sabīl Allāh* (spending in the way of Allah). *Zakāh* is the technical term for mandatory *Ṣadaqah*.

The Rate of *Zakāh*

Zakāh is fixed at 2½ per cent of one's savings, to be paid every year. *Zakāh* is to be paid on gold, silver, livestock, investments and business assets. The assets must be at or above a certain limit called the *Niṣāb*. The *Sharīʿah* has defined different *Niṣāb* for different types of assets.

The Beneficiaries of *Zakāh*

Those who are entitled to be paid out of the *Zakāh* fund are clearly enumerated in Sūrah al-Tawbah (9: 6). They are as follows:

1. the poor
2. the needy
3. those employed to administer the fund
4. those who have been recently reconciled to the Truth so as to win their hearts.
5. those who are in bondage, who must be redeemed.
6. those who are in debt
7. (in the way of Allah – *fī Sabīl Allāh* – is a wide term) which include those who struggle and strive in Allah's cause
8. The wayfarer, that is, travellers stranded on the way.

In this verse the word *Ṣadaqah* is used for the mandatory charity (*Zakāh*).

The Real Spirit of *Zakāh*

As all things in this universe belong to Allah, so does the wealth that is in the possession of human beings. Thus, it is instructive to note that Allah says in the Holy Qur'ān that the poor have a right in your wealth. So if one gives in charity, one is only fulfilling one's duty as a trustee by handing back what already belongs to others: "*And in their wealth and possessions was a portion for the needy who asked and the deprived*" (al-Dhāriyāt 51: 19). "*And those in whose wealth is a recognized right for the needy who ask, and for those who are deprived*" (al-Ma'ārij 70: 24–25).

Nothing should be expected from those who are given charity, nor are they required to show any gratitude. "*And they feed, for the love of Allah, the needy, the orphan, and the captive (saying): 'We feed you for the sake of Allah alone: no reward do we desire from you, or thanks'*" (al-Dahr 76: 8–9). "*Those who spend their wealth for increase in self-purification, and have in their minds no favour from anyone for which a reward is expected in return, but only the desire to seek for the Countenance of their Lord Most High; and soon will they attain (complete satisfaction)*" (al-Layl 92: 18–21).

References

Zakāh: 2: 43; 4: 77; 9: 18; 31: 4; 73: 20.

Ẓann [ظَنّ] (Presumption)

Meanings

Ẓanna means to think, to believe, to assume or to presume. From this root *Ẓann* (pl. *Ẓunūn*) means opinion, assumption, view, belief or supposition.

In the Qur'ān the word *ẓann* is used in two different meanings.

1. It is used for certainty, truth or faith. "*Who bear in mind the certainty that they are to meet their Lord, and that they are to return to Him*" (al-Baqarah 2: 46).
2. It is also used for doubt or scepticism. "*We know not what is the Hour, we only think it is an idea, and we have no firm assurance*" (al-Jāthiyah 45: 32).

Imām al-Rāghib al-Iṣfahānī defines *Ẓann* as what one deduces from the apparent signs. If these signs are strong then it achieves the status of knowledge, whereas if the signs are weak then it is only suspicion or superstition.

Analysis

In the Qur'ān there is no prohibition on having suspicion. What is forbidden is to indulge in making too many assumptions. "*O you who believe! Avoid suspicion as much (as possible): for suspicion in some cases is a sin*" (al-Ḥujurāt 49: 12). The reason is that most suspicions are baseless. This is called *Sū' al-Ẓann,* meaning low opinion and distrust. As against this, it is an admirable quality to have *Ḥusn al-Ẓann* (good opinion) about Allah, His Messenger and the believers.

The other kind of assumption is one that a judge has to make in a court of law where evidence is taken; as he has no direct knowledge of the events, he has to decide what he thinks is the most likely case. This is called *Aghlab al-Ẓann* (that which is mostly probable or most likely).

As the word *Ẓann* has many shades of meaning it is used as the opposite of knowledge, certainty and truth. "*But they have no knowledge therein. They follow nothing but conjecture* (Ẓann); *and conjecture avails nothing against truth*" (al-Najm 53: 28). "*And they (came to) think as you thought, that Allah would not raise up anyone (to judgement)*" (al-Jinn 72: 7).

References

Ẓann: 2: 46; 3: 154; 6: 116; 49: 12; 53: 23.

Ẓulm [ظلم] (Oppression)

Meaning

Ẓalama means to do wrong or evil or to treat someone unjustly. Hence *Ẓulm* is translated as wrong, inequity, injustice, unfairness, oppression or tyranny. Lane in his *An Arabic English Lexicon* defines *Ẓulm* as "the putting of a thing in a place not its own; putting it in a wrong place; misplacing it; either it is by exceeding or falling short, or by deviating from the proper time and place."

The Types of *Ẓulm*

There are three kinds of *ẓulm*. One is the injustice a person does against Allah, his Creator. Associating others with Allah is technically called *shirk*. "Shirk *is indeed the gravest wrong-doing*" (Luqmān 31: 13). It is treated as fabricating a lie against Allah (Hūd 11: 18; al-Zumar 39: 32). The punishment for such transgressors is that they will be denied Allah's mercy on the Day of Judgement. "*Allah forgives not that partners be set up with Him; but He forgives anything else*" (al-Nisā' 4: 48, 116).

The other kind of *Ẓulm* is the wrong that one person commits against another person. "*The blame is only against those who oppress people with wrongdoing and insolently transgress beyond bounds through the land, defying right and justice. For such there will be a grievous penalty*" (al-Shūrā 42: 42).

Finally, there is a wrong that one commits against oneself. Whatever sin one commits one does wrong to oneself. Hence, the Qur'ān has used the term *Ẓālim* (transgressor) for a sinner and *Ẓulm* for a sin. In essence all categories of *Ẓulm* are really the wrong one commits against oneself. On the Day of Judgement such wrongdoers will be told: "*But Allah wronged them not. Nay, they wronged themselves*" (Āl 'Imrān 3: 117).

The Importance of Avoiding *Ẓulm*

There is a *ḥadīth Qudsī* narrated by Abū Dharr al-Ghifārī (may Allah be pleased with him) in which the Prophet (may peace be upon him), relates from his Lord: "O My servants! I have forbidden wrongdoing for Myself and I have made it forbidden for you. Therefore, do not wrong one another" (Muslim). It is clear from this *ḥadīth* that Allah has never committed any form of wrong. This is also mentioned in numerous places in the Qur'ān: "*And Allah means no injustice to any of His creatures*" (Āl 'Imrān 3: 108). "*Allah is never unjust in the least degree*" (al-Nisā' 4: 40).

This *ḥadīth* emphasizes the importance of avoiding any form of *Ẓulm*. *Ẓulm* is the opposite of *'Adl* (justice) which Allah has commanded His believers to observe (al-Naḥl 16: 90). One should realize that committing *Ẓulm* has serious consequences in this world and in the Hereafter. "*Soon will you know who it is whose end will be (best) in the Hereafter. Certain it is that the wrongdoers will not prosper*" (al-An'ām 6: 135). Thus, it is the duty of a believer to avoid *Ẓulm* as well as to stop others from committing *Ẓulm*. The Prophet (peace be upon him) is reported to have said: "Help your brother whether he is the oppressor or being oppressed." One of the Companions was surprised to hear this and asked: "Of course I can help the oppressed but how can I help the oppressor?" The Prophet (peace be upon him) said: "By restraining him from committing oppression. This is (in fact) helping him" (Bukhārī and Muslim).

Ẓulam

Ẓulam, Ẓalām and *Ẓulmah* (pl. *Ẓulumāt*) are very close and similar-sounding words. They mean darkness. The opposite is *Nūr* (light, brightness). Sometimes *Ẓulmah* is used for ignorance and *Shirk* as well as for transgression and wickedness, just as *Nūr* is used for *Īmān* and knowledge as well as good actions. "*Allah is the Protector of those who have faith. From the depths of darkness He will lead them forth into light. Of those who reject faith are the patrons of the evil ones: from light they will lead them forth into the depths of darkness. They will be companions of the fire, to dwell therein (forever)*" (al-Baqarah 2: 257).

There is a very vivid description of the unbelievers struggling in darkness in a very deep ocean:

> *(The unbelievers' state) is like the depths of darkness in a vast deep ocean, overwhelmed with billow topped by billow, topped by (dark) clouds; depths of darkness, one above another. If a person stretches out his hand he can hardly see it! For any to whom Allah gives not the light there is no light.*
>
> (al-Nūr 24: 40)

The Prophet (peace be upon him) has said: "Beware of *Ẓulm*, for *Ẓulm* is darkness on the Day of Resurrection" (Bukhārī).

References

Ẓulm: 6: 82; 11: 117; 22: 25; 31: 13; 40: 17. *Ẓulumāt*: 2: 17; 13: 16; 24: 40; 35: 20; 57: 9.

See also *'Adl*

Bibliography

Tafāsīr

ʿAlī, ʿAbdullah Yūsuf: *The Meaning of the Holy Qur'ān*; new edition, with revised translation and commentary. Brentwood: Amana Corporation, 1992. Many other editions of this work are widely available.

Asad, Muḥammad: *The Message of the Qur'ān*. Gibraltar: Dār al-Andulus, 1980.

Ayoub, Maḥmoud M.: *The Qur'ān and Its Interpreters*. Albany, NY: State University of New York Press, 1984–1992. 2 vols.

Āzād, Abu'l-Kalām: *Tarjumān al-Qur'ān*; edited and translated by Syed Abdul Latif. Delhi: Asia Publishing House, 1990. 4 vols.

Daryābādī, ʿAbdul Mājid: *The Holy Qur'ān*; translated from the original Arabic with lexical, grammatical, historical, geographical and eschatological comments and explanations, and sidelights on comparative religion. Lucknow: Academy of Islamic Research Publications, reprinted by the Taj Company, Lahore, 1957. 2 vols. An abridged version entitled *The Glorious Qur'ān: Text, Translation and Commentary* was published by the Islamic Foundation, Leicester, 2001.

Fārahī, Ḥamīd al-Dīn: *Majmūʿah Tafsīr Farāhī*; translated into Urdu by Amīn Aḥsan Iṣlāhī. Lahore: Markazī Maktabah Jamāʿat-e-Islāmī Pakistan, n.d.

Ibn Kathīr, Ismāʿīl: *Tafsīr al-Qur'ān al-ʿAẓīm*. Beirut: Dār al-Fikr, 1970. 7 vols. The English translation, entitled *Tafsīr Ibn Kathīr (abridged)* was published by Darussalam Publishers, Riyad, 2000, in 10 vols.

Iṣlāḥī, Amīn Aḥsan: *Tadabbur-i-Qur'ān*. Lahore: various publishers, 1967–1980. 8 vols. (Urdu)

Iṣlāḥī, Ṣadr al-Dīn: *Taysīr al-Qur'ān*. New Delhi: Markazī Maktabah Islāmī, 2006. (Urdu)

Kāndhalwī, Muḥammad ʿAlī al-Ṣiddīqī: *Maʿālim al-Qur'ān*. Sailkot: Idārah Taʿlīmāt-e-Qur'ān, 1974–78. 6 vols.

Khan, Irfan Ahmad: *Reflections on the Qur'ān: Understanding Sūrahs Al-Fātiḥah and Al-Baqarah*. Markfield, Leics.: Islamic Foundation, 2005.

Mawdūdī, Abul Aʿlā: *Tafhīm al-Qur'ān*. Lahore: Maktabah Taʿmīr Insānīyat, 1949–1972. 6 vols. (Urdu). English translation by Zafar Ishaq Ansari entitled *Towards Understanding the Qur'ān*, vols. I–VIII up to Sūrah al-Sajdah (Chapter 32). Markfield, Leicester: Islamic Foundation, 1988–2007.

Pānī Patī, Qāḍī Muḥammad Thanā'ullāh: *Tafsīr Maẓharī*; translated into Urdu by Sayyid ʿAbd al-Dā'im Jalālī. Karachi: Dār al-Ishārat, 1991, 12 Vols.

Pirzadah, Shams: *Daʿwat al-Qur'ān*. Bombay: Idārah Daʿwat al-Qur'ān. 4th edition 1973. 3 vols.

al-Qurṭubī, Muḥammad bin Aḥmad: *al-Jāmiʿ li-Aḥkām al-Qur'ān*. Cairo: Dār al-Kitāb al-ʿArabī, 1967. 22 vols.

Quṭb, Sayyid: *Fī Ẓilāl al-Qur'ān*; translated into Urdu by Sayyid Ḥāmid ʿAlī. Lahore: al-Badr Publications, 1987–93. Vols. 1–4 cover *Sūrahs* 1 to 5 and the final volume covers the *Juz'* 30. Another translation in Urdu is by Sayyid Maʿrūf Shāh Shīrāzī. Lahore: Idārah Manshūrāt-i-Islāmī, 1995–97. 6 vols. The English translation by ʿĀdil Ṣalāḥi and Āshūr Shamis entitled *In the Shade of the Qur'ān,* vols. 1–14, covering *Sūrahs* 1–39 and the *Juz'* 30 was published by the Islamic Foundation, Leicester in 1999–2006.

al-Razī, Fakhr al-Dīn: *Al-Tafsīr al-Kabīr wa Mafātīḥ al-Ghayb*. Beirut: Dār al-Fikr, 2002. 17 vols.

al-Ṣābūnī, Muḥammad ʿAlī (ed.): *Ṣafwat al-Tafāsīr*, covers authentic books of *tāfasīr* such as al-Ṭabarī, al-Kashshāf, al-Qurṭubī, al-Ālūsī, Ibn Kathīr, al-Baḥr al-Muḥīṭ and others. Beirut: Dār al-Qur'ān al-Karīm, 1981. 3 vols.

Shafi', Muftī Muḥammad: *Ma'ārif al-Qur'ān*. Karachi: Idārah al-M'ārif, 1975–1976. 7 vols. Urdu.

Concordances, Dictionaries and Encyclopaedias

'Abd al-Bāqī, Fu'ād: *al-Mu'jam al-Mufahras li-Alfāẓ al-Qur'ān al-Karīm*. (Cairo?): Maṭba'at al-Sh'ab, 1378 AH. This is a concordance (an alphabetical arrangement of words) of the Holy Qur'ān that helps to locate the occurrence of words in different parts of the Qur'ān.

Aḥmad Yār, Ḥāfiẓ: *Lughat wa-I'rāb-i-Qur'ān*. Serialized in the journal *Ḥikmat-i-Qur'ān*, Lahore, 1989–90.

Eliade, Mircea: *The Encyclopaedia of Religion*. New York: Macmillan, 1987. 16 vols.

Encyclopaedia of Islam. New ed. Leiden: Brill, 1986–2002. 11 vols.

Esposito, John L.: *The Oxford Dictionary of Islam*. Oxford: Oxford University Press, 2003.

Farāhī, 'Abd al-Ḥamīd [i.e. Ḥamīd al-Dīn]: *Kitāb Mufrādāt al-Qur'ān*. Serai Mir, Azamgarh: Maṭba'at Iṣlāḥ, 1358 AH.

al-Fīrūzābādī, Majd al-Dīn Muḥammad bin Ya'qūb: *Al-Qāmūs al-Muḥīṭ*. (Cairo): Maktabah wa Maṭba'ah Muṣṭafā al-Babī al-Ḥalabī, 3rd edition 1952. 4 vols. in two.

Ibn Manẓūr, Muḥammad bin al-Mukarram: *Lisān al-'Arab*. Beirut: Dār Ṣadar, 1300 AH. 15 vols.

al-Iṣfahānī, al-Rāghib: *Al-Mufradāt fī Gharīb al-Qur'ān*; translated into Urdu by Muḥammad 'Abdahu Fīruzpūrī. Lahore: Shaikh Shams ul-Ḥaq, 1987. 2 vols.

Kassis, Hanna E.: *A Concordance of the Qur'ān* (in English). Berkeley, CA: University of California Press, 1983.

Lane, Edward William: *An Arabic English Lexicon*. London: William and Norgate, 1863. reprinted by Libraire du Liban, Beirut, 1968. 8 vols.

Leaman, Oliver: *The Qur'ān: an Encyclopedia*. London: Routledge, 2006.

McAuliffe, Jane Dammen (ed.): *Encyclopaedia of the Qur'ān*. Leiden: Brill, 2001–2006. 5 vols.

Mir, Mustansir: *Dictionary of the Qur'ānic Terms and Concepts*. New York: Garland Publishing, 1987.

Nadwi, Abdullah Abbas: *Vocabulary of the Holy Qur'an*. Chicago: Iqra International Educational Foundation, 1983 repr. 1996

Nu'mānī, Muḥammad 'Abdul Rashīd: *Lughāt al-Qur'ān*, Lahore: Maktabah Ḥasan Suhail, n.d. 6 vols. Vols. 5 and 6 compiled by Syed 'Abdul Dā'im al-Jalālī (Urdu).

Penrice, John: *A Dictionary and Glossary of the Koran*. London: Curzon Press, 1873. New edition 1971.

Singh, N. K. and Agwan, A. R.: *Encylopedia of the Holy Qur'ān*. Delhi: Global Vision Publishing House, 2000. 5 vols.

Williams, Raymond: *Keywords: A Vocabulary of Culture and Society*. London: Fontana Press, revised ed. 1988.

Reference Books and Monographs

Abdel Haleem, Muhammad: *Understanding the Qur'ān: Themes and Style*. London: I.B. Tauris, 1999.

Abdul-Raof, Hussein: *Exploring the Qur'ān*. Dundee: Al-Maktoum Institute Academic Press, 2003.

Ahmad, Qazi Ashfaq: *Words That Moved the World*. Markfield, Leicester: Islamic Foundation, 1999.

Ali, Sayyid Hamid: *Qur'ānī Iṣṭilāḥāt aur 'Ulamā'-e-Salaf wa Khalaf*. Dehli: Markazī Maktabah Islāmī, 1988.

Denffer, Ahmad von: *'Ulūm al-Qur'ān: An Introduction to the Sciences of the Qur'ān*. Revised edition. Markfield, Leicester: Islamic Foundation, 1994.

Esack, Farid: *The Qur'ān: a User's Guide*. Oxford: Oneworld Publications, 2005.

al-Ghazālī, Abū Ḥāmid Muḥammad: *Iḥyā' 'Ulūm al-Dīn*; Urdu translation by Nadim al-Wajidi. Karachi: Dār al-Ishā'at. n.d. 4 vols.

Mawdūdī, Abu'l A'lā: *Qur'ān kī Chār Bunyādī Iṣṭilāḥen*. Rampur: Maktabah Jamā'at-e-Islāmī Hind, 1952. English translation entitled *Four Key Concepts of the Qur'ān*. Markfield, Leicester: Islamic Foundation, 2006.

Murad, Khurram: 'Introduction' in: *The Islamic Movement: Dynamics of Values, Power and Change*, by Sayyid Abul A'lā Mawdūdī. Leicester: Islamic Foundation, revised edition 1991.

Murad, Khurram: *Way to the Qur'ān*. Leicester: Islamic Foundation, 1985.

al-Nawawī, Muḥyī al-Dīn: *Sharḥ al-Arbab'īn al-Nawawī* – Commentary on the Forty Ḥadīth of al-Nawawī by Jamaal al-Din M. Zarabozo. Boulder: Al-Basheer Company for Publications and Translations, 1999. 3 vols.

Nuqūsh-Qur'ān Number. Lahore: Nuqūsh Press, 1998–2002. 3 vols.

Rahman, Fazlur: *Major Themes of the Qur'ān*. Minneapolis: Bibliotheca Islamica, 1980.

Rippin, Andrew (ed.): *The Blackwell Companion to the Qur'ān*. Oxford: Blackwell Publishing, 2006.

"Sabaeans", article in *Encyclopaedia Britannica,* 11th edition; Cambridge: Cambridge University Press, 1911, vol. 23, pp. 955–958.

Sherif, Faruq: *A Guide to the Contents of the Qur'ān*. Reading: Ithaca, 1995.

al-Suyūṭī, Jalāl al-Dīn: *al-Itqān fī 'Ulūm al-Qur'ān*; trans. into Urdu by Mawlānā Muḥammad Ḥalīm Anṣārī. Karachi: Mīr Muḥammad, n.d. 2 vols.

Walīullāh, Shāh: *Ḥujjatullāh al-Bālighah*. Lahore: Sheikh Ghulam Ali, 1391 A.H.

Index of Arabic Terms

ʿabd, 90, 92-3
ʿābid, 92
ablasa, 219
abrār, 37
***ʿadhāb*, 1-3**, 251
ʿadhb, 1
***ʿadl*, 4-7**, 96, 273
adnā, 50
ʿafā, 153
ʿafuwwun, 153
ʿafw, 153
aghlab al-ẓann, 271
***ʿahd*: 7-10**; *al-ʿahd* 7
ahl al-kitāb: 78, 145-6; as *dhimmī*, 137; and *kufr*, 147; and *shirk*, 221; and *taḥrīf*, 238-9
Aḥmad, 78, 239
***ajal*, 10-11**
ʿajaza, 162
al-ʿājilah, 50
ʿājiz, 162
ʿajiza, 162
akh, 253
ākhā, 253
ākhir, 11
***ākhirah*, 11-14**
***ʿālam*, 14-15**
al-ʿālamīn, 15
ʿalima, 101
Allah, 16-19 and *passim*
***ʿamal*, 19-20**, 48, 99
āmana, 103
***amānah*, 20-2**
ʿamara, 70
***amr*: 22-3**; *al-amr bi al-maʿrūf wa al-nahy ʿan al-munkar*, 23
***anfāl*, 24-5**
anisa, 109
aqsām al-Qurʾān, 184
aqsama, 183
al-ʿarsh, 123
aṣḥāb al-yamīn, 131
al-asmāʾ al-ḥusnā, 19, 37, 105, 113, 119, 153, 181, 222, 265
al-ʿaṣr, 11
aṭāʿa, 207
āthim, 124
athima, 124
al-awāmir wa al-nawāhī, 22
ʿawn, 121
awwal, 11
***āyah*: 25-8**, 188; miracles, 162
āyat al-birr, 36
ʿayn al-yaqīn, 267
ʿazm, 116

bāʿa, 33
badaʿa, 34

badhdhara, 120
baghā, 28
***baghy*, 28-9**
bakhīl, 109
bakhila, 109
balā', 60, 61
***barakah*, 29-30**
bararah, 37
barr, 37
barra, 35
***barzakh*, 30-1**
bashīr, 106, 107
bashira, 106
***bāṭil*, 31-2**
***bay'ah*, 33-4**
***bid'ah*, 34-5**, 221
***birr*: 35-7**; *al-birr*, 37; *birr bi wālidayihi*, 36; cf. *ithm*, 124
bi'sa, 128
bukhl, 109
burhān, 162

da'ā, 39, 48
al-dahr, 11
***ḍalāl*, *ḍalālah*, 37-9**
ḍalla, 37
danā, 50
dār al-ākhirah, 12
dār al-imtiḥān, 14, 51
dār al-khuld, 130
dār al-salām, 130
ḍarar, 93, 95
ḍarra, 93
***da'wah*, 39-40**, 106, 133, 231
dhakara, 40
***dhikr*, 40-2**
dhimmī, 137
***dīn*: 42-7**, 65, 76, 81, 95, 140, 165, 216; and *bid'ah*, 35; and *hijrah*, 80; and *iḥsān*, 96; and *iqāmah*, 113; and Islam, 117-18; and *jihād*, 132, 133; and *millah*, 256; and *naṣīḥah*, 171, 172; *dīn al-ḥaqq*, 76
diyah, 186
***du'ā'*, 48-50**
dunyā, 12, **50-1**

***faḥshā'*, *fāḥishah*, 52-3**
faḥusha, 52
***falāḥ*, 53-5**, 143
falaḥa, 53
faqīr, 55, 56
***faqr*, 55-6**
faraqa, 63
***fasād*, 56-7**
fasada, 56
fasaqa, 58
fasaqah, 58, 59
fāsiq, 38, 58
fatana, 59
faṭara, 61
fatḥ, 54
al-fawz, 53
fay', 24-5
fidyah, 148, 210
fi'l, 20
firdaws, 130
***fisq*, 58-9**, 235
***fitnah*, 59-61**
***fiṭrah*, 61-3**
fu'ād, 182
***al-furqān*, 63-4**, 187

ghāba, 66
***ghaḍab*, 64-6**
ghaḍbān, 64
ghafara, 151
al-ghaffār, 153
al-ghāfir, 153
ghayb, 13, **66-8**, 127, 131, 155, 214, 220
ghusl, 236

ḥadd, 2
hady, 179
hajara, 80
al-ḥajar al-aswad, 212
ḥajj, 50, **68-70**, 72, 92, 105, 112, 178, 202, 204, 211, 212, 213, 216, 242
ḥajja, 68
ḥakama, 82
ḥākim, 84
ḥakīm, 83
ḥalāl, 70
***al-ḥalāl wa al-ḥarām*, 70-2**
ḥalf, 184
ḥalīf, 184
ḥalla, 70
hamazāt, 219
***ḥamd*, 73-4**, 223, 244
ḥamīd, 73, 74
ḥanafa, 75
***ḥanīf*, 75**
ḥaqq: 31, **75-7**; *al-ḥaqq*, 76; *ḥaqq al-yaqīn*, 267
ḥaqqa, 75
al-ḥāqqah 12
***ḥarām*, 70-2**
ḥaraqa, 127
ḥarb, 132, 134
ḥarīq, 127
ḥarrafa, 238
ḥarrama, 70
***ḥasad*, 77-8**
ḥasada, 77
ḥasanatan, 97
ḥāsid, 77
ḥaṣuna, 174
haṭṭama, 127
***hawā*, 79-80**
hāwiyah, 79, 127
ḥayā', 53, 150
hidāyah, 37, 85, 90
***hijrah*, 80-2**, 208
ḥikmah: **82-4**, 217; *al-ḥikmah*, 82, 83
ḥilf, 184
ḥizb, 188
hudā, 37, **85-90**, 187
ḥudūd: 1-2; *ḥudūd Allah*, 2, 201
ḥukm, 83-4
ḥusn al-ẓann, 271
ḥuṭamah, 127

ʿibādah: 24, 54, 70, **90-3**, 113, 121, 221, 231; and *ʿilm*, 101; and *taqwā*, 242; as *dhikr*, 41; *bidʿah* in, 35; *duʿā'* in, 48; in Islam, 118; *jihād* as part of, 134; *ṣalāh* as essential act of, 191; *shirk* in, 205
Iblīs, 136, 218-19
iḍlāl, 38
***iḍṭirār*, 93-5**
iḥrām, 69, 70, 72
iḥsān, 28, **95-7**
iḥṣān, 173-4
iʿjāz, 162
***ikhlāṣ*, 98-100**, 226
ilāh see Allah
***ilḥād*, 100-1**
ilhām, 259
ʿilliyīn, 130
ʿilm: 14, **101-2**, 128, 176; *ʿilm al-tajwīd*, 253; *ʿilm al-yaqīn*, 267
ilqā', 259
īmān: 23, 53, 58, 69, **103-5**, 106, 112, 113, 125, 131, 134, 147, 150, 155, 158, 173, 210, 226, 259, 273; as part of Islam, 118; as part of the *fiṭrah*, 61; belief in *ākhirah*, 13; belief in the *ghayb*, 67; *qalb*, as seat of, 181-2; *yaqīn* as form of, 268
***indhār wa tabshīr*, 106-7**
infāq: **107-9**, 111; *ṣadaqah* as form of, 202
infāq fī sabīl Allāh, 107, 111; *ṣadaqah*, 202; *zakāh*, 269
ins, 109
***insān*, 109-12**

ʿiqāb, 3
iqāmah: **112-14**; *iqāmat al-dīn*, 113; *iqāmat al-ṣalāt*, 112-13, 205
irādah, **114-16**
irtidād, **116-17**
iṣlāḥ, 57
Islam, **117-19** and *passim*
isrāf, **120-1**
istiʿānah: **121-2**; *al-istiʿānah*, 121
iṣṭibār, 201
istighfār, 152
istiqāmah, 113-14, 228
istiwā', **122-3**
ithm, 36, **124-5**
iṭmi'nān, **125-6**

jāhada, 132
jahannam, **126-8**, 232
jahila, 128
jāhiliyyah **128-30**, 209
jahl, 128
jamarāt, 69, 212
janna, 130, 135
jannah: 13, 54, 88, **130-1**, 149, 150, 152, 177, 237, 250; *jannat ʿadn*, 130; *jannat al-ma'wā*, 130, 131; *jannat al-naʿīm*, 130
jazā', 3, 136, 251
jihād, 24, **132-5**, 208, 231; and *hijrah*, 81, 82
jinn, **135-6**, 146, 218
jizyah, **136-7**, 145
juhd, 132
juz', 188

kadhib, 227
kafara, 146
kaffārah, 147-8, 183, 202, 211
kāfir, 38, 147
kalimah: 4, 99, **137-9**, 215, 253; *al-kalimah al-khabīthah*, 138; *al-kalimah al-ṭayyibah*, 138, 215; *kalimah min Allāh*, 138; *kalimāt*, 137, 138-9; *kalimat al-shahādah*, 214-15
kataba, 145
kayd, 154
khāba, 55
khāfa, 143
khalafa, 141
khalaṣa, 98
Khalīfah, 45, 101, 141; *bayʿah* to, 34
al-khannās, 266
khashaʿa, 143
khashyah, 143, 144
khātam: 140; *khātam al-nabīyīn*, 140
khatama, 139
khātim, 140
khatm: **139-40**; *khatm ʿalā al-qalb*, 139-40
khawf 143-4
khayr: 217, 218; *khayr ummah*, 256
khilāfah: 22, 101, **141-2**; *al-khulafā' al-rāshidūn*, 199
khulʿ, 240
khushūʿ, **143-4**
khusrān, 55
kidhb, 227
kirāman kātibīn, 155
kitāb: **145-6**; *al-kitāb*, 145-6, 187; *kitāb maknūn*, 146
kufr: 55, 98, 106, **146-8**, 173; *shukr* opposed to, 222; *ṭāghūt*, 235
al-kursī, 123

laʿib, 149
labisa, 150
laghā, 148
laghw wa lahw, **148-9**
laḥada, 100
laḥd, 100
lahw, 148-9
al-lawḥ al-maḥfūẓ, 145-6
laylat al-qadr, 22, 30, 50, 180

laẓā, 127
***libās*, 150-1**

maghānim, 24, 25
maghḍūb 'alayhim, 65, 66
maghfirah, 131, **151-3**, 196
maḥmūd, 73, 74
makara, 154
***makr*, 154**
***malak*, 155-6**
malaka, 156
malakūt, 158
***malik*, 156-8**
***mālik*, 156-8**
manāsik, 177
manzil, 188
ma'rūf, 23
Marwah, 69, 212, 239
mash'ar al-ḥarām, 213
mashwarah, 223
al-masjid al-ḥarām, 72
maskanah, 56
māta, 159
matāb, 248
mathābah, 251
mathala, 160
mathūbah, 251
mawlā, 263
mawlānā, 263
***mawt*, 159-60**
mighfar, 151
millah, 256
minhāj, 229
miskīn, 56
***mithāl*, 160-1**
mīthāq, 7, 10
mīthāq ghalīẓ, 174
mīzān, 4, 7
mubadhdhirūn, 121
mubārak, 30
muḍārabah, 197
mufsid, 57
Muḥammad: 103, 117, 119, 155, 166, 187; *ḥamd*, 73, 74; *shahādah*, 214, 216
muḥkam: 84; *muḥkamāt*, 27, 84, 146
muḥrūm, 56
muḥsin, 97
muḥṣināt, 174
***mu'jizah*, 162-4**
mukhlaṣ, 99, 100
mukhliṣ, 98, 99, 100
mulk, 157
mu'min: 105; *al-mu'min*, 105
munāfiq, 173
munkar, (evil) 23, (angel) 155
muqarrabūn, 130
al-muqtadir, 181
murshid, 34, 199
muṣābarah, 201
muṣaddiq, 227
al-muṣḥaf, 187
muslim, 117, 118, 119 and *passim*
mustaqīm, 228, 230
muṭahhar: 237; *muṭahharah*, 237
mutashābihāt, 27-8, 84
muttaqīn, 242

na'imā', 175
naba', 164
naba'a, 164
***nabī*, 164-6**
nadhara, 106
nadhīr, 106, 107
nafaq, 172
nafaqa, 107
nafl, 24, 207
nafs: 13, 55, 132, **166-8**, 201; *al-nafs al-ammārah bi'l-sū'*, 167; *al-nafs al-lawwāmah*, 167; *al-nafs al-muṭma'innah*, 125, 126, 167; *anfus*, 166; as part of *jihād*, 132
naḥr, 179
na'īm, 176, 177
nājā, 169

najāt, 169
najwā: **169-70**; *najwah*, 169
nakaḥa, 173
nakāl, 3
Nakīr, 155
al-nār, 127
nasaka, 177
naṣīḥah, **170-2**
nask, 177
naẓāfah, 236
nifāq, 98, **172-3**
nikāḥ, **173-5**
ni'mah, **175-7**, 222
niyyah, 99, 115, 205, 226
nuṣrat, 54
nusuk, **177-9**

qadar, **179-81**
qadara, 179
al-qādir, 181
qadr, 104, 180
qalaba, 181
qalb: **181-2**; *dhikr*, 41; *khatm 'alā al-qalb*, 139-40
qāma, 112, 113
qara'a, 187, 253
qarḍ ḥasan, 108-9
al-qāri'ah, 12
qasam, **183-4**
qaṣaṣ, 185
qaṣṣa, 185
qawwām, 113, 114
al-qayyūm, 113, 114
qirā'ah, 252, 253
qiṣāṣ, **185-6**
qisṭ, 4, 7
al-qisṭās, 4
qitāl, 132, 134
qiyām, 113, 114, 204, 205, 206
al-qiyāmah, 12, 113
Qur'ān, **187-9** and *passim*
qurbān, 178-9

rabā, 196
rabb, **190-2**
rāda, 114
radda, 116
rahbah, 144
rahbānīyah, 144
rāhib, 144
al-raḥīm, 19, 37, **192-6**
raḥmah, 157, 187, 192, 194-6
al-raḥmān, 19, **192-6**
rashada, 199
al-rashīd, 199
rasūl, 164-5, 166
ratila, 253
rāwada, 115
razaqa, 197
al-razzāq, 198
ribā, **196-7**
rizq, **197-8**
rūḥ, 167-8; *al-rūḥ*, 22, 155, 168; *rūḥ al-qudus*, 168
rushd, **199**

sā'a, 232
al-sā'ah, 12, 14
sa'ala, 56
sabaḥa, 243
ṣabara, 200
sabbaḥa, 243, 244
al-sābiqūn, 130
ṣabr, 111, **200-2**, 210
ṣadaqa, 225
ṣadaqah: 197, **202-3**; *infāq*, 107, 108, 109; *qurbān*, 178; *ṣadaqat al-fiṭr*, 202; *zakāh*, 269, 270
ṣadāqah, 227
ṣādiq, 226, 227
Ṣafā, 69, 212
sāḥa, 230, 231
sā'iḥ, 230, 231
sā'il, 56
al-ṣā'iqah, 12

sa'īr, 127
sakīnah, 126
ṣalāh: 36, 54, 111, 143, **203-7**, 242, 244; *dhikr*, 41; *iqāmah*, 112-13, 114; *ṣalāt al-wusṭā*, 206; *ṣalāt al-jumu'ah*, 206; *ṣalāt al-tahajjud*, 206
ṣalāḥ, 57
salām, 117, 118, 119, 204; *al-salām*, 119; *salāmah*, 117
al-salām 'alaykum, 119
ṣalawāt, 207
ṣāliḥ: 57; *ṣāliḥāt*, 19
salīm, 119
sam', 207
***al-sam' wa al-ṭā'ah*, 207-9**
sami'a, 207
saqar, 127
al-saraf, 120
sawā': 123; *sawā' al-sabīl*, 123
sawiya, 122
***ṣawm*, 209-11**
sa'y, 69
sayr, 231
sayyi'ah: 214, 232, 233; *sayyi'āt*, 20
***sha'ā'ir*, 211-13**
shafa'a, 213
***shafā'ah*, 213-14**
shafi', 214
***shahādah*, 214-16**
shāhid, 215, 216
shahīd, 216
shahida, 214
al-shahr al-ḥarām, 72
shakara, 222
shākir, 222, 223
shakūr, 222, 223
sharḥ al-ṣadr, 125-6
sharī'ah: 49, 58, 65, 68, 70, 80, 85, 94, 124, 145, 165, 209, 211, 234, 245, 269; *dīn*, 46-7; *jihād*, 132, 133; *ṣabr*, 200, 201
sharika, 220
***sharr*, 217-18**
shaṭa, 218
shayṭān, 110, 150, 170, 217, **218-19**, 266
shayṭana, 218
shirā', 33
shirākah, 197
shirk: 6, 124, **220-2**, 272, 273; *isti'ānah*, 121-2
shuhadā' 'alā al-nās, 215-16
shukr, 73, 109, 147, **222-3**
***shūrā*, 223-5**, 245
shu'ūr, 211
ṣiddīq, 226-7
ṣidq, 202, **225-7**
siḥr, 163-4
silm, 119
ṣirāṭ, 228
***al-ṣirāṭ al-mustaqīm*, 228-30**
***siyāḥah*, 230-1**
***sū'*: 232-3**; *sū' al-ẓann*, 271
sunnah: 203, **233-4**, 250; *bid'ah*, 35; *sunnah* of Allah, 57, 58, 233-4; *sunnah* of the Prophet, 234
sūrah, 188

ṭā'ah, 82, **207-9**
tāba, 246
taba'a, 140
tabāraka, 30
tabdhīr, 120-1
tabshīr, 106-7
al-ta'dhīb, 1
tafa''ad, 182
ṭaghā, 235
ṭāghiyah, 235-6
***ṭāghūt*, 235-6**
ṭahara, 236
***ṭahārah*, 236-7**
***taḥrīf*, 238-9**
talā, 252
***ṭalāq*, 239-41**
ṭalaqa, 239
talaẓẓā, 127
ṭallaqa, 239

ṭamʿana 125
al-ṭāmmah al-kubrā, 12
taqdīr, 181
taqwā, 36, 124, 131, 144, 150, 153, 169, 178, 208, 210, 215, **241-3**
ṭarīq, 229
tartīl, 253
tasbīḥ, 41, **243-4**
taswiyah, 123
ṭawāf, 69
tawakkul, 231, **245-6**
tawbah: 171, **246-8**; *tawbah naṣūḥah*, 247
tawḥīd, 13, 18, 104, 138, 189; *shirk*, 221
al-tawwāb, 248
tayammum, 94, 236-7
taʿzīr, 1
tazkiyah, 97, 182, **248-50**
thāba, 250
thawāb, **250-1**
thawb, 251
tilāwah, **252-3**

ʿudwān, 36, 124
ukhuwwah, **253-4**
ʿulamāʾ, 102, 105, 121, 143, 264
ūlū al-amr, 22
umm al-kitāb, 146
ummah, 6, 23, 39, 54, 119, 130, 171, 176, 204, 216, 234, **254-6**, 261
ummī, **256-7**
ʿumrah, 70, 72, 259

waḥā, 258
waḥy, **258-9**
wakīl, 246
wakkala, 245
walī, **260-3**
waliya, 260
wilāyah, 260, 261-3
waqā, 241
al-wārith, 265
waritha, 264
waṣiya, 263
waṣiyyah wa wirāthah, **263-5**
al-waswās, 266
waswasa, 265
waswasah, **266-6**
al-wazn, 4
wirāthah, **263-5**
wuḍūʾ, 205, 236

yamīn: 184; *aṣḥāb al-yamīn*, 131
yaqīn: 159, **267-8**; *ʿayn al-yaqīn*, 267; *ḥaqq al-yaqīn*, 267; *ʿilm al-yaqīn*, 267
yaqina, 267
yawm al-dīn 12, 42-3
yawm al-faṣl, 12
yawm al-furqān, 63
yawm al-ḥaqq, 12, 76
yawm al-ḥisāb, 12, 13
yawm al-jazāʾ, 13
yawm al-khurūj, 12
al-yawm al-muḥīṭ, 12
yawm al-qiyāmah, 113
yawm thaqīl, 12

zakā, 248, 268
zakāh: 36, 41, 92, 105, 107, 117, 136, 204, 242, 249, **268-70**; *ṣadaqah*, 202, 203
ẓalama, 272
ẓālim, 38, 272
al-zalzalah, 12
ẓann: 267, **271-2**; *aghlab al-ẓann*, 271; *ḥusn al-ẓann*, 271; *sūʾ al-ẓann*, 271
ẓanna, 271
zaqqūm, 128
zaygh, 140
ẓihār, 240-1
ẓulam, 273-4
ẓulm, **272-4**
ẓulmah: 273; *ẓulumāt*, 102, 273, 274

Index of English Terms

ablution: dry, 94, 236-7; major, 236; minor, 205, 236
Abode: Last, 12; of Eternity, 130; of Peace, 130
Abyss (name of Hell), 79, 127
act of guiding, 37, **85-90**, 187
action: evil, 20, 214, 232, 233; **good**, 28, **95-7**; **intentional**, **19-20**, 48, 99, 103; **of submission**, **117-19**; supererogatory, 24, 207; unintentional, 20
advice: (***naṣīḥah***), **170-2**; (***waṣiyyah***), **263-5**
afraid (v.), 143
agency relationship, 197
agreement, **7-10**
All-Relenting (attribute of Allah), 153
Allah: **16-19**; Book of, 145-6, 187; **Command**, **114-16**; **Judgement**, **114-16**; Kingdom of, 158; Knowledge of, 138-9; Laws of, 57, 58, 133-4; Limits of, 2, 201; Oneness of, 13, 18, 104, 138, 189, 221; Original book of, 146; **Revealed Speech of**, **187-9**; those nearest to, 130; **Wrath of**, **64-6**; wrath, those who incur, 65, 66
Allah-consciousness, 36, 124, 131, 144, 150, 153, 169, 178, 208, 210, 215, **241-3**
Allah-fearing, 242
Allah-inspired tranquillity, 126
alliance, sworn, 184
ally, 184, 246
amusement, 149
angel, **155-6**; recording, 155
anger, **64-6**
apostacy, **116-17**
apprehension, 143, 144
argumentation and proof, 82, 83
ascendancy, **122-3**
ask (v.), 56
astray (v.), 37
atonement, 147-8, 183, 202, 211
authority: 157; those in authority, 22

balance, 4, 7
barrier: (***barzakh***), **30-1**; (*ḥadd*), 2
bath, 236
Battle of Badr, 63
be (creative command), 138
beautiful loan, 108-9
beggar, 56
believe (v.): 103; believer, 105
Beneficent (attribute of Allah), 19, 37, **192-6**
bind (v.), 200
Black Stone, 212

blasphemy, **100-1**
Blast (name of Judgement Day), 12
blessing: **29-30**; blessed, 30, Blessed One, 30
bliss, 176, 177
blood money, 186
book: **145-6**; sacred book, 187
Bottomless Pit of the Fire, 79, 127
bounty, **175**-7, 222
breast, opening of the, 125-6
bringer of glad tidings (attribute of prophethood), 106, 107
brotherhood: **253-4**; brother, 253
burning: **61**; burn (v.), 127; burnt, 182

Calamity (name of Judgement Day), 12
call (v.), 39, 48
calm (v.), 125
certainty: 159, **267-8**; certain (v.): 267; certainty of mind, 267; certainty of sight, 267; certainty of truth, 267
chapter (of the Qur'ān), 188
charity: 107, 111, 202, 269; **compulsory**, 36, 41, 92, 105, 107, 117, 136, 202, 203, 204, 242, 249, **268-70**; **voluntary**, 107, 108, 109, 178, 197, **202-3**, 269, 270
chosen, 98, 99, 100
Christians, 35, 75, 138, 144, 145, 194, 221, 262
circumambulation, 69
cleanliness: (*naẓāfah*) 236, (***ṭahārah***) **236-7**; clean (v.), 236
client, 236
cognizance, 211
command: (***amr***), **22-3**; (*ḥukm*), 83-4
Companions of the Right Hand, 131
compare (v.), 160
compensation, 148, 210
compose in an orderly manner (v.), 253
conceal (v.), 151
confirm (v.), **103**
conflagration, 127
conjecture, 267, **271-2**
conscience: (*al-ḥayā'*), 52-3; (*al-nafs al-lawwāmah*), 167
constitution: (***dīn***) **42**, **43-4**; (*fiṭrah*), 61
consultation: **223-5**, 245
contract (n.): **7-10**; contract (v.), 33
conversion, acceptable, 248
corruption: (***fasād***), **56**-7, (***taḥrīf***), **238-9**; corrupt (v.): 56; corruptor, 57
covenant: 7, 10; strong covenant, 174
cover (v.): (*janna*), 130, 135; (*kafara*), 146
create (v.), 61
credible, 227
Criterion (attribute of the Qur'ān), **63-4**, 187
crookedness, 140
crush (v.): 127; Crusher (name of Hell), 127
cultivate (v.), 53

darkness: 273-4; darknesses, 102, 273, 274
Day: Encompassing, 12; Hard, 12; of Exodus, 12; of Reckoning, 12; of Recompense, 13; of Resurrection, 113; of Separation, 12; of Sure Reality, 12, 76; True, 12, 76
Day of Judgement: (*yawm al-dīn*) 12, 42-3; (*yawm al-ḥisāb*) 13
death: **159-60**; death penalty, 186
deception: (*kidhb*), 227, (***makr***), **154**; deceive (v.), 154
decree (v.): 179; decree, belief in the divine, 104, 180
deeds: **19-20**; bad, 20; evil, 23; good, 19, 23; **shameful**, **52-3**
deliberation, 223

desire, base, 79-80
destiny: (*al-dahr*), 11, (***qadar***), **179-81**; **written destiny, 145**
determination, 116
deviation, error: **37-9**; deviate from goodness (v.), 58
Devil, 136, 218-19 (*see also* Satan)
die (v.), 263
dig a grave (v.), 100
Disaster, Great (name of Judgement Day), 12
disposition, 59-61
distant (v.), 218
diversion, 148-9
Divine Attributes, 19, 37, 105, 113, 119, 153, 181, 222, 265
Divine Proof, 26
Divine Punishment: (***'adhāb***) **1-3**, 251; (*ṭāghiyah*), 235-6
divorce (n.): **239-41**; divorce (v.), 239; pre-Islamic, 240-1
dress: **150-1**; pilgrim's dress, 69, 70, 72 (*see also* garment)
dutiful (v.), 35
Dwellings on High (in Heaven), 130

Earthquake (name of Judgement Day), 12
effort, 132
elevation, 169
endeavour (v.), 132
enjoining good and forbidding evil, 23
entrust (v.): (*waṣiya*) 263; (*wakkala*) 245
envier, 77
envy (n.): **77-8**; envy (v.), 77
equal (v.), 122
equity, 4, 7
error, 37-9
escape, 169
establishment: **112-14**; of prayer, 50, 112-3, 205; of way of life, 113
even, 123
evidence, 26
evil (n.): (***sharr***), **217-18**, (***sū'***), **232-3**; evil (v.), 232
exceed (v.), 235
expiation, 202, 211
extravagance, 120-1

fail (v.), 55
fairness, 4, 7
faith: **103-5**, 106, 245, 252, 257, 262, 264, 271, 273; bearing witness to, 214-15, 253-4; cleanliness as half of, 237; distinction with Islam, 118; heart as seat of, 181; hyprocrisy in, 172-3; in the Unseen, 13, 127, 155, 157-8; love of Allah, 17; marriage and, 174; migration for the sake of, 80-1, 84; recompense for, 130, 175, 177, 251; rejection of, 38, 64, 100, 116, 140, 147, 235; relation to good deeds, 19; sincerity and truthfulness in, 43, 98, 99, 115, 125, 199, 202, 226, 268
fall (v.), **79-80**
falsehood, 31-2
fasting, 209-11
favours, 175-7, 222
fear, 143-4
fighting, 132, 133
Fire (name of Hell), 127
first, 11
flame, blazing: (*laẓā*), 127, (*talaẓẓā*) 127
float (v.), 243
flogging, 1
flow (v.), 230, 231
follow (v.): 252; follow someone's track (v.), 185
forbid (v.), 70
forgiveness: (*'afw*), 153, (***maghfirah***), 131, **151-3**, 196; forgive (v.), 151; Forgiver (attribute of Allah), 153

formation, 123
fraternize (v.), 253
friend of Allah: **260-3**; friend, 226, 227; friendship, 227, 262-3
fright: 144; frighten (v.), 143
frivolity and diversion, **148-9**

Gabriel (Jibrīl), 22, 96, 155, 168, 187, 259
Garden: of Abode, 130, 131; of Comfort and Happiness, 130; of Eden, 130
garment, 251 (*see also* dress)
genie, **135-6**, 146, 218
get up (v.), 112, 113
gift, 85, 179, 202
glad tidings, **106-7**
glorification (of Allah), 41, **243-4**
god, 16 (cf. Allah)
goodness: (*khayr*), 218; (*mubārak*), 30; (*ṣalāḥ*), 57
grace, **175-7**, 222
gratitude, 73, 109, 147, **222-3** (cf. ingratitude)
grave, 100
grow (v.): 248, 268; growth, 196
guard (v.): 241; guardian, 246
guidance: 37, 85, 90; guide (v.), 85; spiritual guide, 34, 199 (cf. misguiding)

harm (n.): 93, 95; harm (v.), 93
hasty, 218
hear (v.), 207
heart: 41, **181-2**; hearts, 166; sealing of the heart, 139-40; seat of faith, 181; sound (of heart), 119
Heaven, 13, 54, 88, **130-1**, 149, 150, 152, 177, 237, 250
Hell, **126-8**, 232
helmet, 151
help (n.): **121-2**; help (v.), 121
Hereafter, **11-14**
hide (v.), 66
high (v.), 164
Holy Spirit (Gabriel), 168
Hour of Resurrection, 12, 14
human being, **109-12**
humble (v.), 143
humility, **143-4**
hypocrisy: 98, **172-3**; hypocrite, 173

idols, **235-6**
Ignorance, Age of: (***jāhiliyyah***), **128-30**, 209, (*ẓulmah*), 273; ignorant (adv.), 128; ignorant (v.), 128
illiterate, **256-7**
immorality, **52-3**
inaccessible (v.), 174
incline (v.), 75
incur loss (v.), 55
increase (v.), 196
indecency: **52-3**; indecent (v.), 52
Inferno (name of Hell), 127
ingratitude, 222 (cf. gratitude)
inheritance: **263-5**; inherit (v.), 264; inheritor, 265
inner peace, 125, 126, 167
innovation, **34-5**, 221
insight, **88**
inspiration: (*ilhām*), 259, (*ilqā'*), 259; inspire (v.), 258
integrity, **199**
intention: (***irādah***), **114-16**; (*niyyah*), 99, 115, 205, 226
intercession, **213-14**
interest, **196-7**
invent (v.), 34
invitation, **39-40**, 106, 133, 231

Jews, 204, 208, 221, 238-9, 259, 262, 268
judgement: (*dīn*), **42**, (*ḥukm*), 83-4; judge, 84
justice, **4-7**, 96, 273

King (attribute of Allah), **156-8**
know (v.), 101
knowledge, 14, **101-2**, 128, 176
Koran see **Qur'ān**

last, 11
law: **43-4**; **lawful and unlawful**, **70-2**; **laws**, **145** (*see also* legal)
lead a life of devotion (v.), 177
leave (v.), 239; leave somewhere (v.), 80
legal: code, 22; discretionary punishments, 1; non-discretionary punishments, 1-2; **process**, **76-7**; **rights**, **76**; witness, 215, 216 (*see also* law)
letter, **145**
liar, 227
life, fleeting, 50
listening and obeying, **207-9**
Lord (attribute of Allah), **190-2**
love, 79
lust, **79-80**

magic, 163-4
Man, 109
marriage, **173-5**; married women, 174; marry (v.), 173
martyr, 216
Marwah, 69, 212, 239
master, our, 263
melt gold to find impurities (v.), 59
Merciful (attribute of Allah): 19, **192-6**; mercy, 157, 187, 192, 194-6
messenger (of Allah), 164-5, 166
migration, **80-2**, 208
miracle: (***āyah***), **25**; (***mu'jizah***), **162-4**
miser: 109; miserliness, 109; miserly, 109
miserable, 128
misguiding, 38 (*see also* error; cf. guidance)
monasticism: 144; monk, 144
month, sacred, 72
Mosque, Inviolable, 72
Most Forgiving (attribute of Allah), 153
Most Praised (Aḥmad), 78, 239
most probable, 271
Munkar, 155
Muslim, 117, 118, 119 and *passim*
Muzdalifah, 213

Nakīr, 155
nations, 15
nature: **disposition**, **61-3**; **of things**, **138**
near (v.): 50; nearer, 50
necessity, **93-5**
news, 164
Night of Power, 22, 30, 50, 180
non-perceptible, 13, **66-8**, 127, 131, 155, 214, 220
norm, **233**

oath: **183-4**; **oath of allegiance**, **33-4**; take an oath (v.), 183
obeying: 82, **207-9**; obey (v.), 207; obeying one's parents, 36
obligation, 7
Oft-Returning (attribute of Allah), 248
Old Testament: 185, 239; as *al-furqān*, **63**
Omnipotent (attribute of Allah), 181
One Who Withdraws (attribute of Satan), 266
opinion, good, 271
oppression: (*baghā*), 28; (***ẓulm***), **272-4**
order: **22-3**; ordering, 181
overcome with grief (v.), 219
overseer, 246
Owner (attribute of Allah): **156-8**; own (v.), 156

parable, **160-1**
Paradise, 130

partnership, **220**
pass judgement (v.), 82
path: (*minhāj*) 229, (*ṣirāṭ*) 228, (*ṭarīq*) 229; even path, 123; **straight path**, **228-30**
patience, 111, **200-2**, 210
pauper, 55, 56
peace: (*salām*) 117, 118, 119, 204, (*silm*) 119; Giver of Peace (attribute of Allah), 119; **giving peace as definition of faith**, **103**; peace be upon you, 119
penance, 147
People of the Book: 78, 145-6; and polytheism, 221; and scriptural distortion, 238-9; and unbelief, 147; as protected persons, 137
people, **254**
perceptible, 67
persecution, **61**
perseverance, 201
person (types of): angry, 64; needy, 56; pious, 57; protected, 137; righteous, 37, 97; unfortunate, 56; **upright**, **75**
piety, 177
pilgrimage: circumambulation, 69; ceremonies of, 177; **greater**, **68-70**, 72, 92, 105, 112, 178, 202, 204, 211, 212, 213, 216, 242; lesser, 70, 72, 259; pilgrim's dress, 69, 70, 72; stoning the pillars, 69, 212
plant, bitter thorny, 128
poll tax, **136-7**, 145
polytheism, 6, 124, **220-2**, 272, 273; seeking help, 121-2
poverty: **55-6**; extreme poverty, 56
Powerful (attribute of Allah), 181
praise (v.): 243, 244; highly praiseworthy (Muḥammad), 73, 74; praised, 73, 74; praiseworthy, 73, 74; **thankful praise**, **73-4**, 223, 244
prayer: 36, 41, 54, 57, 111, 143, **203-7**, 242, 244; Friday prayer, 206; late night, 206; middle prayer, 206; optional, 206-7; standing in prayer, 113, 114, 204, 205-6
precise, 84
predetermine (v.), 179
Preserved Tablet, 145-6
presumption, 267, **271-2**
promise, 7
proof: 63, 81, 163, 167, 184; (***āyah***), **26**; (*burhān*), 162, 187, 202; (***hudā***), **85**
prophet: **164-6**; practice of prophet, 234 (*see also* norm)
proportion, 180
prosperous (v.), 175
prostitute, 29
protection: 260, 261-3; protector, (*mawlā*), 263, (*al-mu'min*) (attribute of Allah), 105
provision: **197-8**; provide with means of subsistence (v.), 197; provider, 113, 114; Provider (attribute of Allah), 198
punishment, 3
purchase (v.), 33
pure (n.): 237; pure (v.), 98; pure and holy, 237; purity, 205, 236; **spiritual purification**, 97, 182, **248-50**

quiet (v.), 125
Qur'ān: **62-3**, **187-9**; compilation, 187-8; contents, 188-9; inimitability of, 162; oaths in, 184; sixtieth of, 188; **recitation of**, 187, **252-3**; script in, 188; seventh of, 188; style of, 189; thirtieth of, 188; **verse of the**, **25-8**, 188

Reality (name of Judgement Day), 12
rebellion: 2, 5, 208; (***baghy***), **28-9**
recitation (of the Qur'ān), **252-3**

recompense (n): 3; recompense (v.), 136, 251
reject (v.), 116
rejoice (v.), 106
religion (*millah*), 256 (cf. way of life)
remember (v.): 40; **remembrance, 40-2**
rendezvous, 251
repentance: 171, **246-8**; sincere repentence, 247
requital, 251
resemble (v.), 160
restoration, 57
Resurrection (name of Judgement Day), 12, 113
retaliation, 185-6
return (v.), 246
revelation: (***ḥaqq***), **76**; (*rūḥ*), 168; (***waḥy***), **258-9**
reverent, 37
reward (n.): **250-1**; reward (v.), 136
right path: be on (v.), 199; stray from (v.), 58
righteousness: **35-7**; Righteous (attribute of Allah): 37, righteous (people), 37
Rightly-guided Caliphs, 199
riot, 59

sacrifice: (***nusuk***), **177-9**; (*qurbān*), 178-9; sacrificial animal: 179; sacrificial camel, 179
Ṣafā, 69, 212
sage, 83
salvation, 53-5, 143
Satan, 110, 150, 170, 217, **218-19**, 266; suggestions of, 219 (*see also* Devil)
satisfaction, 125-6
Scale: (*al-qisṭās*), 4; (*mīzān*), 4, 7
scholars, 102, 105, 121, 143, 264
scorch (v.), 127
seal (n.): **139-40**; seal (v.), 139; Seal of the Prophets, 140; sealing of the heart, 139-40
security, 117
sedition, 59
seduction, 115
seek (v.): 114; seek forgiveness (v.), 152; seek help (v.), 121
self: 13, 55, 132, **166-8**, 201; carnal self, 167; peaceful self, 125, 126, 127; reproaching self, 167
Self-Subsisting (attribute of Allah), 113, 114
sell well (v.), 107
separate (v.): 63; separation, 240
servant, 90, 92-3
share with (v.), 220
sign, 25-8, 188
sin (n.): (***ithm***), 36, **124-5**, (*sayyi'ah*), 214, 232, 233; sin (v.), 124; sinner, 124
sincerity, 98-100, 226; sincere, 98, 99, 100;
slant (v.), 238
slyness, 154
sociable (v.), 109
soul, 167-8
Sovereign (attribute of Allah), **156-8**
speak the truth (v.), 225
species, 15
spending: compulsory, 269; extravagance in, 120; **in Allah's way, 107-9**, 111; voluntary, 107, 202-3
spirit: 167-8; spiritual guide, 34, 199
spoils of war: (***anfāl***), **24-5**, (*maghānim*), 24, 25; spoils: 24-5
spokesman, 215
squander (v.): 120 squanderers, 121; squandering, 120-1
stamp (v.), 139
steadfastness: (*istiqāmah*), 113-14, 228; (*muṣābarah*), 201
stoning the pillars, 69, 212
stop (v.), 1
story, 185
straight (adj.): 228; straight (v.), 113-14, 228

straight path, **228-30**
struggle, **132-5**
submissiveness, **143-4**
succeed someone (v.), 141
supplication, **48-50**
support, 54
surety, 246
surpass (v.), 26
surrender to Allah, **117**
suspicion, 271
Sustainer (attribute of Allah): (*al-razzāq*), 198; (***rabb***), **190-2**
swearing, 184
swim (v.), 243
symbols, **211-13**
synagogues, 207
system of beliefs, **42**, **44**, 118

talk nonsense (v.), 148
temptation: **59-61**; Tempter (name of Satan), 266
Test, Place of (name of Judgement Day), 14, 51
testimony of faith, 214-15
thank (v.): 222; Giver of Thanks (attribute of Allah), 222, 223; thankful, 222, 223
think (v.), 271
thrive (v.), 70
Throne, 123
tidings: 164; **glad tidings**, **106-7**
time, appointed: **10-11**; fleeting, 11
transgress (v.): 28; transgression, 36, 124; transgressor, 38, 58
travel: (*sayr*), 231, (***siyāḥah***), **230-1**; traveller, 230, 231
treaty, 7
trial: (*balā'*), 60, 61; (***fitnah***), **59-61**; Place of Trial (name of Judgement Day), 14, 51
true purpose: **76**; true (v.), 75; true way of life, 76

trust: **20-2**; trust (in Allah), 231, **245-6**
truth: (***ḥaqq***), **75-7**, (***ṣidq***), 202, **225-7**; truthful, 226, 227
tunnel, 172
turn around (v.), 181

Ultimate Reality (attribute of Allah), 76
unbelief: 55, 98, 106, 146-8, 173; and idolatry, 235; as opposed to gratitude, 222; unbeliever, 38, 147
universe, **14-15**
unlawful, **70-2**
unlettered, **256-7**
unseen, 66
untie (v.), 70
upright: 226-7; uprightness, 113

value, 180
verse (of Qur'ān): **25-8**, 188; ambiguous, 27-8, 84; basic, 146; of righteousness, 36; unambiguous, 27-8, 84, 146
vicegerency, 22, 101, **141-2**
vicegerent: 45, 101, 141; pledging allegiance to, 34
victory, 54
visit a venerated place or person (v.), 68

walk between Ṣafā and Marwah, 69
war, 132, 134
warning and glad tidings: **106-7**; warn (v.), 106; warner (attribute of prophethood), 106, 107
waste (v.), 120
way of life: (***dīn***), 44, **45-6**, 76, 165; (**Islam**), 224, 225, 229; way to Allah, 46-7 (cf. religion)
way, clear and straight, **85**
weak (n. and v.), 162
wealth, deprive of, 56

wear (v.), 150
weight, 4
Well-guarded Book, 146
whispering: (***najwā***), **169-70**, (***was-wasah***), **263-5**; whisper to each other (v.), 169
wickedness, **58-9**, 235
will and inheritance, **265-6**
wisdom: (***ḥikmah***), **82-4**, 217; (*ḥukm*), 84
witness (n.): 214-16; witness (v.), 214; witness unto mankind, 215-16
word: 4, 99, **137-9**, 215, 252; evil word, 138; good word, 138, 215; word from Allah (Prophet Jesus), 138; word of guidance, 214-15
world: (***'ālam***), **14-15**; (***dunyā***), 12, **50-1**; worlds, 15
worship: 25, 54, 70, **90-3**, 113, 121, 221, 231; and Allah-consciousness, 242; and knowledge, 101; innovation in, 35; *jihād* as part of, 134; polytheism in, 205; prayer as essential act of, 191; supplication in, 48; worshipper, 92
worship and obedience, **42**
write (v.), 145
wrong (v.), 272